# The Medieval Saga

The north portal of the Urnes stave church, Norway. Photograph by P. G. Maurtvedt. Copyright University Museum of National Antiquities, Oslo, Norway.

# The Medieval Saga

*Carol J. Clover*

CORNELL UNIVERSITY PRESS

Ithaca and London

Cornell University Press gratefully acknowledges a grant
from the Andrew W. Mellon Foundation that
aided in bringing this book to publication.

First published 1982 by Cornell University Press.
Published in the United Kingdom by Cornell University Press Ltd.,
Ely House, 37 Dover Street, London, W1X 4HQ.

International Standard Book Number 0-8014-1447-4
Library of Congress Catalog Card Number 81-17432
Printed in the United States of America
*Librarians: Library of Congress cataloging information
appears on the last page of the book.*

*The paper in this book is acid-free, and meets the guidelines for
permanence and durability of the Committee on Production Guidelines
for Book Longevity of the Council on Library Resources.*

Di molte fila esser
  bisogno parme
a condur la gran tela
  ch'io lavoro.

(I need many different
threads to weave the
wide web I labor on.)

—*Orlando furioso*
  13:81

# Acknowledgments

My first and greatest debt of gratitude is owed to the American Council of Learned Societies, whose support during the academic year 1978–79 made this work possible. For their help in making arrangements for me in Cambridge I am grateful to Dorothy Boerstler, Dorrit Cohn, and Eckehard Simon. Einar and Eva Haugen deserve warmest thanks not only for their willingness to share their small study in Widener Library, but for their cheerful disregard of the crowding and clutter that resulted. Friends who contributed valuable criticism and suggestions are Frederic Amory, Theodore M. Andersson, Joseph Duggan, and Susan Shively.

CAROL J. CLOVER

*Berkeley, California*

# Contents

The Medieval Saga

# Introduction

Aristotle's treatise on poetics appears to have circulated rather widely during the Middle Ages in a Latin translation made in 1256 from the abridged Arabic version of Averroës. As nearly as we can tell, however, it had little if any impact on actual narrative practice. Only in mid-sixteenth-century Italy, with the publication of Robortello's edition and commentary and Segni's Italian translation, did the *Poetics* enter the general literary consciousness.[1] The results are literary history. Although it is probably not fair to say that the *Poetics* alone caused the ensuing literary debates, Aristotle's views did figure prominently, certain authors attacked others on "Aristotelian" grounds, and, by the time the controversy died down, literary neoclassicism was an established fact.

The crux of the controversy was narrative structure—which thus for the first time became the subject of serious theoretical discussion—and the case in point was Ariosto's *Orlando furioso*. The criticism of Ariosto's work was initiated in 1548 with the publication of an epistolary dialogue between Giovanni Battista Pigna and Giovambattista Giraldi Cintio.[2] Pigna's letter spelled out the ways in which *Orlando furioso* failed to conform to the classical precepts of epic (it lacked a proper beginning and end,

---

[1] Joel E. Spingarn, *History of Literary Criticism in the Renaissance*, 2d ed. rev. (New York: Columbia University Press, 1908), esp. pp. 107–24.

[2] A full account may be found in Bernard Weinberg, *A History of Literary Criticism in the Italian Renaissance*, 2 vols. (Chicago: University of Chicago Press, 1916), II, 957–71.

was too long, had no unity of action, had too many characters, was disorderly in its organization, was far too digressive). Giraldi responded, arguing that the "ancient" model of the Greeks was antiquated, that modern times required modern poetry, and that Ariosto was the supreme practitioner of the "new" aesthetic. As the quarrel unfolded, the defenders of Ariosto refined their definition of the "new" aesthetic. They preferred multiplicity to unity, stories telling not of "one action and one man, but many actions of many men,"[3] and a plot that "varies and mingles character just as it varies and mingles actions and persons"[4]—not epic but romance, in a word. The Aristotelians, too, became increasingly theoretical in their defense of classical form and, in the process, increasingly enthusiastic about a poem in the epic mode that met their terms: the *Gerusalemme liberata* by Torquato Tasso. So it was that Tasso's poem came to serve, in Bernard Weinberg's words, as a "foil, a basis of comparison, in the continuing re-evaluation of Ariosto's *Orlando Furioso*" and as "one of the poles in the violent quarrel over the respective merits of the two Cinquecento poets."[5] Tasso's own theories on narrative structure (represented in their final phase in the *Discorsi del poema eroico* of 1594) are firmly pro-epic and pro-Aristotle.

What neither side quite appreciated is that the new literature was not so new as it seemed. Ariosto did not invent the narrative form he used in the *Orlando furioso;* he borrowed it from Boiardo, to whose *Orlando innamorato* he wrote the *Furioso* as a continuation. Boiardo got it from the epic compilations so popular in his time, which in their turn were descended from the cyclic manuscripts of the thirteenth and fourteenth centuries. Ariosto's narrative habits were not new at all, but almost four centuries old. Nor were they peculiarly Italian, nor confined to epic. The most prominent representatives of this sort of writing—prominent in their own time as well as in recent scholarship on medieval literary history—were the French prose romances, above all the so-called Vulgate Cycle (ca. 1215–30). Of the features these books of chivalry had in common with the "new" literature, one, interlace composition, has been called "one of the fundamental aesthetic

---

[3]Gioseppe Malatesta, in ibid., p. 1043.
[4]Malatesta Porta, in ibid., p. 1048.
[5]Weinberg, *History of Literary Criticism*, p. 983.

issues of thirteenth-century prose literature."[6] When the Aristotelians in sixteenth-century Italy attacked Ariosto's sense of structure, therefore, they were in effect attacking a large and central part of medieval literature.[7]

It is a measure of the eventual success of neoclassicism that "romance" became for posterity more or less synonymous with the works of Béroul, Thomas, Marie de France, and Chrétien de Troyes (works, that is, approximating more closely than their prose successors the classical ideal) and was understood only secondarily, if at all, to refer to the popular body of prose works which prevailed from the thirteenth century on. Only recently, largely in consequence of the studies of Ferdinand Lot, Jean Frappier, Eugène Vinaver, and Jean Rychner, has this "other" side of romance been brought up for reconsideration on its own terms. These terms turn out to be crucial to our understanding of the period in general, for they point to a conception of form so pervasive and so consistent that it may be regarded as the majority aesthetic of medieval literary culture—an aesthetic better represented by the *Prose Tristan* than by the *lais* of Marie de France or *Erec et Enide* of Chrétien. The particular value of the Tasso-Ariosto controversy is that it isolated the special properties of this narrative aesthetic and explicated its underlying philosophy at a time when it was still in use, if only in some quarters and in attenuated form.

This "medieval" aesthetic, reflected in its most characteristic form in the prose romances of thirteenth-century France, is the point of departure for the following study of the Icelandic family sagas. The prevailing view of the sagas is that as formal constructions they are peculiarly local products. Hagiography and romance are held accountable in varying degrees for the biographical scheme, the occasional expressions of courtly sensibility, certain words and phrases, and many points of plot. But the style and composition of the sagas, together with their main content and themes, are attributed to native tradition. What foreign debts they owe on the level of form were incurred earlier rather than later

---

[6]Eugène Vinaver, "The Prose *Tristan*," in *Arthurian Literature in the Middle Ages*, ed. R. S. Loomis (Oxford: Clarendon, 1959), p. 345.
[7]See especially, William W. Ryding, *Structure in Medieval Narrative* (The Hague: Mouton, 1971), esp. pp. 9–17.

and to religious writings and chronicle traditions rather than to romance. This book takes a somewhat different view. Its premise is that the Icelandic sagas as formal constructions are not separate from the larger European development of the thirteenth century, but part of it; that the same literary forces that played an important role in the rise of imaginative prose forms in France also played an important role in the evolution of the prose saga in Scandinavia; and that, despite large and obvious differences in temper and style, the Icelandic sagas as literary compositions bear direct comparison with some of the major narrative works of contemporary France and may therefore be classed with them as medieval.

Like recent investigations into medieval narrative and like the sixteenth-century polemics surrounding Ariosto's work, this analysis concentrates on composition: the way parts are put together. The first three chapters consider in descriptive and comparative terms the narrative procedures of the Icelandic sagas: first, how they conform to the principle of coherent multiplicity rather than unity; second, how they conceive of a plot as parallel and interlocking subplots; and third, how they weave together simultaneous lines of action. The final chapter surveys some early texts in the kings' saga tradition in an effort to discern when and in what form ''medieval'' patterns became established in Scandinavian narrative tradition. The chapter concludes with three short sections on the role of Latin history writing in the development of Icelandic prose, the parallel evolution of romance and saga, and the nature of the audience.

This literary emphasis requires a few words of explanation. The impressive evidence that has accumulated around the freeprose/bookprose controversy offers no final answers to the old issue of saga origins, but it has taught us two important lessons about the questions to be asked.[8] One is that we no longer ask whether the saga is literary *or* oral, but what in the received saga can be ascribed to the literary author (whose use of written sources, both native and foreign, is firmly established) and what to a native tradition (the existence of which is the only explanation for the

---

[8] A history of saga scholarship, including its bookprose/freeprose phase, may be found in Theodore M. Andersson's *The Problem of Icelandic Saga Origins: A Historical Survey* (New Haven: Yale University Press, 1964).

survival of traditional material through the preliterate period).
This eclectic view differs from the either/or tendencies current in
those quarters of medieval literary scholarship under the influence of oral-formulaic theory. The second lesson has to do with
the difficulty of assessing the shape of narrative traditions in Iceland before the written saga. The saga's literary loans are identifiable by the usual methods of textual comparison, but its oral
component remains largely unknown and probably unknowable
in any precise sense. The lack of an uncontaminated specimen of
native tradition means that there is nothing to measure the given
saga against. The folktales serve the purpose up to a point, but
they shed no light on the origin and evolution of the long form.
Nor has there been deduced from documented traditions a set of
compositional principles for oral prose, equivalent to those for
oral poetry, which would allow us to speculate by analogy. (The
minority status of prose in oral literature and the theoretical limbo
occupied by the sagas are points that will be taken up in the final
three sections of Chapter 4.) In the absence, therefore, of any
positive means, practical or theoretical, of apprehending the oral
saga, critics have tended to rely on the logic of negative inference:
to identify the literary features of the narrative and to consign the
remainder to native tradition. However reductive that method
might seem, it has yielded some of the more durable results of
saga studies.

This book follows no precise recipe in its treatment of the oral
background. To the extent that it touches directly on the properties of oral prose, it refers in the first instance, like its predecessors, to the classic work, based largely on the evidence of the
folktale, of Axel Olrik and Knut Liestøl. It refers to the burgeon-
ing literature on oral poetry only briefly and on those points
where poetic and prose habits might reasonably be supposed to
intersect. In the same way it refers briefly to the relation of the
rise of literacy and the rise of prose writing in the Middle Ages.
But the chief conclusions follow from the negative inference: if
the admired composition of the Icelandic sagas has origins in
learned sources and analogues in contemporary French prose,
then it cannot be part of the oral legacy. This is as far as the
discussion of the oral background goes. The nature of the preliterary saga and its implications for the aesthetics of oral prose

are not unimportant or uninteresting subjects, but they belong to another book. The first interest of this one is not in sagas that may have been but the place in literary history of those we have.

# CHAPTER 1

# Open Composition

## The Question of Unity

Some years ago Ian Maxwell remarked that when he read a saga for the first time, he leafed through the pages trying to find where the "story" began. Only after he became acquainted with the genre did he realize that he had been looking for the wrong sort of plot: "These were different stories, with rules of their own; and although some made complex and beautiful wholes, their form was not what I should have expected in epic or novel."[1] The observation is telling, and its aptness will be appreciated by anyone who has ever tried to give a synopsis of an Icelandic family saga to a person who has no idea what a saga is. Despite claims of pure plot and economy of action, there is something peculiarly acentric and expansive about the sagas which cannot be explained away as *Stoffreude*. As Andreas Heusler put it, "The design is convoluted and unsurveyable."[2] This is most obvious in such "big" sagas as *Njáls saga* and *Eyrbyggja saga,* but it is also true, albeit it to a lesser degree, of such shorter and tighter works as *Hrafnkels saga.* Even the most biographical sagas drift away at intervals, and sometimes at dramatic length, from the hero, and tell rather of his brother or uncle, or of the affairs of his immediate adversary, or of this or that in the com-

[1]Ian Maxwell, "Pattern in *Njáls saga,*" *Saga-Book of the Viking Society,* 15 (1957–61), 17.
[2]Andreas Heusler, *Die altgermanische Dichtung,* 2d ed. rev. (Potsdam: Athenaion, 1941), p. 221.

munity; or they contain long, unorganic prologues and epilogues; or they may simply include more loose particulars about the hero than the reader of saints' lives or epic is accustomed to expect. Moreover, the tendency of a given saga to overlap matter and to share a common cast of characters with other sagas in the classical tradition is such that it is more reasonable to see the works not as self-contained entities but as interlocking parts of a larger whole. As W. P. Ker said, the sagas are "not rightly understood if they are taken only and exclusively in isolation."[3]

Critics have long been troubled by the sagas' brand of unity. It goes without saying that the sagas do not meet the classical definition, derived from the theory of Aristotle and the practice of Homer and the Greek dramatists, of a well-made narrative with a proper beginning, middle, and end; a narrative characterized by economy, simplicity, and inevitability, and with a single main action to which all parts contribute directly.[4] The sagas, Theodore M. Andersson argues, are built around conflict and proceed in six stages: introduction, conflict, climax, revenge, reconciliation, and aftermath.[5] But the conflict itself can be exceedingly proliferated, and many sagas have more than one conflict. *Eyrbyggja saga* has a sequence of ten conflicts, each one of which stands as a kind of proto-saga.[6] Guðbrandur Vigfússon explained its construction by positing eleven interpolated chapters; Sigfús Blöndal, by positing a much longer original.[7] Whatever the explanation, the result is confusion: as Heusler said, "One can read *Eyrbyggja saga,* with its 170 small octavo pages, six times and still have trouble visualizing the structure."[8] *Grettis saga* is easier to follow, but the structure of its conflict is similarly episodic and diffuse and has no dramatic center. *Vatnsdæla saga*

---

[3]W. P. Ker, *Epic and Romance: Essays on Medieval Literature,* 2d ed. (London: Macmillan, 1908; rpt. New York: Dover, 1957), p. 185.

[4]L. J. Potts, *Aristotle on the Art of Fiction* (Cambridge: Cambridge University Press, 1968), pp. 28–29.

[5]Theodore M. Andersson, *The Icelandic Family Saga: An Analytic Reading,* Harvard Studies in Comparative Literature, 28 (Cambridge, Mass.: Harvard University Press, 1967).

[6]Ibid., p. 161.

[7]From Knut Liestøl, *Upphavet til den islendske ættesaga* (Oslo: Aschehoug, 1929), p. 91.

[8]Heusler, *Die altgermanische Dichtung,* p. 221.

has its share of violence, but lacks a structural conflict and climax. The conflict in *Fóstbrœðra saga* consists of several unrelated episodes. *Víga-Glúms saga* "looks as if it were rather carelessly put together, or perhaps abridged from a fuller version," wrote Ker; "it is a biography with no strong crisis in it," one that "might have been extended indefinitely,"[9] *Hallfreðar saga* has two distinct conflicts separated by a lengthy foreign intermezzo. The conflict of *Ljósvetninga saga* is likewise doubled, the second part duplicating all the phases of the first part in order; it could just as well, in Knut Liestøl's view, be called a conglomerate as a single saga.[10] *Egils saga* has two conflicts in two generations, each one containing independently the "requisite subsections of conflict, climax, and revenge."[11] *Njáls saga* is so emphatically bipartite in construction that it was for years thought to be an amalgam of two originally separate sagas.[12]

But it was, above all, their copiousness that disqualified the sagas as unified narratives in the eyes of the early scholars, who had the classical imperatives more firmly in mind than have succeeding generations. The sagas departed so radically from the ideal of simplicity and economy that they were not considered to be "works of art" at all, but rather loose compilations. Yet even in the arguments for compilation, there emerged a certain distinction that is critical to the understanding of the sagas and to medieval narrative in general: a distinction between traditionally defined unity, which the sagas obviously lacked, and some other kind of unity, which not only held together the narrative mass but made it dramatically intelligible. "No Saga is a jumble of unrelated facts, as real life so often is," wrote Bertha Phillpotts. "There is always a pattern discernible, an effort towards a unity, and unless we are conscious of it we cannot appreciate the Saga to the full." In her view there was no single principle of unity to which the sagas in general subscribed, but different patterns in

[9]Ker, *Epic and Romance*, p. 194.

[10]Liestøl, *Upphavet*, p. 91. In his view, structural aberration is a sign of oral origins (see esp. pp. 90–93).

[11]Andersson, *Icelandic Family Saga*, p. 109.

[12]The bipartition question has been treated most recently by Lars Lönnroth, *Njáls Saga: A Critical Introduction* (Berkeley: University of California Press, 1976), pp. 7–19.

different works. The "refractory material" of *Eyrbyggja saga*, for example, is bound together by a "unity of location" and a "unity of atmosphere."[13] Vigfússon, who argued that *Njáls saga* was a loose compilation of disparate material, perceived an underlying moral design.[14] Ker found the sagas "too immersed in matter" to approximate the classical ideal, yet he, too, conceded an alternative principle (diametrically opposed to that of Phillpotts): "The best of them have that sort of unity which can hardly be described, except as a unity of life."[15] In *Njáls saga*, the perennial test case of the unity debate, this principle was "heroic design": "*Njála*, which is the greatest of all the Sagas, does not make its effect by any reduction of the weight or number of its details. It carries an even greater burden of particulars than *Eyrbyggja*; it has taken up into itself the whole history of the south country of Iceland in the heroic age. The unity of *Njála* is certainly not the unity of a restricted or emaciated heroic play. Yet with all its complexity it belongs to quite a different order of work from *Eyrbyggja*."[16] Maxwell agreed, saying of the sagas in general: "In their own way they are extremely concise and selective, but they seldom select a plot that Aristotle would have approved."[17] In his analysis of six Icelandic sagas, A. U. Bååth showed how episodes that appeared on first glance to be unrelated and superfluous were in fact relevant features of the larger plot or of the governing abstraction. On this basis he judged *Njála* to be the most unified of the sagas, for all its particulars hinged on the idea of an overriding fate: "Such was the author's mastery of the material that he may be assumed to have had the last line firmly in mind when writing the first."[18] From Bååth on, the focus has been on the various patterns and forms of coherence rather than on the traditional precepts of unity. Einar Ólafur Sveinsson has been accused of planting himself "so massively on both sides of the critical fence" of the unity issue "that simple

[13]Bertha Phillpotts, *Edda and Saga* (New York: Holt, 1931), p. 188.
[14]Cited in Maxwell, "Pattern in *Njáls saga*," p. 22.
[15]Ker, *Epic and Romance*, p. 235; see also pp. 184–89.
[16]Ibid., p. 190.
[17]Maxwell, "Pattern in *Njáls saga*," p. 19.
[18]A. U. Bååth, *Studier öfver kompositionen i några isländska ättsagor* (Lund: Gleerup, 1885), p. 159.

readers may well feel bewildered."[19] But Sveinsson has at least ventured a description of the way "unity" works in *Njáls saga:*

> It [*Njála*] has sometimes been called a biography, and more frequently the saga of a district, or even a history of the entire country. But it is none of these. *Njála* is the saga of a complex chain or network of events, and despite the author's "hunger for matter" he is careful not to include too much inappropriate material. In a biography or family saga, the individual or the family always binds together unrelated events, and the thread of the story often tends to become tenuous; in *Njáls saga,* on the other hand, it is the complex connection of events which brings together unrelated individuals.[20]

For Phillpotts, the superfluities of saga plots were only apparent and disappeared as soon as the reader grasped the narrative rules: "Most critics of the Sagas charged them with the introduction of unnecessary or irrelevant incidents. But since the Saga cannot jump backwards in time, it sometimes has to begin a long way back and introduce incidents of which the reason only becomes apparent afterwards, and then only to a reader who realizes that the Saga expects him to understand the relation between cause and effect."[21]

For Andersson, too, confusion is in the eye of the beholder:

> The saga has a brand of unity not unlike the classical injunction against the proliferation of plot in drama. . . . There is no such thing as digression. . . . All the episodes are linked in a sequence leading up to the climax of a saga or leading down from it. This is a fundamental rule and is the key to saga economy. No factor in the plot is superfluous because it either serves to explain the outcome or it derives necessarily from the outcome. Paradoxically, it is the operation of this transparent principle that allows a degree of unexplained obscurity in the plot. . . . Since [the reader] has learned by experi-

[19]Maxwell, "Pattern in *Njáls saga,*" p. 22.

[20]Einar Ólafur Sveinsson, *Njáls Saga: A Literary Masterpiece,* trans. Paul Schach (Lincoln: University of Nebraska Press, 1971), p. 54. This is an adaptation in English of *Á Njálsbúð: Bók um mikið listaverk* (Reykjavík: Hið íslenzka bókmenntafélag, 1943).

[21]Phillpotts, *Edda and Saga,* p. 176. It is hardly true that the sagas "cannot jump backwards in time," however.

ence that saga economy allows nothing superfluous, he makes a
logical connection between a given episode and the climax no matter
how disconnected and far-removed from one another they seem.[22]

The revision of the concept of unity from the classical one to a local
or specialized one is thus complete. The meaning of "unity" here
is quite different from that for a narrative in which the elements
are combined in such a way that "each concerns the other, corresponds to the other, and so depends on the other necessarily or
verisimilarly that removing any one part or changing its place
would destroy the whole,"[23] but is rather one in which the parts
can be shown to relate, however eventually, to a certain climax or
theme. The proof of necessity, in other words, has become a
proof of relevance—conceding by definition narrative copiousness and proliferation. Obviously, any story detail whose function is so obscure as to require extensive explanation is the sort of
element that disqualifies the host narrative as a unity in the classical sense.

The illusion of unity comes in part from the style of the sagas—
the language, which if it is not precisely "oral" is widely considered to be a model of simplicity and exclusion. Here the test of
necessity has some validity: every word counts, and some words,
such as adjectives, count even more than others by virtue of their
underuse. But style is not to be confused with composition. Just
because saga authors do not waste words does not mean that they
do not "waste" scenes and episodes. Nor does the natural surface syntax reflect in any way the organizational patterns of the
larger material. The discrepancy between the naive surface of the
saga and its emphatically literary composition is a basic crux of
the genre.

The illusion of unity is further fostered by the apparent
exclusions—comments to the effect that a matter will not be re-

[22]Andersson, *Icelandic Family Saga*, p. 33.
[23]Torquato Tasso, *Discorsi dell'arte poetica e del poema eroico*, ed. Luigi
Poma (Bari: Laterza, 1964); English translation by Mariella Cavalchini and Irene
Samuel, *Torquato Tasso: Discourses on the Heroic Poem* (Oxford: Clarendon,
1973), p. 78. See Aristotle, *The Poetics*, Loeb Classical Library (Cambridge,
Mass.: Harvard University Press, 1953), Book VIII.

counted because it is extraneous to the story at hand. Thus the narrator of *Eyrbyggja saga* explains:[24]

> Á þessum tímum byggðisk allr Breiðafjǫrðr, ok þarf hér ekki at segja frá þeira manna landnámum, er eigi koma við þessa sǫgu.

> (At this time all of Breiðafjǫrðr was settled; but there is no need to tell here of those people not appearing in this saga.) [chap. 6]

The beginning point of *Bjarnar saga hítdœlakappa* is justified in similar terms:

> En því get ek eigi þeira smágreina, sem milli fóru þeira Bjarnar ok Þórðar, áðr Bjǫrn kom til Skúla, at þær heyra ekki til þessarri sǫgu.

> (But I shall not relate those small matters which passed between Bjǫrn and Þórðr before the point when Bjǫrn came to Skúli, for the reason that they do not belong to this saga.) [chap. 1]

In the case of *Eyrbyggja saga,* the suggestion of formal intention strikes an especially false note, for of all the sagas it lies furthest from any discernible principle of structural unity. The discrepancy between exclusive claim and inclusive practice is also evident in *Grettis saga,* whose author pointedly refrains from recording the activities of Bishop Friðrekr in north Iceland on grounds that they are irrelevant to the saga:

> Mart bar til tíðenda um sameign þeira byskups ok Norðlendinga, þat er ekki kemr við þessa sǫgu.

> (There were many more dealings between the bishop and the men from the north, but they do not concern this saga.) [chap. 13]

The events ensuing on the deaths of Skapti Þóroddsson and Snorri goði are dismissed in similar terms:

> . . . ok mart bar til tíðenda á þessum misserum, þat sem ekki kemr við þessa sǫgu.

---

[24]These and other examples of authorial intrusion are discussed by Paul Schach, "Some Forms of Writer Intrusion in the *Íslendingasögur,*" *Scandinavian Studies,* 42 (1970), 128–56.

(... and many other events occurred that year, but they do not concern this saga.) [chap. 76]

But the same narrator does not hesitate on other occasions to insert matter no less peripheral. Interposed between the point when Grettir leaves Norway (chap. 24) and the moment when he arrives back in Iceland (chap. 28), for example, is what might be called the Sworn Brothers Interlude, a passage of three chapters describing the adventures of Þorgeirr and Þormóðr—an entertaining substory, but hardly pertinent to Grettir's own fortunes. Nor does the saga's "imbecile continuation" (as Ker termed the concluding nine chapters, the so-called *Spesar þáttr*) bespeak a particularly developed sense of aesthetic unity.[25] It may be that the *Grettla* author chose to omit the activities of Bishop Friðrekr on grounds that they had been amply dealt with elsewhere (in *Kristni saga, Þorvalds þáttr víðfǫrla,* and *Laxdæla saga*) and did not bear repeating here; explicit statements to that effect (in which the author defers to other sources) are found here and there in the larger corpus.[26] But the evidence, as a whole, does not support the idea that duplication per se caused the saga authors much alarm; one has the impression rather that territorial considerations are invoked more for the sake of narrative convenience than for any other reason.[27] From the point of view of artistic unity it makes no difference whether statements of exclusion on territorial or any other grounds are true or false; they indicate in either case a form with parameters based on principles other than aesthetic ones—a narrative lacking natural borders and capable of infinite regression into impinging matter. Claims that thus and so will not be related because it is dealt with elsewhere, or would take too long, or does not "belong" to the story at hand, are best not taken at face value, but rather seen as formulaic and arbitrary boundary markers, verbal reminders that every saga represents an individual solution to the fundamental problem of where to draw the line.

Just how far from the main point classical sagas can draw the

---

[25]Ker, *Epic and Romance,* p. 195.

[26]For further examples, see Schach, "Some Forms of Writer Intrusion," esp. pp. 139–44.

[27]See chapter 2, "Stil og varianter," in Liestøl's *Upphavet* (pp. 29–55).

line has not been sufficiently appreciated. Like other European works of imaginative prose from the same period, the sagas subscribe to a principle of open composition. The whole has no fixed shape, but is a flexible structure that can be adjusted to the needs of a particular story or the whims of an individual narrator. These adjustments may consist of deletions (as in Snorri's reworking of sources in his *Óláfs saga helga*), but they consist more commonly of additions: to the extremities in the form of preludes and sequels, and into the interstices in the form of extra details, motifs, scenes, episodes, chapters, *þættir* (short stories). This is the clear lesson of manuscript variants, of the redactions of foreign works (such as the added ending and interpolated chapter of *Erex saga*),[28] and, above all, of the kings' saga tradition, where each new version of the Óláfr biographies represents a renegotiation of the parameters of the form. The tendency toward plot proliferation is so pervasive in the sagas, including the earliest ones, that it must be assumed to be inherent in the art; certainly it is a central factor in the evolution of the form from shorter and simpler plots to longer and more complex ones. The Icelandic sagas in particular can be copious to the point of opacity, embracing sizable chunks of narrative matter which are marginal by any logic and superfluous by the traditional terms of unity. The otherwise well-integrated *Laxdæla saga,* for example, includes two lengthy elements on the slenderest of pretexts. One is the quarrel between Hǫskuldr and Hrútr (chap. 19), and the other an account of Hrappr Sumarliðason (chap. 10 and 17–18), which has been justified on grounds that it "provides information on the land where Hjarðarholt is later built, Kjartan's home and the scene of much of the saga."[29] *Reykdæla saga* contains a subplot of such dimensions that it is sometimes mentioned separately as *Skútu saga.* Chapters 14–16 of *Kormáks saga,* which recount the adventures of Bersi following his divorce from Steingerðr, have no bearing on either Kormákr's or Steingerðr's stories and may be considered a clear digression. The travels of Hallfreðr constitute an unnecessary, though not uninteresting, expansion in the plot of

[28]See Foster W. Blaisdell, "The Composition of the Interpolated Chapter in the *Erex saga,*" *Scandinavian Studies,* 36 (1964), 118–26; and Jane A. Kalinke O.P., "The Structure of the *Erex saga,*" *Scandinavian Studies,* 42 (1970), 343–55.

[29]Andersson, *Icelandic Family Saga,* p. 172.

his saga. The equivalent tour in *Gunnlaugs saga* is likewise "digressive and unintegrated . . . in structural terms, at least, an intercalation."[30] *Fóstbrœðra saga* contains a number of apparently pointless episodes (the killing of Ljótr, the Loðinn incident, the capsizing of Þormóðr's boat), superfluous characters (the foster brothers Eyjólfr and Þorgeirr, Helgi selseista, and Gestr/ Steinarr), and an unnecessary sequence involving Þormóðr's erotic entanglements (chaps. 9–11)[31]—in addition to the notorious briefer "digressions" of a learned nature, once regarded as later interpolations, but now thought to be original.[32] Nor, in *Njáls saga,* does the feud between Bergþóra and Hallgerðr, however colorful it may be as a display of temperament, have any direct consequences in the plot. The Conversion and Clontarf episodes constitute genuine digressions.

This is the sort of matter—there are many more examples—that modern plot summaries are likely to bracket or omit altogether as irrelevant to the "story." Discussions of saga form have tended to focus on main actions and key scenes and to consign the remainder to the category of deviant or unintegrated material, no matter how many pages that remainder may occupy in a given saga, and no matter how regularly such remainders crop up in text after text. However much this neoclassical approach may tell us about the narrators' sense of drama and the moral climate they are trying to evoke, it tells us next to nothing about the mechanics of proliferation and the logic of inclusion—and, by extension, the concept of a significant event and the causal chains leading up to it. It is in the structural marginalia that we are able to come to terms with the sagas' "own brand" of unity and to place Icelandic narrative art in its medieval context.

Let us look more closely at an extended passage of an intrinsically marginal nature. The passage comes from *Njáls saga* (chaps. 75–90) and may be called the Atlantic Interlude, for it involves the

---

[30]Ibid., p. 127.
[31]Ibid., pp. 191–92.
[32]See Jónas Kristjánsson, *Um Fóstbræðrasögu* (Reykjavík: Stofnun Árna Magnússonar, 1972), pp. 13–96.

foreign journeys of several men and lies between the two Icelandic halves of the saga.[33] It begins in chapter 75, with the departure from Iceland of Þráinn (story A) and Grímr and Helgi Njálsson (story B), the decision of Gunnarr to stay (story C), the departure of Kolskeggr (story D), and the arrival of Kolbeinn, whose story is quickly displaced by that of Hrappr (story E). It ends in chapter 90 with the return to Iceland of four of these men (Þráinn, Hrappr, Grímr, and Helgi), and the arrival of a fifth (Kári Sǫlmundarson). The narrative stretch between these two points can be diagramed as in the chart on page 30 (the numbers indicating the narrative order of the elements).

The rationale behind the Atlantic Interlude—that it forms a necessary nexus between Gunnarr's saga and Njáll's saga—is reflected in its component parts, each of which serves either a reflexive or an anticipatory function or both. Gunnarr's story (C) carries over from the earlier part of the saga, here rising to its climax (his slaying at Hlíðarendi), moving to a revenge (the killing of Tjǫrvi by Skarpheðinn and Hǫgni), and ending on a note of equilibrium as Njáll negotiates a settlement. Its reflexive and anticipatory relevance is self-evident and requires no further comment. The story of Kolskeggr tells how, in accordance with the terms of his outlawry, he goes abroad, and in accordance with his vow never to return to Iceland should Gunnarr die, spends the rest of his life in foreign lands, ending up in the Byzantine guard. If this biographical appendix seems unnecessary, it, too, has its reflexive function, for Kolskeggr's absence, together with those of Þráinn and the Njálssons, is construed as an immediate cause of Gunnarr's death. "Now people were saying that the district was being emptied of its best men," the author remarks in chapter 75, and again, one page later, "They all felt that it would be easy to catch Gunnarr, now that Kolskeggr and Þráinn and many other friends of his were away."

The story of Kolbeinn/Hrappr is the one that best illustrates the circumstantial logic in which sagas, above all *Njáls saga,* specialize. Hrappr first appears in the saga in a rowboat, ap-

---

[33]Cf. Lars Lönnroth's division in his *Njáls Saga,* esp. p. 24.

| | A: Þráinn | B: Grímr and Helgi | C: Gunnarr/Iceland | D: Kolskeggr | E: Hrappr/Kolbeinn |
|---|---|---|---|---|---|
| Summer I | 1. Leaves Iceland. 15. Arrives in Norway; goes to Earl Hákon's court. | 2. Leave Iceland. 21. Encounter storm at sea. 22. Fight vikings; join Sigurðr against Scots. | 3. Decides to stay in Iceland. | 4. Argues with Gunnarr; leaves. | 27. Kolbeinn comes to Iceland. |
| Autumn I | | | 5. Stays at home autumn and winter. | 10. Arrives in Norway. | " |
| Winter I | | 23. Stay winter in Orkneys. | " | 11. Stays winter in Norway. | 28. Stays winter in Breiðdalr. |
| Spring I | 17. Kolr incident. | " | 6. Declines Óláfr pá's invitation. | | " |
| Summer II | 18. Accompanies earl on trip to Sweden. | 24. Go raiding with Kári. | 7. Althing plan to attack Gunnarr. | 12. Goes to Denmark. 13. Goes to Russia. | 29. Kolbeinn takes Hrappr to Norway. Hrappr seduces Guðrún and is outlawed. |
| Autumn II | " | " | 8. Attacked and killed. | | |
| Winter II | 19. Stays winter with Earl Hákon. | 25. Stay winter with Earl Sigurðr in Orkneys. | | 14. Stays winter in Russia. Goes to Constantinople, where he stays until his death. | |
| Spring II | 20. Hears of Gunnarr's death and delays return to Iceland. | 26. Leave for Norway. | 9. His revenant is seen. Tjǫrvi killed in revenge. Njáll negotiates a settlement. | | |
| Summer III | 31. Prepares for return to Iceland. 34. Escapes with Hrappr and goes to his farm in Iceland. | 30. Trade in Norway. 33. Refuse Hrappr passage. 35. Pursued and captured by Earl Hákon. Escape and sail to Orkneys. | | | 32. Hrappr burns temple, solicits passage, stows away with Þráinn. Lives with Þráinn for a year. |
| Autumn III | | 36. Stay with Eiríkr. | | | |
| Winter III | | 37. Spend winter with Earl Sigurðr. | | | |
| Spring III | | 38. Go raiding. | | | |
| Summer IV | | 39. Return to Iceland. | | | |

proaching the departing Kolbeinn and begging passage to Norway on his ship. Kolbeinn takes him on, but when they arrive, Hrappr refuses to pay. Kolbeinn seems to exist in the saga for no other reason than to be cheated by Hrappr and to proffer the ominous advice that Hrappr never betray his master. Hrappr obliges without delay the literary law that injunctions exist only for the breaking by seducing the daughter of his mentor Guðbrandr. From that point on, his story falls like a row of dominoes. The Guðrún episode leads to Hrappr's outlawry; which leads to his desecration of the temple; which leads to his desperation to escape the country and hence the harbor incident, in which he stows away with Þráinn, leaving the Njálssons to bear the brunt of the earl's wrath; which gives rise to the Njálssons' subsequent demands for compensation; which in turn results, after some hostile byplay, in the battle at Markár, in which both Þráinn and Hrappr are killed; all of which has yet further consequences up the line in the feud plot rising toward its climax at Bergþórshváll.

The Njálssons' story (B) fits the classic Travel Pattern.[34] Grímr and Helgi leave Iceland (*útkoma*), enter into service at a foreign court (that of Sigurðr in the Orkneys), and prove their capacity for raiding, warfare, and viking fights (Tests). Their story climaxes with a capture and escape and is brought to a point of quiescence when, after their Return (*útanferð*), they settle in at Bergþórshváll. The reflexive dimension of their story lies, once again, in their absentee status with respect to Gunnarr. The anticipatory dimension lies in part in the revelation of their character during their foreign adventures (their valor, loyalty, and adherence to the heroic code), which prefigures the behavior they will display as the Icelandic part of their story unfolds. Their viking battle in chapter 84 has an additional outcome, however: it leads to the chance intervention of Kári Sǫlmundarson, which in turn results in their introduction into the service of Earl Sigurðr; which throws Kári and the Njálssons into a firm alliance; which in turn explains how he happens to accompany them to Iceland— where, of course, as the chief survivor of the climactic burning at Bergþórshváll he will move to the saga's center stage.

[34]On the Travel Pattern, see Anna Cornelia Kersbergen, *Litteraire Motieven in de Njála* (Rotterdam: Nijgh & van Ditmar's Uitgevers-Maatschappij, 1927), esp. p. 119; Joseph C. Harris, "Genre and Narrative Structure in Some *Íslendinga þættir*," *Scandinavian Studies*, 44 (1972), 1–27; and Lönnroth, *Njáls Saga*, pp. 71–76.

Þráinn's story also fits the Travel Pattern. He comes to Norway, enters the service of Earl Hákon (in which he proves his mettle by killing a renegade viking and sailing with unparalleled skill), and finally, after his narrow escape with Hrappr, returns to Iceland. The double relevance of his story deserves further comment, for it takes a particularly elegant form. Its latter half (his aiding and abetting of Hrappr both in the flight from Norway and after their arrival in Iceland) has obvious consequences in the later plot: it leads to the suit for damages and, eventually, the bloodshed at Markár. But its former half (his stay at the court of Earl Hákon in Norway) is a last, oblique reflex of the saga's first half. From the moment he arrives at Hákon's court, Þráinn is equated with his kinsman Gunnarr of Hlíðarendi. Gunnarr is mentioned by name no fewer than eight times in chapter 82, in the form of admiring comments on his prowess, fearlessness, taste for the ornate, and special place in the earl's affection. Þráinn's role is clearly that of Gunnarr's surrogate, though for just what purpose is not clear until the end of the chapter, when the reports of Gunnarr's death reach Norway:

> Þá spurðusk tíðendi af Íslandi, er mǫrgum þótti mikil: lát Gunnars frá Hlíðarenda. Þá vildi jarl eigi, at Þráinn fœri út, ok var hann með honum eptir.

> (Then from Iceland came the news, which many thought of moment, of the death of Gunnarr of Hlíðarendi. Now the earl did not want Þráinn to return to Iceland, so he stayed behind with him.) [chap. 82]

Andersson has noted the saga custom of inserting at the time of the hero's death a brief characterization of his physique, personality, or prowess.[35] Gunnarr thus gets not one such necrology, but two: an Icelandic one, on the occasion of his death, and a Norwegian one, by analogy with Þráinn, just preceding the news of his death, at the earl's court. This oblique second eulogy is as much a tribute to the *Njála* narrator's fondness for duplication as it is to Gunnarr's heroic stature.

If the Atlantic Interlude as a whole is diffuse and acentric, the individual stories it embraces are plain enough. Unraveled from its context and set together single file, each story traces a familiar plot (Gunnarr's being a Feud story, Hrappr's an Outlaw tale, and

---

[35]Andersson, *Icelandic Family Saga*, pp. 60–62.

Þráinn's and the Njálssons' Travel *þættir*) and comes to an ending of sorts. Moreover, the author has gone to some lengths to make each story temporally complete: time is reckoned by seasons, and each season is accounted for in each story. In other words, the unity that is lacking on the level of the saga as a whole is found, at least in approximate form (interweaving aside), on the level of its smaller parts (scene, episode, *þáttr*). As Ker put it: "It is in the short story, the episodic chapter, that the art of Icelandic narrative first defines itself. This is the original unity; it is here, in a limited, easily comprehensible subject-matter, that the lines are first clearly drawn. The Sagas that are least regular and connected are made up of definite and well-shaped single blocks. Many of the Sagas are much improved by being taken to pieces and regarded, not as continuous histories, but as collections of separate short stories."[36] The completeness of these stories, as well as the fact that there are not one or two but five of them and that they have been elaborately synchronized, proves the author's aesthetic intention. There is no effort to simplify the story; on the contrary, it is deliberately complicated. Plot proliferation is not only not avoided, it is actively pursued. Finally, as the following chapters emphasize, natural order is eschewed in favor of an interlace system of chance encounters and temporal correspondences. The passage that appears to the neoclassical glance to be one of the least orderly in the saga turns out, on closer inspection, to be one of the most patently contrived in the entire corpus.

It is clear, in other words, that if *Njáls saga* does not operate on a system of unity, it operates on a no less firmly defined system of coherence. Things are related not directly but circumstantially by a process that may be termed entailment: a given particular contributes not immediately to the main plot, but to another particular, which in turn contributes to one beyond that—and so on, until the narrowing sequence arrives at the central action of the story.[37] E. Ó. Sveinsson describes the process in metaphoric terms:

[36]Ker, *Epic and Romance*, p. 189.

[37]The structural logic of the sagas is captured in the Mother Goose rhyme that traces the relation between the kingdom and the horseshoe nail. See Iona and Peter Opie, eds., *The Oxford Dictionary of Nursery Rhymes* (Oxford: Clarendon, 1951), p. 324. See also C. M. Bowra, *Heroic Poetry* (New York: St. Martin's Press, 1964), p. 350.

From beginning to end *Njála* is an articulated, unified complex of events, all of which precipitate others. The initial impulse is not a single event, but many individual and originally unrelated events which appear somehow to be harmless and insignificant. Each one draws its nourishment from its own roots and its own soil. It grows and develops, and soon sends out shoots which take root far from their point of origin, and then become entwined and entangled with other unrelated events. Through this a new course of events is initiated, which acquires a new content and a new direction through contact with other apparently unrelated and innocuous events, and thus the saga continues.[38]

The underlying fascination is with the possibility of infinite regression, and the graphic form is the result of what Ian Maxwell called the "principle of the integrity of episodes," by which something considered worth reporting at all is worth recording in full scenic detail: "Sagas prefer to deal with whole episodes, not pieces or aspects or reflections of them."[39] The same can be said of characters: sagas prefer to give prehistories and outcomes even to lesser figures. The impulse to give prehistories can be seen clearly in the case of Hrappr in *Njáls saga*. Hrappr's first significant appearance is in chapter 88, when his role as a stowaway precipitates the harbor incident. But the author is not content to let an unknown character rush out of the woods. We must first learn of his desecration of the temple, and before that his seduction of Guðrún, and before that his cheating of Kolbeinn out of his fare after approaching him in a rowboat and begging to be taken aboard, and before that—but here the scenic treatment ends and the narrator simply reports the bare facts—that he was the son of a certain Ǫrgumleiði and that he had killed a man. This cutoff point is, of course, entirely arbitrary, presumably dictated by symmetrical concerns: as it stands, Hrappr's entry into the saga as a fugitive from Iceland prefigures his dramatic flight from the Norwegian authorities. But the author was at least theoretically free to pursue Hrappr's story even further back—to his birth, perhaps, or to the life and times of his parents or grandparents.

    This is the logic of embedded *þættir:* a side character's story, or

[38]Sveinsson, *Njáls Saga,* p. 54.
[39]Maxwell, "Pattern in *Njáls saga,*" p. 25.

an incidental happening, is rendered in such complete terms that it constitutes a separable subplot. So, for example, *Sǫrla þáttr, Vǫðu-Brands þáttr*, and *Ófeigs þáttr* in *Ljósvetninga saga*. The relation of *þættir* to the sagas is a vexed question with a long history in saga scholarship. It will suffice here to point out that the separability of *þættir*—the fact that they appear either in the immediate context of a family saga or in the context of a later compilation—documents their semi-independent status and, more important, demonstrates that no matter how neatly they may be integrated into their host narrative, they constitute distinct and lengthy structural digressions.

It is in light of these patterns that the encyclopedic phenomenon of the late saga period is properly viewed. Far from being a thing apart from the Icelandic sagas, *Flateyjarbók* is their logical extension—a hypertrophied example of the techniques so much admired in their moderate, "classical" form. *Flateyjarbók* consists in the main of two biographies, the *Longest Saga of Óláfr Tryggvason* and an expanded version of the *Óláfs saga helga*, each of which has been rendered, the preface says, in its most saturated form:

> þar næst fra Olaafi konungi Tryggua syni medr ollum sinum þaatum. þui næst er sagha Olafs konungs hins helga Haralldz sunar med ollum sinum þaattum ok þar med sǫgur Orkneyia jarla.

(Next [is told the saga] of King Óláfr Tryggvason with all its *þættir;* next is the saga of King Óláfr Haraldsson the Saint with all its *þættir,* including the sagas of the Orkney earls.) [*Flateyjarbók,* preface]

There are inserted into the royal biographies no fewer than forty-eight detachable substories, many known from other sources, ranging from brief wholesale entries or *þættir* (e.g., *Sǫrla þáttr* and *Rauðúlfs þáttr*) to saga-length narratives interspersed nonconsecutively in the longer text (e.g., *Fóstbrœðra saga, Hallfreðar saga*, and *Jómsvíkinga saga*). These intercalations account for about 350 of the 550 pages of the *Longest Saga* and some 300 of the 520 pages of *Óláfs saga helga*.

The logic of inclusion is clearly that of entailment: whatever item bears or can be brought to bear, no matter how distantly or

obliquely, on the royal biography, is included. Some of the substories are extended anecdotes of a semi-independent nature in
which the king himself figures as a secondary figure (e.g., *Nornagests þáttr*), but others are tangential to the biography and involve, rather, political developments in the Orkneys or the life
and adventures of certain lesser figures. The skald Hallfreðr, for
example, is the subject of a piecemeal digression whose dimensions (37 pages) and form are such that it amounts to a separate
saga—and is preserved as such elsewhere. Hallfreðr's relation to
the *Longest Saga* is, therefore, much the same as that of Þráinn
to *Njáls saga;* and in like wise the relation of *Fóstbrœðra saga* to
*Óláfs saga helga* is much the same as the Sworn Brothers Interlude to *Grettis saga*. The difference is one of degree, not kind.
*Flateyjarbók* gives complete and detailed renditions of these pendant stories, which for that reason stand out all the more clearly
as intercalations, whereas the Icelandic sagas tend to summarize
and subordinate them in such a way as to ameliorate the impression of outright digression (although the Atlantic Interlude clearly
documents the story-within-a-story impulse at the classical saga
stage, for the *Njála* narrator has pursued the threads much more
fully than the larger story warrants).

The narrative brinkmanship of the *Longest Saga* is acknowledged outright:

> N<V>þo at margar ræður ok fra sagnir se skrifadar iþessu mali. þær
> er eigi þickia miök til heyra sögu Olafs konungs TryGva sonar þa þarf
> þat eigi at vndraz. þviat sva sem rennandi vötn fliota af ymissvm vpp
> sprettum. ok koma oll i einn stað niðr. til þeirar sömu likingar hafa
> þessar fra sagnir af ymisligv vpp hafi eitt endimark at ryðia til þeira
> at burða sem Olafr konungr verðr við staddr eðr menn hans. sva sem
> enn man synaz iþvi er eptir feR.

> (Now it is not to be wondered at that many of the tales and stories
> written here seem not to belong to the saga of Óláfr Tryggvason. For
> just as running water flows from various sources yet all comes to-
> gether in a single place, so, in like wise, do all these stories from
> various sources have a common goal—to clear the way for those
> events which concern King Óláfr and his men, as will become ap-
> parent in what follows.) [chap. 177]

The "network of streams" metaphor is of some historical interest, as I shall suggest in chapter 6, for it appears in one of those parts of the *Longest Saga* (chap. 177) attributed to Gunnlaugr Leifsson, in which case the original referent was a Latin biography from the late twelfth century.[40] In any event, it stands as a metaphorical description of the proliferating patterns of entailment that we find in varying degrees in saga literature as a whole. Not only the body of the saga but also its beginning and ending are subject to expansion by means of entailment. Andersson noted the tendency of the introduction and aftermath sections in particular to "admit various marginalia," becoming "biographical and even antiquarian": "This is apparently not owing to some lapse in the author's art, since introduction and conclusion are ubiquitous and are somehow felt to be necessary adjuncts to saga form. No saga is without a prologue (except the imperfect manuscript of *Heiðarvíga saga*) and only three sagas conclude without affixing some sort of nonfunctional epilogue (*Bjarnar saga, Reykdæla saga,* and *Valla-Ljóts saga*)."[41] It is no surprise that these introductions tend to have the character of regressive sequences—backward extension into the history of the family even into previous generations. Some are brief and consist only of report narrative, but others are prolonged and scenic and amount to separable substories. *Fóstbrœðra saga* begins with the dramatic account of Þorbjǫrg's bold intervention on behalf of Grettir Ásmundarson, who is thus saved from the gallows. The episode, also told in *Grettis saga,* is inorganic and may be an interpolation (it is not found in all manuscripts); but whether it is original or an early addition, it tells us something about the thirteenth-century attitude toward beginning a saga with dramatic matter unrelated to the main story and involving characters other than the principals. The same pattern holds for *Laxdœla saga,* the first seven chapters of which are devoted to the life and adventures of Unnr in djúpúðga. Her ostensible connection with the main saga is genealogical: two of the major heroes, Kjartan and Bolli, count

---

[40]Bjarni Aðalbjarnarson, *Om de norske kongers sagaer,* Skrifter utgitt af Det Norske Videnskaps-Akademie i Oslo, II, hist.-fil. kl., vol. 2 (1936), 104.
[41]Andersson, *Icelandic Family Saga,* p. 26.

her as an ancestor by marriage. But this relationship hardly explains the narrative detail devoted to her story and in particular to her remarkable death scene. It seems, rather, that the author has elected to tell her story for its own sake. The result is a miniature biography of semi-independent status which stands as a preface to the longer saga.[42] Another prefatory subplot, though not precisely a genealogical one, is the story of Hrútr and Unnr at the beginning of *Njáls saga*. Its connection with Gunnarr's saga is clear enough: it introduces Hallgerðr, Hrútr's kinswoman and Gunnarr's future wife; and it brings Unnr, after her divorce, to Gunnarr for help in recovering her dowry. Yet the story is considerably overdeveloped in proportion to its actual function. The author appears yet again to have pursued it for its own sake and for its proleptic value on the question of failed marriages. Thus the bipartite *Njáls saga* has a presaga in the Hrútr/Unnr story and a sequel of sorts in the Kári story.

*Ljósvetninga saga* offers a similar example. It, too, is bipartite, distributing two major climax plots over two generations (the first between Guðmundr and the Ljósvetningar, the second between Eyjólfr and the Ljósvetningar), and it, too, has a prefatory subplot: a tale involving the two brothers Sǫlmundr and Sǫxólfr, who are outlawed for bad behavior, go to Norway, return to Iceland in hope of reinstatement, and are overtaken in an ambush that results in the deaths of Sǫlmundr and one of his assailants. The subplot is clearly cultivated for its own sake and comes to an end with the mediation of the case. After this clear pause, the saga proper—that is, the first climax plot, having to do with Guðmundr and the Ljósvetningar—commences.

In *Egils saga*, an entire generational saga is played out before Egill is born, one-third of the way into the narrative. This tale centers on his uncle Þórólfr, who dies at the hands of the king and is avenged by Skallagrímr and Kveld-Úlfr (Egill's father and grandfather), who then flee to Iceland and establish a family there. The relation of this plot to the second plot, Egill's own

---

[42]"By the energy of the story of Kjartan, the early story of Laxdale is thrown back and left behind as a mere prelude, in spite of its length," wrote Ker (*Epic and Romance*, p. 192).

story, is well known. The genetic opposition between the
brothers Skallagrímr and Þórólfr is duplicated in Egill and Þórólfr
Skallagrímsson in such a way as to prefigure not only the nature
of the fraternal relationship in the second generation, but also
their differing fates: the royalist brother dies, whereas the indi-
vidualist brother, Egill, survives to an advanced age, as had his
father and grandfather before him. The "shape" of *Egils saga*—
bipartite saga, or presaga plus main saga—is in the eye of the
beholder. But in either case we are dealing with two complete,
distinct, and structurally duplicate narrative entities.

It is particularly instructive to look at the two cases where
variant beginnings have been preserved—or, rather, where later
authors have tried to improve on existing versions of certain
sagas by supplying more elaborate prologues.[43] One such example is *Brandkrossa þáttr*, which is an elaboration on the beginning
of *Droplaugarsona saga*. The original beginning is itself an unorganic subplot involving the antecedents of Helgi Droplaugarson;
the *Brandkrossa þáttr* simply compounds the situation by adding
certain information about the antecedents of Helgi Ásbjarnar-
son. The second example is more drastic, for it involves the generation of an entire saga, *Þorsteins saga hvíta*, out of a very brief
preface in the standard version of *Vápnfirðinga saga*. *Þorsteins
saga hvíta* is thus in medieval terms a product of cyclic composition, and in modern terms a spin-off.

The sagas' tendency toward plot proliferation is even more
pronounced in the epilogues. By Andersson's count, twenty-one
of twenty-four family sagas affix some sort of nonfunctional
epilogue.[44] Many of these (e.g., *Fóstbrœðra saga*, *Hallfreðar
saga*, *Heiðarvíga saga*, and *Þorsteins saga hvíta*) involve later
adventures in the lives of the heroes. Others recount adventures
in the lives of other characters, for example, the last chapter of
*Gunnlaugs saga*, in which Helga marries a second husband and
dies on his breast. The last twenty-eight chapters of *Njáls saga*
are devoted to Kári Sǫlmundarson, and although they play out

[43]For an analysis of the motivation behind the attachment of prologues and
sequels, see Kathryn Hume, "Beginnings and Endings in the Icelandic Family
Sagas," *Modern Language Review*, 68 (1973), esp. 593–606.
[44]Andersson, *Icelandic Family Saga*, p. 26.

the revenge and reconciliation phases of the larger plot, they are protracted to a degree that invites separate consideration as Kári's saga.

The most notorious continuation is the elaborate one of *Grettis saga,* in which Þorsteinn goes first to Norway and then to Constantinople in pursuit of his brother's slayer. He finds him, kills him, and is imprisoned for the deed. At this point the revenge phase is complete and a new plot involving illicit romance initiated: Þorsteinn is ransomed by the married lady Spes and becomes her lover. After some fabliaulike episodes involving narrow escapes from a suspicious husband, an equivocal oath borrowed from the Tristan legend, and a subsequent divorce, Þorsteinn and Spes marry and return to Norway. At the end of their lives they make a pilgrimage to Rome and die there as Christian penitents. The link connecting this frivolous romance plot with the sober tragedy of the saga proper is, of course, the figure of Þorsteinn. *Spesar þáttr* thus stands in the same relation to *Grettis saga* as Kári's story does to *Njáls saga,* Bolli Bollason's story (*Bolla þáttr*) to *Laxdœla saga,* and Jǫkull Búason's story (*Jǫkuls þáttr Búasonar*) to *Kjalnesinga saga:* a secondary character (son or brother of the hero or survivor of the climax) moves to center stage and becomes the subject of a sequel. The force of the sequel tendency is indirectly confirmed in the Norse translation of *Perceval.* Chrétien's poem, which weaves the parallel stories of Perceval and Gawain, breaks off in the midst of a Gawain portion. The Norse redactor has solved the problem by casting the story up to verse 6518 as *Parcevals saga* (supplying a brief ending), and then appending the dangling Gawain adventure as a separate *Valvers þáttr* (supplying both a beginning and an ending). However whimsical this procedure may seem from the point of view of the original tale, it is fully explicable in terms of the classical saga practice of casting secondary biographies as sequels.

The saga ending is thus the analogue of the saga beginning: the one elaborates the careers of ancestors and the other the careers of progeny or other surviving kin. If to these extremities are added further genealogical lists, as is commonly done, the result, in the case of the family sagas, is a span of history connecting the

present-day audience with its premigration point of origin.[45] The
exercise is realized most completely in the kings' saga tradition.
Structurally, *Heimskringla* is a "saga" in which each generational stage in the backward and forward extensions from the
center, *Óláfs saga helga*, is itself amplified to full-saga status,
*Ynglinga saga* standing at the head as the ultimate genealogical
list into mythic antiquity. This analytic picture of *Heimskringla*
in fact accords with what we know about its evolution.

It is by now clear that no Icelandic saga conforms to the Aristotelian concept of unity and that the best of them, *Njáls saga,* is
the least unified of all. Indeed, to measure the sagas against the
classical model is something of a negative exercise. But to discern
what a work is not is also a way of clarifying what it is. The sagas
seem not to favor simple structure, but lean toward compound
forms and bipartite forms in particular. They are characterized
not by simplicity and "one action" but by multiplicity and plot
proliferation. A large proportion of their material is included not
for its actual plot value, but for its reflexive or anticipatory value.
The idea of natural order is violated regularly and deliberately in
the interweaving of stories. The sagas lack fixed beginning and
ending points, but accumulate preludes and sequels. Moreover,
for all their individual "completeness," the sagas share characters, dovetail matter, and refer and defer to one another in a way
that suggests that they were not conceived as self-contained
wholes but as interrelated or interdependent members of a larger
undertaking—the dramatic chronicle of the Icelandic settlement
period in the case of the family sagas ("the Commonwealth
makes one epic out of the multiplicity of Sagas"[46]) and the history
of the Norwegian dynasty in the case of the kings' sagas. They
resemble, in short, the category Aristotle disparaged as the very
antithesis of proper epic: history. "A history has to give an account not of one action, but of a single period and everything that
happened during it to one or more persons, no matter how disconnected the several events may have been."[47] When epic displays the characteristics of history, it is bad epic.

[45]See Hume, "Beginnings and Endings," esp. pp. 604–6.
[46]Phillpotts, *Edda and Saga*, p. 149.
[47]Aristotle, *Poetics*, part 4.

## The European Context

Bad epic, from the point of view of the neo-Aristotelians, was a specialty of the Middle Ages. Although longer literary forms were cultivated on a wide scale during the medieval period (prose as well as poetry, romance and hagiography as well as epic), they were constructed according to a set of rules having nothing to do with the Homeric standard. The extent to which the neoclassicists were cognizant of this set of rules is unclear; although there is implicit in the Tasso-Ariosto controversy a recognition that the barbarisms of medieval epic were not random or idiosyncratic but patterned and consistent, the ad hominem and generally negative quality of the debate was not conducive to an assessment of the earlier practice on its own terms. Only in recent decades have literary historians systematically identified the peculiar attributes of medieval narrative. Particularly relevant to the case of the Icelandic saga are their observations about compound structure, amplification, and cyclic composition.

*Compound structure.* It has been proposed that medieval narrative can be classified in three roughly chronological groups: simple, compound, and complex.[48] Simple structure is best seen in the shorter forms (the Breton *lais,* the fabliaux) and does not concern us here. A compound work is one which has more than one integral part. Bipartition has long been recognized as a favored form in medieval works,[49] and its frequent and artful use by the ablest writers of the period suggests that it was not accidental, but "a standard structural device whose esthetic propriety was in some sense taken for granted."[50] An early and obvious example

---

[48]William W. Ryding, *Structure in Medieval Narrative* (The Hague: Mouton, 1971), pp. 162–68.

[49]See, e.g., W. T. H. Jackson, *The Literature of the Middle Ages* (New York: Columbia University Press, 1960), pp. 56–57 and 108–9. Intentional bipartition in *Beowulf* was first argued by J. R. R. Tolkien, "*Beowulf:* The Monsters and the Critics," *Proceedings of the British Academy,* 22 (1936), esp. 271–72; rpt. in Lewis E. Nicholson, ed., *An Anthology of Beowulf Criticism* (Notre Dame: University of Notre Dame Press, 1963), esp. pp. 81–83; in *Perceval* by Wilhelm Kellermann, "Aufbaustil und Weltbild Chrestiens von Troyes im Percevalroman," *Beihefte zur Zeitschrift für romanische Philologie,* 88 (1936), esp. 94–95; and in the Alexis biography by Ernst Robert Curtius, "Zur Interpretation des Alexiusliedes," *Zeitschrift für romanische Philologie,* 56 (1936), esp. p. 124.

[50]Ryding, *Structure in Medieval Narrative,* p. 116.

is *Beowulf*, where one part tells a coherent story of his heroic youth in the service of a king and the other part a coherent story of his own career as king. The shape, as William W. Ryding puts it, is that of a dumbbell: two halves connected by a brief nexus (in this case very brief, the transition being accomplished in ten lines).[51] Another early example is the eleventh-century *Vie de Saint Alexis,* which falls into symmetrical halves with the hero's death marking the transition.[52] The Middle High German *Spielmannsepik* tends toward bipartition;[53] *König Rother* in particular falls into halves (possibly influenced by the split structure of the *Aeneid*).[54] The *Nibelungenlied* is obviously bipartite, the first half (sts. 1-1142) telling of Siegfried and ending with his death and the second half (sts. 1143-2379) relating the fall of the Burgundians; Kriemhilt's marriage to Etzel forms a brief transition. The pattern by which the death of a young hero serves at the same time to end one epic action and to begin a second one, a revenge phase, can also be seen in the Oxford *Roland* and in the *Chanson de Guillaume* (both of which have been suspected of being amalgams of two originally independent stories). According to Ryding, the idea is "to concentrate misfortune at the center and then make the sequel a violent retaliation against those responsible for the misfortune."[55] In addition, the first halves of both the *Roland* and the *Guillaume* focus on young, impetuous heroes (Roland and Vivien), whereas their second halves focus on the older and wiser statesmen who serve as their mentors (Charlemagne, Guillaume). Thus while the two parts are structurally independent, they are thematically connected and form a diptych. In *Tristan* the diptych is generational. It has been suggested that the story in its original form had only to do with Tristan and Isolde[56] and that an unknown adapter added a parental prelude telling of the ro-

---

[51]Ibid., p. 112.
[52]See Curtius, "Zur Interpretation des Alexiusliedes," pp. 117–18; and A. G. Hatcher, "The Old French Poem Saint Alexis: A Mathematical Demonstration," *Traditio,* 8 (1952), 156.
[53]See Walter Johannes Schröder, *Spielmannsepik,* Sammlung Metzler (Stuttgart: Metzler, 1967), pp. 33–34 and 47–49; also Jackson, *Literature of the Middle Ages,* pp. 108–9.
[54]See Ryding, *Structure in Medieval Narrative,* p. 135.
[55]Ibid., p. 125.
[56]See Friedrich Ranke, *Tristan und Isold* (Munich: Bruckmann, 1925), p. 6.

mance of Rivalen and Blanchefleur, their marriage, and the death of Blanchefleur during the birth of Tristan, whose name and destiny reflect the pain of his entry into the world. But it is in Chrétien's works that the diptych idea gets a pointedly moral application. A clear example is *Cligès,* the first third of which tells the story of the inarticulate romance of Alexander and Soredamors, leading to their marriage and the birth of a son, Cligès, and concluding with their death. The second two-thirds tells of Cligès's life and adventures—including, most centrally, his love for, and eventual marriage to, Fénice. By putting the stories of Soredamors and Fénice side by side, Chrétien appears to be making a point about the proper relation of love and marriage—in contradistinction to *Tristan,* on which it is visibly calqued.[57] Here the genealogical diptych is a device by which the juxtaposition of structurally independent narratives confers a special significance on the whole.[58]

That such constructions were not accidental but deliberate seems clear from the fact that there are so many of them, they account for some of the first-class narratives of the period, they are found over the generic range (heroic epic, saints' lives, romance), and such masters as Chrétien appear to have remolded unipartite sources into compound structures. The existence of monocentric, well-made forms (particularly the fabliaux and the Breton *lais*) makes all the more pointedly obvious the doubling and trebling tendencies of the longer genres. From the point of view of the literary aesthetic, it is immaterial whether the compound structure of, for example, the *Chanson de Guillaume* is original or the result of reworking or amalgamation.

The relevance of the bipartite aesthetic to the sagas is self-evident. If, as has been argued, a revenge plot is by definition bipartite,[59] then bipartition is a given of the Icelandic family

---

[57]The view that *Cligès* was conceived as a rebuttal to *Tristan* has been urged by Jean Frappier, *Chrétien de Troyes: L'homme et l'œuvre,* Connaissance des lettres, 50 (Paris: Hatier-Boivin, 1957), pp. 107–8; and Anthime Fourrier, *Le courant réaliste dans le roman courtois en France au moyen-âge* (Paris: Nizet, 1960), I, 112–78.

[58]On the genealogical diptych in the context of medieval rhetorical writings, see Edmond Faral, *Les arts poétiques du XIIe et du XIIIe siècle: Recherches et documents sur la technique littéraire du moyen âge* (Paris: Champion, 1958), p. 60.

[59]Ryding, *Structure in Medieval Narrative,* p. 126.

sagas, for like the *Nibelungenlied* they typically develop post-climactic matter into subplots of independent dimensions. The protagonist dies; his death initiates a fresh plot in which a new protagonist undertakes a fresh action; this in turn rises to another climax. However naturally the revenge plots may seem to follow on the climaxes of *Hrafnkels saga, Reykdœla saga, Valla-Ljóts saga, Bandamanna saga* (M version), *Hávarðar saga ísfirðings, Grettis saga, Fóstbrœðra saga,* and above all *Laxdœla saga,* they are in fact in structural terms second stories—stories, moreover, that often duplicate in briefer compass the phases of the preceding or "main" story. In the case of *Grettis saga,* the independent character of the revenge plot is underscored by the geographical relocation to Constantinople and a shift of modal gears from heroic to romantic.

The case for inherent bipartition by virtue of subject matter might be arguable were the sagas otherwise simple in their structure. But reflexive doublets (along with other kinds of symmetrical multiplication clearly intended to create meaningful juxtapositions) are too frequent a feature on all levels of the saga for us to doubt the existence of an underlying aesthetic. On the level of scene, the tendency toward doubling is clear (to return to the Atlantic Interlude) in the two Gunnarr necrologies (one direct, one reflexive) and in the story of Hrappr, twice an outlaw and twice a stowaway. Reflexive doublets and symmetrical series are a particular specialty of *Njáls saga* (e.g., the three slaps in Hallgerðr's three marriages), but they are by no means restricted to it. In *Gísla saga* the murders of Vésteinn and Þorgrímr are neatly counterpoised versions of one another, as are the ceremonial acts performed at both funerals (at Vésteinn's funeral, Þorgrímr ties Hel shoes on the dead man, saying, "If these come untied, I don't know how to tie Hel shoes," and at Þorgrímr's funeral, Gísli heaves a boulder onto the burial ship, saying, "If the weather loosens this, I don't know how to anchor ships"). The manneristic use of contrasts, proleptic dreams, echo scenes, and sequential repetitions in *Laxdœla saga* is well known and needs no elaboration. The elements of parallel, contrast, and repetition are also exploited in *Gunnlaugs saga,* notably in the scene in which Gunnlaugr and Hrafn engage in a poetic competition in front of the king of Sweden, each commenting on the other's performance.[60] In *Heiðarvíga saga* there is a curious pattern whereby a series of standard preparatory activities (reconnaissance, arming, strategic planning, enlisting of allies, harangues in the form of taunts, and provisioning) is rendered not once but twice, the first time briefly and the second time emphatically and in a different order.[61]

Compounding occurs also on the level of larger phases, in particular those saga parts designated by Andersson as the conflict and revenge. *Laxdœla saga* has not one but two lengthy revenges (i.e., revenge and counterrevenge) in which the second echoes and duplicates themes or features of the first. In the same way, *Hallfreðar saga* and *Kormáks saga* have double conflicts. In *Grettis saga, Eyrbyggja saga,* and *Bjarnar saga hítdœlakappa,* the conflict is further multiplied into a chain of episodes in which none takes precedence over others; they are polycentric. The six "parts" of the saga are thus best seen not as fixed structural entities, but as "moves" subject to considerable protraction and multiform variation, in which bipartition is the rule and further multiplication a possibility.

Doubling on yet a larger scale is seen in *Ljósvetninga saga, Egils saga,* and *Njáls saga.* In *Ljósvetninga saga,* the story is distributed over two generations so that there are two conflicts, two climaxes, two vengeances, and two reconciliations—a very nearly doubled plot. In *Egils saga* the doubling is complete and has the form of a diptych. There are, in structural terms, two distinct sagas: one focusing on the father and set in Norway, the other focusing on the son and set mostly in Iceland. What is noteworthy here is not the mere fact of bipartition, but the fact—as in *Cligès* and *Tristan*—that the two parts comment on each other in such a way as to give rise to an abstract idea or meaning that embraces both of them and gives special depth to the second. The individualist/loyalist opposition between Skallagrímr and Þórólfr reasserts itself, with much the same results, in Egill and Þórólfr. In light of the history of the first generation, the outcome in the second generation is a foregone conclusion, with the repetition indicating the author's intentionality.

---

[60]Andersson (*Icelandic Family Saga,* pp. 43–49) gives other examples of such symmetries.
[61]Ibid., pp. 47–48 and 150–51.

The most impressively bipartite of the saga is, of course, *Njáls saga*. Here it is not a question of a generational diptych, but of a double social tragedy. The pattern is strikingly like that of the *Roland* and the *Guillaume*: a younger, brasher hero comes to an untimely end and is replaced, in the narrative eye, by an older, wiser, statesman figure. Here, too, the shape is that of a dumbbell, with the Atlantic Interlude serving as the joining nexus. Further, the two halves stand in a diptych relation to one another, each commenting on the other either directly or indirectly. The thematic reciprocity throughout is perhaps most pointedly illustrated in the climactic sequences: the attack on Gunnarr at Hlíðarendi and the attack on Njáll and his family at Bergþórshváll. The attackers at Hlíðarendi are frustrated time after time in their attempts to overcome Gunnarr with arms, and Mǫrðr Valgarðsson proposes that they set fire to the house instead.[62] Gizurr replies, "That shall never happen, even if I knew my own life depended on it." After another unsuccessful sally, Mǫrðr repeats his suggestion and Gizurr his refusal: "I don't know why you insist on something that no one else wants; that shall never happen." But if Mǫrðr was about to urge his incendiary solution yet a third time, he is cut short by a sudden reversal of circumstances: Þorbrandr succeeds in slashing Gunnarr's bowstring, and it is only a matter of time before they bring him down. When, similarly thwarted in his efforts to overcome Njáll and his family by arms alone, Flosi announces in ringing tones his decision to attack with fire, he completes the epic triad that has been left conspicuously open-ended for the space of 150 pages:

> "Eru nú tveir kostir, ok er hvárrgi góðr: sá annarr at hverfa frá, ok er þat várr bani, en hinn annarr at bera at eld ok brenna þá inni, ok er þat þó stór ábyrgð fyrir guði, er vér erum kristnir sjálfir. En þó munu vér þat bragðs taka."

> ("We now have two choices, neither of them good: one is to turn back, and that would mean our own death, and the other is to attack with fire and burn them to death indoors, and that is a great respon-

---

[62]Lönnroth (*Njáls Saga*, pp. 199–200) takes the proposal to attack Gunnarr with fire in chapter 77 as evidence that the medieval audience already knew in detail the story of the Bergþórshváll burning.

sibility before God, since we ourselves are Christians. But this is the
course we must take.") [chap.

128]

Whether Flosi has the Hlíðarendi attack immediately in mind is
not clear, but the analogy is certainly foremost in the minds of
Njáll and Skarpheðinn:

"Þat mun ekki," segir Njáll, "ok vil ek, at menn gangi inn, því at illa
sóttisk þeim Gunnarr at Hlíðarenda, ok var hann einn fyrir. Eru hér
hús rammlig, sem þar váru, ok munu þeir eigi sótt geta." "Þetta er
ekki þann veg at skilja," segir Skarpheðinn; "Gunnar sóttu heim
þeir hǫfðingjar, er svá váru vel at sér, at heldr vildu frá hverfa en
brenna hann inni. En þessir munu sœkja oss með eldi, ef þeir megu
eigi annan veg, því at þeir munu allt til vinna, at yfir taki við oss.
Munu þeir þat ætla, sem eigi er ólíkligt, at þat muni þeira bani, ef oss
dregr undan."

("I don't think so," says Njáll, "and I want everyone to go indoors,
because they had great difficulty overcoming Gunnarr at Hlíðarendi,
and he was one against many. The buildings here are just as strong
as the ones there, and they won't be able to overcome us." "That's
not the way to look at it," says Skarpheðinn. "The chieftains who
attacked Gunnarr at his home were of such excellent character that
they would rather turn back than burn him to death indoors. But
these men will attack us with fire if they cannot defeat us in any
other way, because they will do anything to gain the upper hand
against us. They perceive, as well they might, that if any of us
survives, it will be their death.") [chap. 128]

The reference forward from Hlíðarendi to Bergþórshváll was implicit, but the reverse reference, from Bergþórshváll to
Hlíðarendi, is overt and fully conscious, enunciated by the
characters themselves. If either climax is read without reference
to the other, the question is simply a literal one of whether or not
to attack with fire. But taken together, they bring into focus the
opposition on which the saga as a whole is constructed: between
morality according to a traditional code of personal honor on one
hand, and a pragmatic social consciousness on the other. Njála's
special richness grows out of the ironic playing on this opposition.
The traditional code requires the pursuit of honor to the last resort; but the last resort in the pursuit of honor, burning, is dishon-
orable. The honor code kills the most honorable; solutions that by

the traditional terms are least honorable (compromise, the payment and acceptance of recompense whether it seems immediately equitable or not) are finally the only socially tenable ones. As in *Egils saga,* and medieval bipartite narrative in general, the whole of *Njáls saga* is greater than the sum of its two parts. Aesthetically, it makes no difference whether the bipartition is original (as we assume is the case in *Egla*) or the result of artful amalgamation (as has been argued in the case of *Njála*). The result in either case is a two-part structure in which the two parts stand in a double-reflex arrangement that confers an abstract "meaning" on the whole. As Vinaver wrote of a similar arrangement in the *Prose Lancelot,* "once the two events become simultaneously present in our minds, each acquires an added depth through the other and their interaction brings to the fore, as no other device could have done, the underlying tragic theme."[63]

*Amplification.*   One of the chief differences between classical and medieval treatises on the art of poetry is the insistence of the latter on amplification.[64] "Amplification is the heart of the matter; it is the principal function of the writer," says Edmond Faral in reference to the rhetorical documents of the twelfth and thirteenth centuries.[65] It is a commonplace that the medieval author did not conceive of his or her task as creating fresh stories, but of finding and improving old ones. Of her own literary originality, Christine de Pizan wrote: "Architects and masons do not make the stones and other material they use for their buildings, nor do embroiderers make their silk and gold. What counts is the imagination that enables the artist to use the materials."[66] Whatever

[63] Eugène Vinaver, *The Rise of Romance* (New York: Oxford University Press, 1971), p. 85.

[64] The rhetoricians pay lip service to brevity as a narrative virtue, but treat amplification in greater length and in more enthusiastic tones. Geoffrey of Vinsauf's *Poetria nova,* for example, devotes 470 lines to amplification but only 40 to abbreviation. The bias is reflected in literary practice. Abbreviation "does not appear to be of much interest to vernacular literature, not only because not all the methods it recommends are applicable, but also because brevity is seldom sought after," writes Faral (*Les arts poétiques,* p. 85).

[65] Faral, *Les arts poétiques,* p. 61; pp. 60–85 are devoted to the techniques of amplification.

[66] From Enid McLeod, *The Order of the Rose: The Life and Ideas of Christine de Pizan* (London: Chatto & Windus, 1976), p. 103.

else improvement may have entailed in the individual case, it also involved, as a matter of course, increasing the material, sometimes by several fold. The *Aliscans* is more than twice as long (8,500 verses) as its predecessor, the *Chanson de Guillaume* (3,554 verses), which may itself have been put together from shorter pieces. Benoît de Sainte-Maure turned about 30 pages of Dares's prose history of Troy into a verse romance of 30,000 octosyllables. Marie de France's *Lai du Fresne,* 534 verses in length, is blown up into a full-scale romance (*Galeran de Bretagne*), 7,812 verses in length.[67] The growth phenomenon is best known from the Arthurian tradition (*Perceval,* for example), where shorter and simpler stories are reworked (in German as well as French versions) into longer and more complex ones, which are in turn finally woven together into the compilations of the thirteenth century.

One of the chief ways shorter texts were turned into longer ones was simply by adding blocks of new material either onto the ends of the story or into its middle. But there were also finer internal processes by which matter was amplified along horizontal lines. Of the amplification devices recommended by the medieval rhetoricians, digression is the one of which "the Middle Ages made lavish use."[68] It was advocated in particular by Martianus Capella, Cassiodorus, Geoffrey of Vinsauf, and John of Garland.[69] Digression "expands and adorns the matter,"[70] wrote Geoffrey of Vinsauf (whom C. S. Lewis called "almost embarrass-

[67]See Ryding, *Structure in Medieval Narrative,* chap. 3 ("The Question of Length"), esp. p. 63.

[68]Ernst Robert Curtius, *European Literature and the Latin Middle Ages,* trans. Willard R. Trask (New York: Harper and Row, 1963), p. 71.

[69]Ibid., pp. 490–93; also Faral, *Les arts poétiques,* pp. 74–75; Eugène Vinaver, ed., *The Works of Sir Thomas Malory* (Oxford: Clarendon, 1967), pp. lxvii–lxviii; and the same author's *Rise of Romance,* esp. pp. 74–76.

[70]Geoffrey of Vinsauf, "Documentum de modo et arte dictandi et versificandi" in Faral, *Les arts poétiques,* p. 274. Even treatises on letter-writing reflect the distinction between unity and multiplicity. Anonymous of Bologna writes that letters may contain two kinds of narration: simple and complex. "A narration is simple that is completed by the narration of only one matter. A narration is complex, on the other hand, in which several matters are recounted" (Anonymous of Bologna [Alberic of Monte Cassino], "The Principles of Letter-Writing [Rationes dictandi]," in *Three Medieval Rhetorical Arts,* ed. James J. Murphy [Berkeley: University of California Press, 1971], p. 18 [pt. 7]).

ing'' on the subject).[71] But it is clear from both his major treatments of the topic that Geoffrey had in mind something different from the classical definition of digression. In the *Poetria Nova* he put it this way:

> Si velit ulterius tractatus linea tendi,
> Materiae fines exi paulumque recede
> Et diverte stylum. . . .
> Est etiam quaedam digressio quando propinqua
> Transeo, quod procul est praemittens ordine verso.
> Progressurus enim medium quandoque relinquo
> Et saltu quodam quasi transvolo; deinde revertor
> Unde prius digressus eram.

(If the lines of the treatise need to be stretched out still farther, step outside the confines of the subject matter and give a little ground and divert your stylus. . . . Indeed, it is a kind of digression when I pass over things which are near, presenting in an inverted order what is at a distance. For now and then, being about to proceed to the middle, I leave off, and by a leap as it were, I vault over a certain matter; then I revert to the point whence I had before digressed.) [*Poetria nova*, vv. 527–36]

The procedure is clarified in *Documentum de modo et arte dictandi et versificandi*, in which he specifies two forms of digression: *ad aliud extra materiam* (introducing outside matter—a ''digression'' proper) and *ad aliam partem materiae* (moving to another part of the same matter).[72]

That rhetorical theory and literary practice correspond on this and other central points is undeniable; but how to explain that correspondence is less than clear. Recent discussions of the character of medieval narrative seem to take for granted that rhetoric had a prescriptive force—that interlace narrative, for example, was ''one more application of the digressive principle and an offshoot of Rhetoric.''[73] But we are far from certain to

---

[71]C. S. Lewis, *The Discarded Image: An Introduction to Medieval and Renaissance Literature* (Cambridge: Cambridge University Press, 1964), p. 192.

[72]''Unus modus digressionis est quando digredimur in materia ad aliam partem materiae; alius modus quando digredimur a materia ad aliud extra materiam'' (Geoffrey of Vinsauf, ''Documentum'' in Faral, *Les arts poétiques*, p. 274).

[73]C. S. Lewis's summary (*Discarded Image*, p. 193) of Vinaver's views as expressed in his edition of Malory (pp. xlviii–lviii).

what extent medieval authors even knew the treatises, much less used them.[74] It is more likely, as Charles Sears Baldwin says, that the manuals from the late twelfth century on represent little more than "the passive voice of poetic, not its active"[75]—not so much causing as responding to, and attempting to codify, the structurally unorthodox literature fast rising to prominence, especially in France. The emphasis in the treatises on amplification, digression, artificial order, and the like thus represents the effort of the rhetoricians to parse this new literature according to the terms of the old system—a system on which they remained conceptually dependent even as it was being rendered obsolete.[76]

The idea of structure that emerges from the *artes poeticae* is foggy at best. It is commonly claimed that the medieval rhetoricians did not address structure ("composition for them goes no further than the adjustment of a sentence"[77]) and that apparent statements about structure, such as the distinction between artificial and natural order, amount to expressions of antistructure, providing a pattern "not to promote composition, but to obviate its necessity."[78] This is the heart of the neo-Aristotelian objection to "medieval" literature: not only did it produce monsters rather than well-proportioned figures (to borrow the Canon of Toledo's formulation), it did so not by accident but by design.[79] The monsters in question were the often vast and vastly popular prose romances, best known to posterity in the form of the *Prose Tris-*

[74]A catalogue (as yet unpublished) of Geoffrey manuscripts compiled by John McKinnell does not suggest a wide circulation.

[75]Charles Sears Baldwin, *Medieval Rhetoric and Poetic* (New York: Macmillan, 1928; rpt. Gloucester, Mass.: Peter Smith, 1959), p. 196.

[76]"The basic principle of medieval rhetoric is a frank pragmatism, making highly-selective use of ideas from the past for needs of the present" (Murphy, ed., *Three Medieval Rhetorical Arts*, p. xiv).

[77]Baldwin, *Medieval Rhetoric*, p. 196; also Curtius, *European Literature*, esp. pp. 70–71. For a closer analysis of the problem, see Douglas Kelly, "The Scope of the Treatment of Composition in the Twelfth- and Thirteenth-Century Arts of Poetry," *Speculum*, 41 (1966), 261–78.

[78]Baldwin, *Medieval Rhetoric*, p. 196.

[79]"I have never seen a book of chivalry with a whole body for a plot, with all its limbs complete, so that the middle corresponds to the beginning, and the end to the beginning and middle; for they are generally made up of so many limbs that they seem intended rather to form a chimaera or a monster than a well-proportioned figure" (Cervantes, *Don Quixote*, trans. J. M. Cohen [Harmondsworth, Middlesex: Penguin, 1950], Book I, chap. xlvii.)

*tan* and the monumental Vulgate Cycle (some 2,800 large pages in modern edition). Viewed structurally, the *Lancelot* and the *Queste del saint graal* (the third and fourth parts of the Cycle) lack a "story" altogether—or, rather, have an acentric story consisting of little more than the sum of its interlaced digressions. Intramural digression in these works, in other words, is not an occasional embellishment, but their basic operating procedure and the key to their construction and evolution. It is important to realize that it was in this form, not in the simpler forms of their verse predecessors, that the romances were in many cases best known from the thirteenth century on and that the modern popularity of the early poetic versions is in large measure the result of a scholarly revival. The *Prose Tristan,* for example, was considerably more influential than the poetic versions, which fell out of favor at an early date.[80] It was, moreover, exactly this kind of polycentric and digressive compilation and its underlying aesthetic of thematic cohesion rather than thematic unity that came under attack by the neoclassicists during the Italian literary debates in the latter half of the sixteenth century.

It is against the theoretical background of amplification (above all, digression) and the literary practice of thematic proliferation that the patterns of saga composition come into full relief. The copiousness of the sagas echoes the tendency toward narrative inclusiveness in medieval literature in general. Such passages as the Clontarf episode in *Njáls saga* and the Sworn Brothers Interlude in *Grettis saga* qualify as digressions proper, and what have been termed entailment sequences fit remarkably well the theoretical definition of a digression *ad aliam partem materiae* and the corresponding literary practice, especially in the prose romances, of lateral excursion. This is not to say that the Icelandic authors knew the rhetoric manuals (it is far from clear that their French and English cousins had a firsthand acquaintance with such writings), still less that they drew a technical distinction between types of digression. But their enthusiastic use of "digressive" material in all denominations witnesses to the sagas'

---

[80]See especially Eugène Vinaver, "The Prose *Tristan,*" in Roger Sherman Loomis, ed., *Arthurian Literature in the Middle Ages: A Collaborative History* (Oxford: Clarendon, 1959), esp. pp. 346–47. The forty-eight manuscripts of the *Prose Tristan* attest to its popularity in its own time.

participation in the aesthetic manifested in the literature and formulated by the rhetoricians of the time. A saga, like the prose romances, is conceived as an acentric bundle of interlocking subplots. Its "own brand" of unity, like that of the prose romances, is not the traditional unity of theme (where each part is related to the main action), but the characteristically medieval cohesion of themes (where each part need only relate to another part), the formal result being a brachiate plot including a considerable portion of matter which is neither strictly necessary nor strictly superfluous but something in between.[81] Narrative overloading to this degree is not associated with folk narration, nor is the interweaving of story lines it presupposes. From the evidence of their composition, it would appear that the sagas were literarily conceived along common medieval lines.

*Cyclic composition.* The Old French *Roman d'Enéas* offers an object lesson in the working assumptions of a twelfth-century redactor, for to the source, Virgil's *Aeneid,* is attached not only a preface of 800-odd lines giving a synopsis of Trojan history (extracted from Aeneas's later apologue, which was shortened accordingly), but also a lengthy and structurally unnecessary suffix, evidently fabricated out of whole cloth, telling of Lavinia's love story. The fact that Virgil's *Aeneid* was the touchstone of the medieval rhetoric manuals did not deter its medieval "translator" from making whatever improvements seemed appropriate, even at the expense of the widely celebrated beginning *in medias res.*[82] For the medieval author, the extremities of a work, no matter how aesthetically satisfying they may have seemed in the received version, were the natural frontiers for further expansion. Many medieval authors, indeed, did nothing but compose preludes, sequels, and further adventures for already existing lives, and forge links between previously unrelated stories. In this literary climate, needless to say, the Aristotelian notion of an artistic unity with a preconceived beginning and end is meaningless.[83]

---

[81]The distinction between unity of theme and cohesion of themes is the underlying premise of the documents contained in Faral, *Les arts poétiques.* See also Vinaver, *Rise of Romance,* p. 74; and Curtius, *European Literature,* pp. 501–2.

[82]Ryding, *Structure in Medieval Narrative,* pp. 39–40.

[83]"Whether or not it was attached to one of the cycles, a conventional long romance could thus aggregate. *Bevis of Hampton* or *Guy of Warwick* might be

Such is the case with the enormous proportion of medieval narrative which can be classified as cyclic.[84] The first major example of the cyclic impulse is in the French epic tradition in the form of an ever-widening complex of tales concerning Guillaume d'Orange. Although the evolutionary details are disputed, it would seem that an early epic on Guillaume's major adventures inspired spin-off epics on his *enfance,* his younger years (*Le couronnement de Louis, La prise d'Orange, Le charroi de Nîmes*), his brothers, uncles, nephews, and cousins, and his father, his grandfather, and finally his great-grandfather, Garin de Monglane, whose *geste* thus came to head the cycle. The component epics circulated independently but were eventually collected in compendiums, undergoing linguistic and formal renovation in the process (in the fifteenth century the entire cycle was recast in prose). The largest manuscript contains eighteen epics, a total of some 80,000 lines. The cyclic idea becomes clearer in this context. If the structural principle of the separate works was biographical, the structural principle of the compendium is genealogical. Taken as a whole, it amounts to a vast dynastic chronicle, of which the formerly independent epics are seen as contributing chapters. Whole works are construed as preludes, sequels, or thematic or material complements to neighboring works.

What the family is to the Guillaume cycle, Arthur's court and the Grail quest are to the prose Vulgate Cycle. (The cyclic idea is also present in the romances of Chrétien, but only in the prose renderings does it attain encyclopedic dimensions.) The Vulgate Cycle has five parts, of which the third and central one, the *Lancelot* proper, recounts a series of interwoven adventures of Lancelot and others of the round table knights. This is followed by the *Queste del saint graal,* an account in a rather more pious mode of Galahad's search for the Grail. The final part, *La mort le roi Artu,*

---

longer or shorter without the slightest narrative difference. It is long because it is interminable. Even in better hands the medieval long romance prevails part by part, as it was read. It was not composed as a single narrative. Such singleness as the middle age cultivated in romance must be sought in the parts considered as separate stories, and will be found oftener in the shorter romances that remained by themselves" (Baldwin, *Medieval Rhetoric,* p. 268).

[84]See Georges Doutrepont, *Les mises en prose des épopées et des romans chevaleresques du XIV^e au XVI^e siècle,* Mémoires de l'Académie royale de Belgique, classe des lettres, 40 (Brussels, 1939), pp. 475–85.

tells of Arthur's death and the collapse of the Arthurian world.
These three form the original corpus; at a somewhat later date
were attached *L'estoire del saint graal*, a "retrospective sequel"
with early information on the Grail,[85] and *Merlin*, with early information on Arthur (a lengthy rendition in prose of Robert de
Boron's poetic version).[86] Together with the *Livre d'Artus*, these
run, in H. R. Sommer's edition, to seven large-page volumes.

The composition of the Vulgate Cycle is one of the perennial
puzzles of medieval literary studies; for if it is on one hand a vast,
sprawling compilation, it is on the other hand remarkably coherent, bound together from beginning to end by a system of "forecasts and concordances" suggesting a strong grasp of the
whole.[87] The *Lancelot* looks forward to events in the *Queste* and
the *Mort Artu*, and events in the *Mort Artu* are directly related to
events in the *Lancelot*. Ferdinand Lot accounted for this "diver-
sité dans l'unité"[88] by positing a single author (of the original trilogy),[89] whereas Albert Pauphilet and others attributed the
connecting devices to later redactors and interpolators.[90] Jean Frappier, on the other hand, argued (by analogy with medieval building procedure) for a committee of three of whom one, the "architect," wrote some or all of the Lancelot proper and provided
the master plan for the trilogy as a whole.[91]

The influence of both the matter and the form of the Vulgate
Cycle was profound and far-reaching, affecting developments in

[85]Jean Frappier, "The Vulgate Cycle," in Loomis, ed., *Arthurian Literature of the Middle Ages*, p. 313.

[86]For a brief introduction to the prose Arthurian matter, see ibid., chaps. 22–27.

[87]Frappier, "Vulgate Cycle," pp. 295–96.

[88]The phrase serves as title of the first chapter of Jean Frappier's *Etude sur la mort le roi Artu*, 2d ed. (Geneva: Droz, 1961).

[89]Ferdinand Lot, *Etude sur le Lancelot en prose* (Paris: Champion, 1918), p. 64 and passim.

[90]Albert Pauphilet, *Le legs du moyen âge: Etudes de littérature médiévale* (Melun: Librairie d'Argences, 1950), pp. 212–17.

[91]Frappier, *Etude sur la mort le roi Artu*, pp. 122–46. "The best solution is to content ourselves with the hypothesis of the single architect and not to resort to the hypothesis of the single author: *La queste* and *La mort Artu* would thus be composed by particular authors, but within the framework of a general plan estab-lished in advance. It requires an effort of historical imagination for us to grasp a creative process that subordinates the individual to a group; we have difficulty conceiving that a team spirit might induce authors to abandon their independence in favor of a collaborative effort that subsumed them" (p. 142).

Italian, Spanish, Portuguese, English, Dutch, Irish, and Welsh traditions—as well, of course, as subsequent French practice.[92] That the medieval Scandinavians were conversant with cyclic forms of literary composition is self-evident from the organization of thirteenth- and fourteenth-century manuscripts. A considerable portion of Norse literature is preserved in cyclic form, for example, the *Codex Regius*, *Mǫðruvallabók*, *Flateyjarbók*, *Morkinskinna*, and *Heimskringla*—not to speak of *Karlamagnús saga* and *Þiðreks saga*. The similarities in conception between these works and certain of the Continental cyclic works are many and striking. *Heimskringla*, like the Guillaume cycle, began as the biography of a single man, Óláfr Haraldsson, but was reconceived shortly thereafter as a dynastic history by a process of backward and forward extensions—a process that involved, as is well known, the relocation of certain beginning and ending material into adjacent sagas in the interest of a more precise chronology (thus Óláfr's *enfance* was moved into the saga of Óláfr Tryggvason). In other words, a work originally conceived as an independent whole, with its own beginning, middle, and end (built approximately on the hagiographic pattern), becomes in its cyclic adumbration one of several biographical chapters in a universal chronicle of the kings of Norway beginning with the mythic past and ending with Magnús Erlingsson. The genealogical chronicle had its synoptic precedent in *Fagrskinna* and *Morkinskinna*, and biography its precedent in *Sverris saga* and the preclassical sagas of the two Óláfrs, but it remained for Snorri Sturluson to combine the two traditions in cyclic form. It is worth noting that *Heimskringla*, by virtue of its sheer bulk and excellence of construction, has been subject to the same sort of speculation as that aimed at the Vulgate Cycle—the question of whether it is to be attributed to a single person or to a literary atelier under the supervision of an "architect."[93]

If the redactor(s) of *Heimskringla* rewrote and extensively

[92]James Douglas Bruce, *The Evolution of Arthurian Romance from the Beginnings Down to the Year 1300*, 2d ed. (Baltimore: Johns Hopkins Press, 1928), I, 126–27 and 146; II, 39–41. Lot (*Etude sur le Lancelot en prose*, pp. 280 ff.) also devotes a chapter to the wider influence on later literatures of the Vulgate Cycle.

[93]Lönnroth, "Tesen om de två kulturerna: Kristiska studier i den isländska sagaskrivningens sociala förutsättningar," *Scripta Islandica*, 15 (1964), 83–97.

edited the works that stood as sources, the compiler of
*Mǫðruvallabók* let the material stand in something closer to its
original form—abbreviating somewhat, but not to a degree that
threatened the idiosyncratic qualities of the individual works. The
formal and material similarities of the works selected for
inclusion—Icelandic family sagas—suggest a certain generic
consciousness. A chronological structure is not possible because
the component parts are roughly contemporaneous, and the author resorted rather to the organization of *Landnámabók,*
whereby the entries were put into a geographical order, starting
with the locale of *Njáls saga* in the southwest and working
clockwise in seven "stops" around the island. If there is no larger
frame story to contain the parts, and if their beginnings and endings are more fixed than those in the Norwegian cycle, it is
nonetheless clear that the parts interlock (by overlapping material, sharing a common cast of characters, and referring to one
another) in such a way as to form a cyclic whole, the symbolic
and approximate geographic center of which is Þingvellir. As
Phillpotts wrote, "Just as each Saga has its own story and its own
chief characters, the Sagas as a whole compose another story....
The Commonwealth makes one epic out of the multiplicity of
Sagas."[94] Whatever the structural differences between
*Heimskringla* and *Mǫðruvallabók,* they proceed from a common
impulse: to assemble a whole and coherent national chronicle.
Like their European counterparts, the encyclopedic works are
not complete records of the entire cycle, but partial collections. It
is convenient to see all those texts we know as the family sagas as
branches of an Icelandic cycle, the fullest extant manuscript of
which is *Mǫðruvallabók.* By the same token, we may speak of
smaller proto-cycles pertaining to the Orkneys, the Faeroes, and
Greenland/Vinland.

The most completely realized encyclopedia in Scandinavian
tradition (and the most extreme example of narrative acquisitive-
ness) is *Flateyjarbók* (the main part of which is dated to the late
fourteenth century). The ostensible backbone of the three-volume
work is the dynastic succession of four Norwegian kings (Óláfr

94Phillpotts, *Edda and Saga,* pp. 149 and 311.

Tryggvason, Óláfr Haraldsson, Sverrir, and Hákon Hákonarson), but this is preceded, followed, and frequently interrupted by substories so removed in time, place, and theme as to constitute digressions. The adjacent sagas of the two Óláfrs contain, in addition to the "main story" (the biography proper), forty-eight detachable substories, of which eleven are interspersed piecemeal (see list in chapter 2). The compiler did not rewrite or edit but simply set or wove together an extraordinarily eclectic group of existing texts in what was presumably their received form: poetry and prose, religious and secular, *þættir* and sagas, historical and legendary. Of some interest from the historical perspective is the fact that *Flateyjarbók* overlaps and shares characters and material with the Icelandic cycle (and the proto-cycles of the Faeroes, Orkneys, and Greenland) to the point where it may be said to have absorbed them. The tendency of the Icelandic and Norwegian cycles to overlap on certain points (particularly through the medium of the skalds) is, of course, evident at the outset; but with *Flateyjarbók* the two cycles have, for all practical purposes, coalesced into a single supercycle, the point of departure of which is Norwegian, but a not inconsiderable portion of whose matter is colonial.

If whole manuscripts reflect the medieval cyclic impulse, so, as this chapter has tried to show, do the individual works themselves. The single Icelandic saga is conceived as a central action or series of actions from which emanates contingent matter in forward and backward unfoldings in the form of prologues, epilogues, genealogical expansions, pendant *þættir*, and the like. The impulse may be seen even at the Eddic stage, where the story of Brynhildr and Sigurðr has already acquired its backward extension in the form of Sigurðr's childhood and its forward extension in the laments; by the time of *Vǫlsunga saga*, the regressive sequence extends to the fifth generation, with the stories of Sigurðr's parents and grandparents constituting miniature sagas (the generational theme in this instance, played out at each stage, has to do with sexual union, usually of an irregular sort—a fitting background for Sigurðr's own fatal dealings with women). That this habit must be literary was argued by Heusler ("The narrative parameters, the scope of the work . . . exceed the limits of oral

performance") although the immediate model he proposed was
the chronicle.[95] Again, if to the size of the individual saga's compass is added its tendency to interlink with other sagas—both
family sagas and kings' sagas—the cyclic nature of the larger
enterprise comes into full relief. The Icelandic sagas cannot indeed be rightly understood in isolation—neither in isolation from
each other, nor from other kinds of sagas, nor from the encyclopedic compilations of which they are commonly a part, nor,
finally, from contemporary literary developments on the Continent, above all, the rise of the prose cycles in thirteenth-century
France. Whatever its special properties, saga literature as a phenomenon rests firmly on the larger foundation of the Middle
Ages.

[95]Andreas Heusler, "Die Anfänge der isländischen Saga," rpt. in Heusler's
*Kleine Schriften,* 2 vols., ed. Stefan Sonderegger (Berlin: de Gruyter, 1969), II,
441 (originally published in *Abhandlungen der Königlich Preussischen Akademie
der Wissenschaften,* phil.-hist. Kl. [1913], pp. 1–87). See also his *Die altgermanische Dichtung,* p. 221: "The parameters of the matter, the question of 'how
much' betrays the saga's origin in chronicle."

# CHAPTER 2

# Stranding

In 1908 the folklorist Axel Olrik drew up a list of "epic laws" or general principles of folk narrative. One of his points, the law of single-stranded narration, cites Icelandic saga practice as a counterexample:

> Modern literature is fond of entangling the threads of the plot. Folk narrative holds the single strand fast: it is always single-stranded. [Its plot proceeds steadily forward to the nearest point both in time and in the logical chain.] Folk narrative does not double back to pick up missing links in the narration. [It does not break off in order to return to prior events, and it does not shift scenes unless the course of the plot requires such a shift.] When one encounters, in the Icelandic sagas, such phrases as "Now the two stories run along together" (*Nú ferr tvennum sǫgum fram*), one has left the realm of oral narrative—this is literature. [The art of the Icelandic saga verges on that of the modern novel or story, and by its very nature differs fundamentally from oral narrative.] The folktale tells only one story at a time. [Its linear nature is the defining characteristic of genuine folk narrative.][1]

[1]The classic version of Axel Olrik's "laws" is the German version: "Epische Gesetze der Volksdichtung," *Zeitschrift für deutsches Altertum*, 51 (1909), 1–12. An English translation of this essay may be found in Alan Dundes, ed., *The Study of Folklore* (Englewood Cliffs, N.J.: Prentice-Hall, 1965), pp. 129–41. The "laws" appeared first in Danish, in somewhat different form, under the title "Episke love i folkedigtningen," *Danske studier*, 5 (1908), 69–89. Yet a third version appeared in *Nordisk tidskrift* (1908), pp. 547–54. The translation here is my own, based on the German version but including, in brackets, some phrasings from the original Danish version.

This formulation has figured prominently in the few general attempts—there are surprisingly few—to relate Olrik's set of "epic laws" to the sagas. Walther Heinrich Vogt, a contemporary of Olrik's, detected multi-ply narration in the first half of *Egils saga* and judged it to be literary on that account; conversely, he felt that the single-ply second half was reflective of oral tradition.[2] He tried on similar grounds to distinguish the traditional from the literary layer in *Bjarnar saga hítdœlakappa*.[3] Reinhard Prinz, using more or less the same scheme, found instances of stranded composition and hence a literary sensibility in *Gísla saga*.[4] Liestøl, like Heusler, preferred to reduce Olrik's "law" to a "tendency" on grounds that cases of simple stranding are sometimes found in folktales, but he nevertheless affirmed the underlying principle.[5] Heusler considered as clear signs of literary structure ("buchmässiger Aufbau") the sagas' copiousness, polycentricity, and broken chronology: "Snorri's *Óláfs saga helga* meshes complex and polycentric narrative masses into a whole that advances chronologically in such a way that a thread is interrupted and resumed several pages later. This sophisticated procedure lies far beyond the capacity of the preliterary saga tellers. In addition, the narrative parameters, the scope of the work, exceeds the limit of oral performance."[6] Maarten van den Toorn arrived at much the same conclusion by using the tools of modern narrative theory.[7]

---

[2]Walther Heinrich Vogt, *Zur Komposition der Egils saga Kpp. I-LXVI* (Görlitz: Hoffmann and Reiber, 1909). Ole Widding tempered Vogt's judgment: "Perhaps it is not as sharp a difference as Vogt suggests, but that the sections [are] woven together to a greater extent—completely in keeping with the medieval rules of literary borrowing." See his "Islændingesagaer" in Hans Bekker-Nielsen, Thorkil Damsgaard Olsen, and Ole Widding, *Norrøn fortællekunst* (Copenhagen: Akademisk forlag, 1965), p. 85.

[3]Walther Heinrich Vogt, "Die Bjarnar saga Hítdœlakappa: Lausavísur, frásagnir, saga," *Arkiv för nordisk filologi*, 37 (1920), 27–79.

[4]Reinhard Prinz, *Die Schöpfung der Gísla saga Súrssonar* (Breslau: Ferdinand Hirt, 1935).

[5]Knut Liestøl, *Upphavet til den islendske ættesaga* (Oslo: Aschehoug, 1929), pp. 101–2. Liestøl does not, however, address directly the degree and complexity of the practice in the sagas.

[6]Andreas Heusler, "Die Anfänge der isländischen Saga," rpt. in Heusler's *Kleine Schriften*, ed. Stefan Sonderegger, 2 vols. (Berlin: de Gruyter, 1969), II, 440–41; originally published in *Abhandlungen der Königlich Preussischen Akademie der Wissenschaften*, phil.-hist. kl. (1913).

[7]Maarten Z. van den Toorn, "Zur Struktur der Saga," *Arkiv för nordisk filologi*, 73 (1958), 140–68; and "Zeit und Tempus in der Saga," *Arkiv för nordisk filologi*, 76 (1961), 134–52.

Einar Ólafur Sveinsson refers to the composition of *Njáls saga* as a "web" or "network of events" and distinguishes it from the more straightforward patterns of biography or chronicle.[8] Anne Heinrichs has recently termed "intertexture"[9] the technique of binding together the narrative mass by a system of "forecasts and concordances" (as Frappier described the same phenomenon in the Vulgate Cycle).[10] Lee Hollander, in an ingenious essay on the "exceedingly multifarious" composition of *Eyrbyggja saga*, charted the interweaving of plots and concluded that because the device could easily be eliminated, it must be deliberate. He compared it with the practice of sentence intercalation in skaldic poetry and concluded that they were manifestations of the same aesthetic.[11] Andersson focuses on the macrostructure of the Icelandic family sagas but notes several puzzling instances of "unnecessarily complicated" plot organization.[12] He speculates that the author of *Eyrbyggja saga*, for example, "had chronological sources that called for the interspersing of these episodes."[13] Phillpotts distinguished a subgroup of "two-strand" sagas (*Reykdœla saga, Hrafnkels saga, Vápnfirðinga saga, Þorsteins þáttr stangarhǫggs, Gunnlaugs saga, Kormáks saga,* and *Bjarnar saga hítdœlakappa*) and one "three-strand" saga (*Laxdœla saga*) and guessed that they developed naturally out of the biographic form.[14] Sigurður Nordal considered double-stranded nar-

[8]Einar Ólafur Sveinsson, *Njáls Saga: A Literary Masterpiece,* trans. and adapted by Paul Schach (Lincoln: University of Nebraska Press, 1971), pp. 53–55; originally published as *Á Njálsbúð: Bók um mikið listaverk* (Reykjavík: Hið íslenzka bókmenntafélag, 1943).

[9]Anne Heinrichs, "'Intertexture' and Its Functions in Early Written Sagas: A Stylistic Observation of *Heiðarvíga saga, Reykdœla saga,* and the Legendary Olafssaga," *Scandinavian Studies,* 48 (1976), 127–45.

[10]Jean Frappier, "The Vulgate Cycle," in *Arthurian Literature in the Middle Ages,* ed. Roger Sherman Loomis (Oxford: Clarendon, 1959), pp. 22–23.

[11]Lee M. Hollander, "The Structure of *Eyrbyggja saga,*" *Journal of English and Germanic Philology,* 58 (1959), 222–27.

[12]Theodore M. Andersson, *The Icelandic Family Saga: An Analytic Reading,* Harvard Studies in Comparative Literature, 28 (Cambridge, Mass.: Harvard University Press, 1967), esp. pp. 148–52, 160–62, and 208–10.

[13]Ibid., p. 162.

[14]"Two-strand" sagas consist of "the inter-actions between two men or two families, where their relations are friendly or hostile." They are "not simply double biographies, or periods in the lives of two men: they eschew all mention of incidents which do not bear on the relations between them. They are quite a distinct form" (Bertha Phillpotts, *Edda and Saga* [New York: Holt, 1931], p. 200).

ration an "excellent trait in the construction" of *Hrafnkels saga,*
but noted "one curious use" that "must surely be considered a
defect of craftsmanship"—a passage involving an unnecessary
reversion to an earlier point in time:

> After Hrafnkell's humiliation at Aðalból the Saga describes his pur-
> chase of land and his rise to power in the first *years* at
> Hrafnkelsstaðir. After returning to describe events at Aðalból in the
> first *days* after Hrafnkell's departure, it *then* describes Hrafnkell's
> reception of the reports about the destruction of Freyfaxi and the
> temple-burning—events which, of course, took place a few days
> after his departure. It would have been more natural if the saga had
> told first of Hrafnkell's departure, then of the activities of Sámr and
> the sons of Thjóstarr, followed by Hrafnkell's reception of the news,
> and in this way had avoided splitting in two the section describing
> his second rise to power. Such an arrangement would have had the
> additional merit of resembling more closely the method of narration
> employed in popular oral recitation.[15]

He concluded that the author must have had some special aim
relating to Hrafnkell's ultimate fate.

In general it may be said that the nature of the inquiry into this
aspect of saga composition has been conditioned, directly or indirectly, by the terms of Olrik's original formulation: critics share
the underlying assumption that, because the sagas emerged out of
oral culture at some point, the proper standard against which to
measure a saga is a folktale, and any differences that emerge
indicate the degree of "literary" interference. Whatever merit
there is in this view, its local bias has inhibited us in pursuing just
what the other half of Olrik's equation, "sophisticated literature," might actually mean in historical and comparative terms.
This is the point of departure for the following two chapters. This
chapter is an attempt to describe stranded composition in the
sagas and to view it in a contemporary European context. Chapter 3 concentrates on narrative synchrony, again with an eye to
Continental developments. The distinction is an artificial convenience, and the chapters, like the processes they describe, should
be understood to be dependent on one another.

[15] Sigurður Nordal, *Hrafnkels saga Freysgoða,* trans. R. George Thomas (Car-
diff: University of Wales Press, 1958), pp. 35–36.

## Stranded Narrative

Stranding refers to a shift of narrative focus from part to part, usually in a way that entails the discontinuous telling of something that could just as well, and more naturally, be told all at once. A strand is the "something" in question, and its component parts, to stay within the conventional metaphor, may be termed "stitches." A strand may be brief and enclitic or it may be a full biography or anthology of events which, separated from its context, itself constitutes an independent narrative entity. In the latter case, an episode is interrupted to be resumed at a later point in the midst of a second episode, whose further development is thus postponed—to be continued, in its turn, in the midst of still a third episode. Or a strand may be a person, or a group of people (family, berserks, band of attackers), or a place (Bergþórshváll, a ship, a royal court), or an abstract vector in the plot (as in *Eyrbyggja saga* or *Heiðarvíga saga*)—whatever, indeed, one might expect to be narrated in a single unit but is instead rendered piecemeal.

Nor are strands fixed in form: they divide and merge according to the vicissitudes of plot (as, for example, in *Njáls saga,* where certain individual character-strands join to form the composite strand of the "burners" and, after the climactic event, diverge into individuals who go, eventually, their separate ways). Moreover, matter that is integral in one context may be subdivided in another. A dramatic example is *Hallfreðar saga,* which is a strand in the *Longest Saga of Óláfr Tryggvason* (intercalated in eight parts) but an integral saga, or chapter, of *Mǫðruvallabók.* Finally, although they in no sense constitute separable stories, certain leitmotifs in the sagas may also be counted as manifestations of the stranding aesthetic: the weapon Grásíða, for example, which "cuts a ragged swath" through *Gísla saga,*[16] Hallgerðr's hair and Skarpheðinn's grin in *Njáls saga,* and the headdress in *Laxdœla saga.* The principle of inseparability implied by this system of cross-references (or intertexture) has been a crux in the theories concerning the origin and transmission of the sagas.

[16]Theodore M. Andersson, "Some Ambiguities in *Gísla saga:* A Balance Sheet," *Bibliography of Old Norse-Icelandic Studies* (Copenhagen: The Royal Library, 1968), p. 14.

But the exact content or size of a strand is not so important as the process of stranding itself: the rhythmic movement of the story in fits and starts, the folding back on itself of the plot, the patterns of delays and detours, the preference over straightforward arrangement for one in which "the themes run parallel, or entwined, or are brought together as in a chequer of knotting and plaiting."[17] Strands are not, it should be emphasized, ornamental tendrils, but contributing parts of the ongoing plot, taking place in or around the narrative present. The saga is the sum of its interwoven strands, a "verbal braid" whose meaning is not stated outright but is implied in the juxtapositions and intersections.[18]

Stranding by character is, not surprisingly, most frequent in the so-called district chronicles, where the course and logic of the story lie in no single individual but in the interaction of dozens or hundreds of characters over the space of two or more generations. But it is similarly represented to a surprising degree even in such patently biographical sagas as *Grettis saga* and *Egils saga*. A short example (about fourteen pages) of character stranding at an unadorned minimum may be found in *Þorsteins saga hvíta*. The plot revolves around the slaying of Einarr (kinsman by marriage of Þorsteinn hvíti) by his onetime trading partner Þorsteinn fagri. Þorsteinn fagri is betrothed to Helga but goes with Einarr to Norway, where an illness prevents his timely return. Einarr returns alone to Iceland, where he circulates false reports of Þorsteinn's death and marries Helga. Meanwhile, back in Norway, Þorsteinn recovers, returns to Iceland, seeks out Einarr, and kills him in his house. In revenge, Einarr's father collects men and they kill Þorsteinn fagri's brothers and drive Þorsteinn himself into exile. After five years, Þorsteinn returns and lives under the sponsorship of Þorsteinn hvíti. When Einarr's nephew Brodd-Helgi reaches a threatening age, Þorsteinn returns to Norway and spends the rest of his life there.

If Þorsteinn fagri is the saga's main character, he is hardly a

---

[17]William Worringer, *Form in Gothic*, trans. and ed. Herbert Read (London: Putnam, 1927), p. 41; cited by Eugène Vinaver, *The Rise of Romance* (Oxford: Clarendon, 1971), p. 77.
[18]The term "språklig flettverk" is used in reference to skaldic diction by Hallvard Lie, *"Natur" og "unatur" i skaldekunsten, Avhandlinger utgitt av Det Norske Videnskaps-Akademi i Oslo, II, hist.-fil. kl. (1957)*, p. 28.

freewheeling, independent hero in the style of a Lancelot or a Beowulf. He is rather a function of, and exists as a hero only in relation to, his family and his local district in Iceland. (His three Norwegian sojourns are, with the exception of his developing illness, empty spots in the plot.) Nor is he a particularly dominant figure in the narrative: only about 35 percent of the text focuses exclusively on him, the rest being devoted to the parallel destinies of such figures as Einarr, Þórir, and Þorgils and to the brief appearances of numerous minor characters. *Þorsteins saga hvíta* boasts about forty named characters (making it about twice as densely populated per page as *Njáls saga* with its six hundred characters), of whom most are introduced in the following fashion:

(A) Hrani hét maðr ok var kallaðr gullhǫttr. Hann var fóstri Þorgils, en frændi Ásvarar. Hann var hávaðamaðr mikill ok var heimamaðr at Hofi ok var kallaðr grályndr. (B) Þorkell hét maðr ok var kallaðr flettir. Hann var heimamaðr at Hofi ok frændi þeira Hofverja, mikill ok sterkr. (C) Þorbjǫrn hét maðr. Hann bjó i Sveinungsvík. Þat er á milli Melrakkaslèttu ok Þistilsfjarðar. Þorbjǫrn var drengr góðr ok rammr maðr at afli, vinr góðr Þorsteins hvíta. (D) Maðr er nefndr Þorfinnr. Hann bjó at Skeggjastǫðum í Hnefilsdal. Hann átti ok enn annat bú. Þorgerðr hét kona hans. Þau áttu þrjá sonu, ok hét Þorsteinn sonr þeira ok var kallaðr fagri, annarr Einarr, þriði Þorkell. Allir váru þeir mannvænligir. Þorsteinn var fyrir þeim brœðrum. Hann var fullkominn at aldri, er hér er komit sǫgunni. (E) Kraki hét maðr, ok bjó hann á þeim bœ, er heitir á Krakalœk. Kraki var vel auðigr maðr, kvángaðr maðr, ok hét kona hans Guðrún. Þau áttu dóttur eina barna, er Helga hét ok var allra kvenna fríðust, ok þótti sá kostr beztr í Fljótsdalsheraði.

(A) Hrani was the name of a man, nicknamed gullhǫttr. He was the foster son of Þorgils and a kinsman of Ásvǫr. He was a farmhand at Hof. He was a rowdy man, said to be malicious. (B) Þorkell was the name of a man, nicknamed flettir. He too was a farmhand at Hof and was a kinsman of the Hof people, a large man and strong. (C) Þorbjǫrn was the name of a man. He lived at Sveinungsvík, which lies between Melrakkaslétta and Þistilsfjǫrðr. Þorbjǫrn was a good fellow, very strong, and a close friend of Þorsteinn hvíti. (D) A man was named Þorfinnr. He lived at Skeggjastaðir at Hnefilsdalr, although he also owned another farm. Þorgerðr was the name of his wife. They had three sons, one of whom was named Þorsteinn, nicknamed fagri, the second Einarr, and the third Þorkell. They were all promising men. Þorsteinn was the most outstanding of the brothers. He was fully grown at this point in the saga. (E) Kraki was the name of a man, and he lived on that farm called Krakalœkr. Kraki was quite a wealthy man, married to a woman named Guðrún. They had a daughter named Helga who was the most beautiful of women and was considered the best match in the Fljótsdalr district.) [chap. 3]

To the untrained eye, this passage is little more than a blurred census list, rather like a random page of *Landnámabók*. But the practiced audience knows that five distinct lines of the story are being plaited into the saga (above and beyond the three major lines developed in chapters 1 and 2) and held in temporary abeyance until such time as the plot requires their individual participation—in the case of strand D, 5 lines later; strand E, 56 lines later; strand A, 66 lines later; strand C, 138 lines later; and strand B, 181 lines later (or 125 lines before the end of the saga). It is characteristic of such cluster introductions that roughly equivalent space is devoted to major and minor characters.[19] Of Þorsteinn fagri (strand D) it is said only that he was the foremost of three brothers and full grown when the saga took place, and of Þorkell flettir (strand B) that he resided at Hof, was related to that family, and was a large and strong man. The cluster introductions thus form a kind of selvage in which all threads, large and small, are evenly secured, and from which they emanate in parallel lines to form the warp of the story. It is only in the subsequent interweavings that their relative relationships, and the design of the story, become fully clear. Þorsteinn emerges as the hero, but Þorkell flettir turns out to be a marginal character who reappears only once, very briefly, toward the end of the saga.

The treatment of Þorkell flettir illustrates one of the dramatic consequences of stranding as a narrative technique. The sum total of his role in *Þorsteins saga hvíta* is his introduction (above) and the following brief account of his contribution to the revenge attack on Þorsteinn's brothers:

[19]Their relative importance is indicated, rather, in the adjectives used to describe them. See Lars Lönnroth, "Rhetorical Persuasion in the Sagas," *Scandinavian Studies,* 42 (1970), 164–70.

Þá bauð Þorkell flettir at fara á bak húsinu ok hlaupa af vegginum ofan milli Þorbjarnar ok duranna ok bera hann svá frá durunum ok ofan fyrir brekkuna. Þorgils bað hann svá gera. Síðan breytti Þorkell svá, at Þorbjǫrn varð með þessari atferð borinn frá seldurunum.

(Then Þorkell flettir offered to go to the back of the building and jump down from the wall in such a way as to land between Þorbjǫrn and the door and so drag him outside down over the slope. Þorgils told him to go ahead. In this way Þorkell managed to get Þorbjǫrn out of doors and away from the shed.) [chap. 7]

The advance introduction of characters (and, in longer sagas, their nonconsecutive development over the course of the stranding process) is thus, among other things, a device that enables the narrator to execute a climactic sequence entirely free of explanatory clutter. The burning at Bergþórshváll is a brilliant example: its sustained representation of immediate and unadulterated action and its affective impact despite utter authorial silence are the dramatic fruits of a literary technique. The narrative marshals through the tragic scenes no fewer than thirty-one named men and women, all of whom have been introduced and to some degree fleshed out in advance, and at least twelve of whom are distinct personalities with a particular set of reasons for being in that place at that time. The picture bears little resemblance to the medieval artist's depiction of a crowd as identical people acting in unison. Nor is it one of those literary situations whose tragic dimension must be explained or urged by the narrator. When Flosi arrives at Bergþórshváll in chapter 128, the audience is fully cognizant of the intention and significance of the situation and of the complex causal facts leading up to it; no further explanation is required.

Þorkell flettir constitutes something less than a narrative presence in Þorsteins saga hvíta, yet his introduction and suspension in chapter 3 and his retrieval in chapter 7 serve as a rudimentary illustration of the technique of saga stranding. Once introduced, characters can be recalled into the action, as either central or side actors, whenever and as often as the story requires or the narrator wishes. In Njáls saga, the Mǫrðr Valgarðsson thread surfaces and recedes twenty times between chapters 25 and 145. Likewise, Snorri goði appears as a major figure in Eyrbyggja saga some

three dozen times, and as an auxiliary figure in *Laxdœla saga*
fifteen times, and in *Njáls saga* six times (his shared presence
suggests the cyclic relation of those works). A saga is the sum of
such threads, and the narrator's art lies, above all, in playing out
the lines in the most dramatically effective manner.

Although stranding is subject to variation in kind and degree,
certain standard patterns obtain, the chief of which are represented in *Þorsteins saga hvíta*. Chapters 4–6, for example, contain back-to-back the two narrative situations most amenable to
stranded treatment in the sagas (perhaps in literature in general):
the parting of ways of major characters and attack sequences. At
the point Einarr leaves his ailing partner Þorsteinn in Norway, the
story forks and follows both histories in turn until they rejoin:
first Einarr's arrival in Iceland, marriage to Helga, and settlement
in Atlavík; then Þorsteinn's recuperation and return; and finally
their convergence at Atlavík. The scene-switching between the
two strands before and during the attack sequence is equally typical:[20] focus is first on Þorsteinn (his route and arrival at the door);
then on Einarr (still in bed); then on Þorsteinn (his exchange with
Ósk); then on Einarr (his exchange with Ósk, his climbing out of
bed and dressing, and his emergence from the sleeping room); and
finally on both of them as they confront one another and
Þorsteinn cuts Einarr down. Such scene-shifting is a common,
though by no means an exclusive, property of climactic sequences. It is simply a more rapid, more finely tuned, and hence
more obviously artificial version of an ongoing narrative manner.
Shifting of focus is predicated on a stranded story; and a stranded
story, whether its changes are fast or slow, is in turn predicated
on an aesthetic of delay and suspense.

Certain ongoing actions serve as standard points of transition
from one strand to another. The illness of Þorsteinn fagri is a
classic example: the narrator leaves an ill or wounded character
and returns to him only when he has recuperated sufficiently to
rejoin the action. Other stock actions include journeys abroad
(e.g., viking expeditions), spending uneventful time at certain
places (e.g., winter at a foreign court), or, in the shorter range,
protracted conversation, hiding, eating, or drinking (e.g., ban-

[20]See Andersson, *Icelandic Family Saga*, p. 58.

quets), sleeping or resting, and riding from one point to another. Ambush passages follow a predictable pattern: the ambushers come to a halt, dismount, rest, and often eat a meal before proceeding with their attack, at which point the narrative shifts to give an account of the other side. The principle in all cases is that of equilibrium: leaving one side of the story in a state of suspended animation in order to pursue another line of action. *Þórðar saga kakala* (*Sturlunga saga*) provides a novel example. Þórðr and Svarthǫfði elude pursuers by taking cover in a snowdrift. The narrator then turns to the pursuers and spends a full three pages telling not only how they ride past the snowbank in question, but also how they subsequently engage in a battle in a churchyard, beat a dangerous retreat, and drive their horses to exhaustion. Only after this entire sequence of events is summarized and concluded does the narrator retrieve Þórðr and Svarthǫfði from their chilly lair:

Nú er at segja frá þeim Svarthöfða ok Þórði Bjarnarsyni, er þeir lágu í fönninni, þar til er flokkr Kolbeins var um fram riðinn.

(Now it is to be told of Svarthǫfði and Þórðr that they lay in the snowdrift until Kolbeinn's band had ridden past.) [chap. 11]

There is a certain humor, presumably deliberate, in this grim version of the rule of equilibrium.

In chapter 24 of *Grettis saga*, Grettir flees Norway; in chapter 28 he arrives in Iceland. The intervening chapters are taken up with the Sworn Brothers Interlude, in which Þorgeirr Hávarsson slays a man in a dispute over whale rights and is outlawed. The episode takes place during the year preceding Grettir's return and is not immediately pertinent to his own fortunes. Rather, like its functional counterpart the cluster introduction, it serves to bring into the saga characters who will later have occasion to cross paths with Grettir. The episode marks a new phase of the saga—a long stretch of narrative compositionally distinct from what precedes and follows it in that it embraces five story lines or subplots, each one of which is spliced at least once by parts of the others. Four of these subplots or story lines consist of relationships between Grettir and other men: Þorgeirr Hávarsson (A),

Barði Guðmundarson (B), the cohorts Þorbjǫrn ferðalangr and
Þorbjǫrn øxnamegin (C), and Þórir Skeggjason (D). The fifth subplot is "no plot at all, but the account of Glámr's curse and
Þorsteinn's promise of revenge."[21] What is noteworthy is not so
much the proliferation per se but the discontinuity in the presentation of these stories, which may be roughly outlined as follows:

A[1]   Ásmundr's relative Þorgils is slain by Þorgeirr Hávarsson; Ásmundr
       outlaws Þorgeirr.
B[1]   Grettir seeks out Auðunn and wrestles with him; Barði Guð-
       mundarson separates them; Grettir promises to aid Barði in his
       revenge.
C[1]   Grettir injures an opponent during a horse fight and kills several
       men in the ensuing skirmish.
B[2]   Barði Guðmundarson fails to call on Grettir for assistance; Grettir
       tries to avenge the slight, but is forced to withdraw.
E[1]   Þórhallr Grímsson's farm is haunted; his shepherd Glámr is killed
       mysteriously, becomes a revenant, and kills his two successors;
       Grettir overcomes and kills Glámr; Glámr predicts outlawry,
       loneliness, and death for Grettir.
C[2]   Þorbjǫrn ferðalangr accuses Grettir of cowardice; he extends his
       scorn to Ásmundr; Grettir kills him.
D[1]   Grettir sails to Norway. He fetches fire for his shipmates and un-
       wittingly burns down a house together with its inmates. He tries
       to attest his innocence by ordeal, but is prevented from completing
       the test. He kills a berserk who challenges his host.
E[2]   Grettir's brother Þorsteinn vows to avenge him should the need
       arise.
C[3]   Þorbjǫrn ferðalangr's companion Þorbjǫrn øxnamegin ambushes
       Grettir's brother Atli unsuccessfully. The matter is settled at the
       Thing. Atli harbors one of Þorbjǫrn's workers and Þorbjǫrn kills
       him.
D[2]   Þórir Skeggjason, whose sons died in the fire set by Grettir, has
       Grettir outlawed in Iceland.
C[4]   Grettir kills Þorbjǫrn øxnamegin and his son.
A[2]   Grettir takes refuge with Þorsteinn Kuggason, Snorri goði, and
       Þorgils Arason. Þorgils harbors Þorgeirr and Þormóðr at the same
       time and keeps the outlaws in leash.
C[5]   During the litigation after Þorbjǫrn øxnamegin's slaying, Snorri
       goði and Skapti Þóroddsson try unsuccessfully to lift Grettir's
       outlawry.

[21]Ibid., p. 209 (from which also the plot outline is adapted).

This sequence is not, of course, a haphazard concatenation of events. The episodes all devolve either directly or indirectly on Grettir and serve to illustrate his progressive victimization. Yet the pattern of their occurrence strikes an artificial note, particularly when compared with the rather more straightforward procedure elsewhere in the saga. One has the impression that in this section the author's taste for the baroque has been given free rein. Certainly the following short passage from chapter 42 constitutes a gratuitous complication:

Þar er nú til at taka, er áðr var frá horfit, at Þorbjǫrn øxnamegin spurði víg Þorbjarnar ferðalangs, sem fyrr var sagt; brásk hann við reiðr mjǫk ok kvezk vilja, at ýmsir ætti hǫgg í annars garði.

(Now to pick up a line of the story that was set aside earlier, in which Þorbjǫrn øxnamegin learned of the slaying of Þorbjǫrn ferðalangr, as was told before; he reacted very angrily and said he hoped there would be a retaliation from more than one quarter.) [chap. 42]

But what follows is not a settling of the score, or indeed about Þorbjǫrn øxnamegin at all. Instead, the narrator turns abruptly to another side of the story, telling how Ásmundr grows ill, dies, and is buried, and how Atli assumes the family property and thereafter undertakes a journey to Snæfellsnes to buy dried fish. Only then does the story return to Þorbjǫrn. The above notice is therefore isolated, presumably deliberately, from both of its natural contexts: the past event it recalls (the slaying of Þorbjǫrn ferðalangr) five chapters earlier and the revenge it anticipates one chapter later. It is in such lonely stitches that we glimpse most clearly the mechanics of interlace.[22]

The pattern here is not unlike that of the Atlantic Interlude of *Njáls saga*. Here, too, the author develops five stories, each one comprising a recognizable and temporally complete subplot and all covering the same period of time (see chart on p. 30 above). The stories are played out in the following order:

[22]Heusler, countering the *þáttr* theory ("Die Anfänge," p. 452), argued that *Grettis saga* was constructed not on the pattern a + b + c but rather the pattern G + a + G + b + G + c. Either pattern indicates open composition and a sort of interlace form.

A¹  Þráinn leaves.

B¹  Grímr and Helgi leave.

C¹  Gunnarr decides to stay.

D¹  Kolskeggr leaves.

C²  Gunnarr spends an uneventful winter and declines a spring invitation from Óláfr pá. The plans for the attack on Hlíðarendi are laid at the Althing in the summer and carried out that autumn. Gunnarr's revenant puts in an appearance. Skarpheðinn and Hǫgni slay Tjǫrvi in revenge for Gunnarr's death. Njáll negotiates a settlement.

D²  Kolskeggr goes to Norway and spends the winter there. The following summer he goes to Denmark, where he is baptized in consequence of a dream vision. He moves on to Russia and from there to Constantinople, where he becomes a leader in the Varangian guard.

A²  Þráinn arrives in Norway and winters with Hákon. He kills Kolr. He accompanies the earl to Sweden, spends the following winter with him, hears of Gunnarr's death in the spring, and delays his return to Iceland on that account.

B²  Grímr and Helgi are caught in a storm at sea. They fight with vikings and engage in a battle in Scotland. They stay the winter, spring, and part of the summer in the Orkneys. They go raiding with Kári the following summer. They spend a second winter in the Orkneys and leave for Norway in the spring.

E¹  Kolbeinn, having arrived in Iceland, stays the winter in Breiðdalr. He takes Hrappr to Norway the following summer. Hrappr is outlawed after the Guðrún episode.

B³  Grímr and Helgi arrive in Norway and begin trading.

A³  Þráinn prepares for his return to Iceland.

E²  Hrappr burns the temple and tries to get passage to Iceland.

B⁴ + A⁴ + E³  The Njálssons reject Hrappr, but Þráinn takes him aboard. The two of them escape to Iceland and settle down together on Þráinn's farm.

B⁵  Grímr and Helgi flee Norway with Hákon in pursuit. They stay with Eiríkr, sail to the Orkneys, winter with Sigurðr, go raiding in the spring, and return with Kári in the summer.

The narrative bulk of Gunnarr's and Kolskeggr's stories is, within the framework of the Atlantic Interlude, for the most part straightforwardly told (in C² and D²). But the other three stories are broken apart and interbraided in such a way as to bring out certain contrivances of destiny—the three-plot convergence in Norway in the summer of the second year, for example, or the synchronic idea that while Gunnarr is being attacked in his home, Hrappr is in Norway involved in a liaison with Guðrún, Þráinn is in Sweden, Kolskeggr is in Russia, and Grímr and Helgi are raiding off the Orkney coast. This preoccupation is particularly apparent in two brief stitches (B³ and Λ³) inserted in the middle of Hrappr's story (E¹ and E²):

Nú er þat at segja, at um sumarit fóru Njálssynir af Orkneyjum til Nóregs ok váru þar í kaupstefnu um sumarit. Þráinn Sigfússon bjó þá skip sitt til Íslands ok var þá mjǫk albúinn. Þá fór Hákon jarl á veizlu til Guðbrands. Um nóttina fór Víga-Hrappr til goðahúss þeira jarls ok Guðbrands ok gekk inn í húsit.

(Now it is to be told that in the summer the Njálssons left the Orkneys for Norway, where they spent the summer trading. Þráinn Sigfússon was preparing his ship for a voyage to Iceland at the time and was almost ready to sail. Earl Hákon, meanwhile, was attending a feast at Guðbrandr's estate. During the night, Víga-Hrappr came to the earl's and Guðbrandr's temple and went inside.) [chap. 88]

Neither notice is necessary because the information in both cases is given elsewhere (the Njálssons' presence in Norway was mentioned in B², and Þráinn's imminent departure is mentioned in A³); they form, moreover, a patent interruption in the otherwise integral story of Hrappr. The idea, of course, is to put into the mind of the audience a picture of three actions about to intersect: Hrappr, fleeing the earl's men, will make for the harbor, where he will encounter the Njálssons and Þráinn in the process of pulling up their gangplanks.

From the point of view of a medieval author bent on amplifying the story, the advantages of such plot braiding are obvious. New material is not embedded abruptly in an existing text, but is spliced into it, the ending strands of one part being woven together with the beginning strands of another part in such a way as to make the transition between the two imperceptible. The Atlantic Interlude is the largest example of the process, serving to suture two entire sagas. But the same knitting patterns are evident on a smaller scale throughout the corpus. The Unnr and Hrútr prelude is not freestanding, for example, but is spliced firmly together with Hallgerðr's story, which in turn merges with Gunnarr's story. Broken down by chapter, the passage works as follows:

| Unnr/Hrútr prelude | | Gunnarr's saga | |
|---|---|---|---|
| Chap. 1a | Hrútr is introduced. | | |
| | | Chap 1b | Hǫskuldr and Hrútr discuss Hallgerðr's "thief's eyes." |
| Chap. 2 | He is betrothed to Unnr. | | |
| Chap. 3 | He goes to Norway and becomes involved with Gunnhildr. | | |
| Chap. 4 | He leaves Norway in quest of his inheritance. | | |
| Chap. 5 | He vanquishes vikings, and with Gunnhildr's intervention he retrieves his inheritance. | | |
| Chap. 6 | He returns to Iceland and marries Unnr, who becomes unhappy. | | |
| Chap. 7 | Unnr, on Mǫrðr's advice, divorces Hrútr. | | |
| Chap. 8 | Hrútr sustains the divorce and retains the dowry. | | |
| | | Chap. 9 | Hallgerðr is betrothed to Þorvaldr against her wishes. |
| | | Chap. 10 | They marry. |
| | | Chap. 11 | They set up household. Hallgerðr taunts Þorvaldr; he slaps her and is killed by Þjóstólfr. |
| | | Chap. 12 | Hallgerðr dissolves the household, and Hǫskuldr brings about a settlement. |
| | | Chap. 13 | Again against her wishes, Hallgerðr is betrothed a second time (to Glúmr). |
| | | Chap. 14 | They marry and have a daughter. |

That the author has employed intertwining not solely as a splicing device but as literary effect is clear from three of the stitches: chapters 1a, 1b, and 18. The three-sentence introduction of Unnr with its comment on her nubile state belongs logically to chapter 2, where she is betrothed to Hrútr. The scene in which Hallgerðr's thievish eyes are discussed (chapter 1b) belongs logically to the fuller description of her person and the story of her marriages in chapters 9–17. And in exactly the same way, the three-sentence notice of Mǫrðr's death and Unnr's subsequent financial plight (chapter 18) belongs logically to the duplicate information (and her actual effort to retrieve her dowry) in chapter 18 and following. Because these extra stitches could easily be eliminated, they must be deliberate. As it is, they serve as yet further witness to the baroque propensities of the *Njála* author. From the point of view of the listening audience, beginning the saga with two dangling prefixes, made all the more emphatic by the transitional phrase at their conclusion ("Now the saga turns west to Breiðafjarðardalir"), must have seemed a flamboyant touch indeed. Even Finnur Jónsson acknowledged the artificiality of the procedure: "As *Njála* now begins, no original saga ever began."[23]

A more elaborate and sustained use of stranding is found in *Eyrbyggja saga*, whose structural peculiarities have long puzzled

[23]Finnur Jónsson, *Den oldnorske og oldislandske litteraturs historie*, 3 vols., 2d ed. (Copenhagen: Gad, 1920–24), II, 523.

critics. It is, among other things, a saga without a main character.
If Snorri goði emerges as such, he does so only by dint of
ubiquity, not because his biography has been developed in any
normal sense. His history is spotty at best (his last eighteen years
being a "perfect blank"[24]), and he is not treated to the usual
sympathetic perspective. Moreover, the saga lacks entirely the
usual organization of the matter around a climax. Its "exceedingly multifarious"[25] structure has the appearance of a compilation of several loosely related episodes, each of which might be,
"if properly expanded, enough to constitute in itself a saga."[26]
But the incidents are not made into sagas, nor are they rendered
as *þættir* set end to end, nor are they even ordered consecutively
within the longer narrative. Instead they are subdivided into parts
and interspersed in the larger story. The artificiality of the exercise was noted by Hollander: "As a rule, the Family Sagas follow
a linear construction of one thing after, or leading to, another;
with no important or extensive matter intervening between cause
and effect, and events chronologically following one another. Not
so Eyrbyggja."[27] Hollander's picture of a "normal" saga may not
bear close scrutiny, but his perception of *Eyrbyggja* as excep-
tionally puzzled in its composition is well taken. He distinguishes
in chapters 15–55 seven major story lines (and a number of minor
ones, which he discounts) interwoven in the order: $A^1$ $B^1$ $A^2$ $B^2$
$C^1$ $B^3$ $D^1$ $C^2$ $D^2$ $B^4$ $E^1$ $F^1$ $G^1$ $E^2$ $G^2$ $E^3$ $G^3$ $E^4$ $F^2$ $E^5$. He concludes
that the "interbraiding, like the intercalation of sentences in
Skaldic poetry, is hardly fortuitous; rather, it shows conscious
planning on the part of an author who has in mind an audience
that is constantly on the *qui vive* and able to follow this method of
presentation. He does not merely string along the traditions of his
countryside artlessly—popular tradition does just that—but arranges them to suit his purpose"—that purpose being the creation
of suspension "similar to the premonitions and predictions which
are so frequently used in the sagas."[28] Andersson agrees that the

[24]Eiríkr Magnússon's introduction to his translation in *Saga Library*, II (1892),
quoted by Hollander in "Structure of *Eyrbyggja saga*," p. 222, note 2.
[25]Hollander, "Structure of *Eyrbyggja saga*," p. 222.
[26]Andersson, *Icelandic Family Saga*, p. 161.
[27]Hollander, "Structure of *Eyrbyggja saga*," p. 223.
[28]Ibid., p. 227. Hollander's approach to *Eyrbyggja* has been expanded somewhat by Jean-Pierre Mabire, *La composition de la Eyrbyggja Saga*, Publication
du Centre de Recherches sur les Pays Nordiques de l'Université de Caen (Caen,

organization of *Eyrbyggja saga* seems contrived, but offers a somewhat different explanation: "What is puzzling in the saga is the involution of conflicts. The Vigfúss, Styrr, Bjǫrn Breiðvíkinga-kappi, and Þorbrandssynir strands are picked up and dropped, sometimes twice, before finally being unraveled. This interweaving of plots is not normal saga procedure and there is no apparent reason for it. It could in fact be easily eliminated: If the Styrr ... and Bjǫrn Breiðvíkingakappi ... plots were gathered together, the narrative would be straightened and a normal order restored. Perhaps the author has chronological sources that called for the interspersing of these episodes."[29] But the interweaving in *Eyrbyggja saga* is not abnormal, it is merely more elaborate. It is also a more exposed example because it is not absorbed in a larger climax structure: the interweaving cannot be construed as the intricate working out of a climactic prehistory, but is a contrived effect, complete in itself.

A similar pattern is found in *Heiðarvíga saga* (chaps. 15–26), although here it is not the characters' actions or the story lines, but the typical preparatory moves involved in climactic staging, that are artificially broken up and interlaced together. The climax in this case is the slaying of Gísli Þorgautsson in chapter 27. The preceding twelve chapters are, in usual fashion, given over to "reconnaissance, arming, strategic planning, enlisting of allies, harangues in the form of taunts, and provisioning."[30] But each move is divided into two or three substeps and reported nonconsecutively. For example, provisions are stocked in chapter 19 but not collected until chapter 23; allies are enlisted in chapter 17 and assembled in chapter 21; intelligence is prepared in chapter 15, gathered secondhand through agents in chapter 20, and finally

---

1971), esp. pp. 45–57. Mabire objects to Hollander's purely "aesthetic" analysis: "But there is yet another reason why the author has interlaced different actions. In fact—and this Lee M. Hollander has not made clear—our author has chosen the most natural way in the world for setting out the events—that is, he presents them to us in the chronological order of their occurrence. But this method of presentation created a serious problem for him when he had to deal with two simultaneous events; in such cases, he resorted to an order of his own personal choice" (pp. 55–56). A perceptive discussion of narrative chronology can be found in W. P. Ker's comparison of the Icelandic sagas and Joinville's *Histoire de Saint Louis* in *Epic and Romance*, 2d ed. (London: Macmillan 1908; rpt. New York: Dover, 1957), pp. 269–74.

[29] Andersson, *Icelandic Family Saga*, p. 162.
[30] Ibid., p. 150.

assembled by the principals in chapter 25. Two matching taunts are placed at a remove from one another (Þórðr melrakki's in chapter 18 and Þuríðr's in chapter 22), and a good omen in chapter 23 is posed against bad omens in chapter 26. The passage may be outlined as follows: $A^1 B^1 C^1 D^1 E^1 F^1 A^2 D^2 E^2 F^2 G^1 B^2 A^3 G^2$. Here it is not merely a question of continuing an action, but of intensifying it (or duplicating it, as with the taunts) for dramatic effect. Björn M. Ólsen saw the pattern of suspension and delay in *Heiðarvíga saga* as a kind of *oflist,* or hyper-art.[31]

In *Hrafnkels saga,* Sigurður Nordal suggested, the author's "method of dealing with single or double-stranded narrative when two stories are being unfolded simultaneously but neither can be carried through immediately to its proper conclusion" is also used as a device for revealing the psychology of the characters and hence the intention of the author: "After Einarr releases Freyfaxi and sees him rush off down the dale, he tries unsuccessfully to catch him. At that moment Einarr must have known that his own death was near. But we are not told his fears or whether he thinks of escape. The saga follows the horse. Einarr is not mentioned again until Hrafnkell meets him as he lies idly on the wall of the sheepfold counting his sheep. He has not attempted to flee from danger any more than he thinks to avoid telling the truth. This is very effective and makes his slaying appear all the more deplorable." Likewise the account of Hrafnkell's ride to the Althing: "We follow him south to Síða. He arrives at the Assembly after Sámr, is informed of Sámr's arrival and thinks it amusing. After this we learn nothing of his behaviour until Sámr brings the case against him before the court. 'Men rushed to Hrafnkell's booth and told him what was about to happen.' This silence shows best what Hrafnkell thinks of Sámr's antics, and how he discounts them; at the same time it explains how his careless contempt allowed his own affairs to drift beyond any apparent point of recovery."[32] The idea that structure indicates intention may be extended to the saga as a whole. *Hrafnkatla* is not multi-stranded, but strictly two-stranded; and with few exceptions (such as the Einarr/Freyfaxi episode noted by Nordal) the two strands

[31]Björn M. Ólsen, "Um Íslendingasögur," *Safn til sögu Íslands,* 6 (1937–39), 208.

[32]Nordal, *Hrafnkels saga Freysgoða,* pp. 35–36.

consist of Hrafnkell's actions and those of his opponents. The latter strand (Einarr, Sámr, Bjarni, Þorbjǫrn, Þorkell, Þorgeirr) changes composition during the course of the saga, but its function as the opposing force remains constant. If *Hrafnkatla* is elusive, that is because of its archaic social morality, not its structure. Next to the "Gothic wildness and multiplicity of motives"[33] of, for example, *Njála* and *Eyrbyggja, Hrafnkels saga* has, in its simple structural dualism, something of the character of a Christian exercise.

Although its component parts have been studied, some in considerable detail, *Flateyjarbók* has seldom been treated as a whole work, still less a work related compositionally to classical saga narrative. In fact, the processes of compilation in *Flateyjarbók* duplicate, on a much larger scale, the processes of stranding in classical saga narrative—making them more clearly visible in the process. In *Flateyjarbók,* "strands" emerge as such by virtue of their size, their detachability (their presence in other manuscript contexts indicates their semi-independent status), their marginal relation to the "main plot" (the compilers were for the most part casual about supplying logical connections, with the result that the digressive nature of the subplots is clear), and, of course, their status in the manuscript itself (they are often marked off with capital letters or rubrics). If we follow the Vigfússon-Unger edition, we get a gross reading of forty-eight component threads that, in addition to matter from the royal biographies proper, make up the sagas of the two Óláfrs. If to these are added an indeterminate number of substrands (the longer *þættir* are themselves stranded), we begin to get an idea of the scope of the project.

The insertion of integral narrative units (for example, *þættir*) is, of course, common practice in the sagas and standard procedure in *Flateyjarbók*. Less common—or less obviously common—is the incorporation in discontinuous segments of episodes, *þættir,* or entire sagas that are known or may be assumed to have existed elsewhere in continuous if not independent form. *Hallfreðar saga,* for example, is preserved as a unit in *Mǫðruvallabók* but, in *Flateyjarbók,* is divided into eight parts and inserted piecemeal into the biography of Óláfr Tryggvason (the *Longest Saga*).

[33]Rosemond Tuve, *Allegorical Imagery: Some Mediaeval Books and Their Posterity* (Princeton: Princeton University Press, 1966), p. 343.

82 The Medieval Saga

Hence the very story whose first existence was in the form of a side strand in the Óláfr biography achieved, at some point in the thirteenth century, independent status—only to be reabsorbed as a discontinuous strand, itself stranded, in the *Longest Saga*. Similarly intercalated in the *Longest Saga* are the ongoing accounts of Kjartan Óláfsson (five segments), the Jómsvíkings (two segments), Stefnir Þorgilsson (three segments), and the Vinland voyages (two segments). Into the adjacent *Óláfs saga helga* have been interlaced *Fóstbrœðra saga* (five segments) and *Ásbjarnar þáttr selsbana* (two segments). Distributed over both royal biographies are the sagas of the Faeroes (five segments) and the Orkneys (four segments). The scope and pattern of this procedure can be seen in the following list of the digressions, in order of their occurrence, in both sagas (interstitial passages of royal biography proper are excluded):[34]

Óláfs saga Tryggvasonar (Flateyjarbók)

A¹ Jómsvíkinga saga
B¹ Otto þáttr keisara
C¹ Færeyinga saga
A² Jómsvíkinga saga (continued)
D¹ Þorleifs þáttr jarlaskálds
E¹ Orkneyinga saga
F¹ Albani þáttr ok Sunnifu
G¹ The Icelandic settlement
H¹ Þorsteins þáttr uxafóts
G² The Icelandic settlement (continued)
I¹ Sǫrla þáttr
J¹ Stefnis þáttr Þorgilssonar
K¹ Rǫgnvalds þáttr ok Rauðs
L¹ Hallfreðar þáttr vandræðaskálds
M¹ Kjartans þáttr Óláfssonar
L² Hallfreðar þáttr vandræðaskálds (continued)
L³ Hallfreðar þáttr vandræðaskálds (continued)
M² Kjartans þáttr Óláfssonar (continued)
M³ Kjartans þáttr Óláfssonar (continued)
L⁴ Hallfreðar þáttr vandræðaskálds (continued)
N¹ Ǫgmundar þáttr dytts
M⁴ Kjartans þáttr Óláfssonar (continued)
M⁵ Kjartans þáttr Óláfssonar (continued)

[34]The list is adapted from the table of contents in the Vigfússon/Unger edition.

L⁵  Hallfreðar þáttr vandræðaskálds (continued)
O¹  Nornagests þáttr
P¹  Helga þáttr Þórissonar
J²  Stefnis þáttr Þorgilssonar (continued)
C²  Færeyinga saga (continued)
Q¹  Þorvalds þáttr tasalda
R¹  Sveins þáttr ok Finns
S¹  Rauðs þáttr ins ramma
T¹  Hrómundar þáttr halta
U¹  Þorsteins þáttr skelks
V¹  Þiðranda þáttr ok Þórhalls
W¹  Kristni þáttr
X¹  Eiríks þáttr rauða
X²  Eiríks þáttr rauða (continued)
Y¹  Vínlands saga
Z¹  Svaða þáttr ok Arnórs kerlingarnefs
W²  Kristni þáttr (continued)
L⁶  Hallfreðar þáttr vandræðaskálds (continued)
a¹  Eindriða þáttr ilbreiðs
L⁷  Hallfreðar þáttr vandræðaskálds (continued)
J³  Stefnis þáttr Þorgilssonar (continued)
b¹  Halldórs þáttr Snorrasonar
c¹  Orms þáttr Stórólfssonar
L⁸  Hallfreðar þáttr vandræðaskálds (continued)
Y²  Vínlands saga (continued)
C³  Færeyinga saga (continued)
E²  Orkneyinga saga (continued)
d¹  Hálfdanar þáttr svarta
e¹  Haralds þáttr hárfagra
f¹  Hauks þáttr hábrókar

Óláfs saga helga (Flateyjarbók)

g¹  Haralds þáttr grenska
h¹  Óláfs þáttr Geirstaðaálfs
i¹  Styrbjarnar þáttr Svíakappa
j¹  Hróa þáttr heimska
k¹  Fóstbrœðra saga
l¹  Eymundar þáttr Hringssonar
m¹  Tóka þáttr
n¹  Ísleifs þáttr byskups
k²  Fóstbrœðra saga (continued)
o¹  Eymundar þáttr af Skǫrum

E³   Orkneyinga saga (continued)
p¹   Eindriða þáttr ok Erlings
k³   Fóstbrœðra saga (continued)
q¹   Ásbjarnar þáttr selsbana
q²   Ásbjarnar þáttr selsbana (continued)
C⁴   Færeyinga saga (continued)
r¹   Knúts þáttr ins ríka
s¹   Steins þáttr Skaptasonar
t¹   Rauðúlfs þáttr
u¹   Vǫlsa þáttr
k⁴   Fóstbrœðra saga (continued)
k⁵   Fóstbrœðra saga (continued)
C⁵   Færeyinga saga (continued)
E⁴   Orkneyinga saga (continued)
v¹   Nóregs konungatal
w¹   Brenna Adams byskups

If the intertwining appears in some cases to have been introduced in the interest of a proper chronology (temporally, it is
more natural to thread the biography of Hallfreðr onto the biography of Óláfr at intervals than it would be to embed it as a single
unit), it seems in other cases to be gratuitous. The short (about
eleven pages) *Ásbjarnar þáttr selsbana*, for example (q¹ and q² in
the list), is dramatically interrupted when the narrator reverts to
the main topic and tells something of Óláfr's conversion activities
in Norway (chap. 176) and the birth of Magnús inn góði (chap.
177). Only then is the digression resumed, as it were, and
Ásbjǫrn's story concluded (chap. 178). The interruption has no
chronological justification and could just as easily have been delayed a page. But its interposition serves to remind us that the
compiler, like the classical saga narrator, put a premium on suspense through interruption.

*Flateyjarbók* is thus an object lesson in the workings of
baroque exposition and in the role of narrative stranding in the
expansion of the form. The conception of the narration as a complex moving tapestry allows for almost infinite amplification by a
simple process of weaving tangential themes onto the edges of the
main theme, and yet other themes onto the tangential themes, all
by the logic of entailment. The compiler, it will be recalled (see p.
36 above), offered (or retained) as a defense for narrative mul-
tifariousness an analogy with nature: "Just as running water

flows from various sources yet all comes together in a single place, so, in like wise, do all these stories from various sources have a common goal.'' The dynamic image of a network of streams joining to form a swelling mainstream is particularly appropriate not only to the encyclopedic compilation, but to saga composition in general. *Flateyjarbók* is often regarded as a mechanical exercise, a thing apart from classical saga, but it is better seen as a more extreme rendition, the logical end point, of a literary technique that is evident, in lesser and varying degrees, over the generic range.[35]

## The Language of Stranding

The question arises how the sagas can maintain such an elaborate and artificial structure and at the same time appear so narratively naive. How does it happen that a compositional form that would seem by definition to be predicated on extensive authorial intervention enjoys an almost universal reputation as the most extreme example in Western tradition of figural narration? The incompatibility is striking and invites a reconsideration of the doctrine of nonintrusion. The obvious starting point is the narrative mechanics of the saga at those junctures where authorial directions would seem to be required—at those moments, that is, when strands are initiated, suspended, retrieved, and terminated, and where the author might reasonably be expected to offer narrative guidance.

In many cases, particularly in shorter sagas or when the narrative interval in question (the narrated time between suspension and retrieval of a strand) is short, these transitions are accomplished silently or by means of such neutral and functionally ambiguous phrases as ''svá er frá sagt (thus is it said of)'' or ''nú er frá því at segja (now to tell of this).'' Elsewhere they are effected by means of phrases that are specific to the technique—phrases that recur as functional elements in similar contexts. These phrases make up what might be called the language of stranding.

Examples of phrases used to introduce a strand for the first time include:

---

[35]On interlace composition in *Þiðreks saga,* see Hans Friese, *Thidrekssaga und Dietrichsepos: Untersuchungen zur inneren und äusseren Form,* Palaestra, 128 (Berlin: Mayer & Müller, 1914).

Þorgnýr er greindr til sǫgunnar (Þorgnýr is added into the saga)
Sá maðr er nefndr til sǫgunnar, er Arnórr hét (That man is brought
into [lit. "named to"] the saga who was called Arnórr)
Nú víkr sǫgunni vestr til Breiðafjarðardala (Now the saga turns west
to Breiðafjarðardalir)

Examples of phrases indicating a temporary suspension of a
strand include:

sem enn mun sagt verða síðar (of which more will be told later)
sem enn mun heyra mega síðar í sǫgunni (of which one will be able to
    hear more later in the saga)
er síðar var getit (as will be [lit. "has been"] brought up later)
munu vér hér fyrst hverfa frá (let us now turn away [from this
    matter] for a while)
koma þeir allir við þessa sǫgu síðan (they all appear in this saga
    later)
hverfum hér frá at sinni (we turn away [from this episode] for the
    time being)
nú verðr þar at hvílask (there [this action] will rest for now)

The retrieval of a suspended strand is a more complex negotia-
tion, requiring an act of memory, sometimes a major one, on the
part of the audience. Retrieval phrases are especially conspicuous in the sagas, not least because they are often syntactically
overloaded with "recall" information—recapitulation of an earlier action and renaming of character, time, and place.

Nú er at segja frá Snorra goða, at hann fór til féránsdóms í Bitru
    norðr, sem fyrr var ritat (Now it is to be told of Snorri goði that he
    went to the court of confiscation north in Bitra, as was written
    before)
Nú þar til at taka, er áðr var frá horfit, at laugardaginn eptir reið
    Vermundr (Now [the story] takes up at that point, where it left off
    before, when Vermundr rode, on the following Saturday)
Þórir, sonr Ketils flatnefs, er fyrr var frá sagt, at vá Áskel goða
    (Þórir, son of Ketill flatnefr, of whom it was said before that he
    killed Áskell goði)
Nú er at segja frá sýslu Þórðar, hversu honum endisk (Now it is to be
    told of Þórðr's activity, and how it turns out for him)
Nú er þar til máls at taka er þeir skilðu með vináttu, sem fyrr er ritat

(Now it is time to take up the story where they parted on friendly terms, as was written before)

Sometimes the suspension of one strand and the retrieval of another are negotiated in single or adjacent phrases:

Nú verðr þar frá at hverfa um stund, en taka til út á Íslandi ok heyra, hvat þar gerisk til tíðenda, meðan Þorkell er útan. (Now we must leave [this matter] for a while and take [the story] up again out in Iceland, to hear what was happening there while Þorkell was abroad.)
Hermundr hét sonr hans Eyvindar ok Hrómundr inn halti, er síðar verðr getit. Látum þar nú fyrst líða um, en segjum nǫkkut frá Hrolleifi. (Hermundr was the name of Eyvindr's son, and also Hrómundr inn halti, who will be mentioned later. Let us pass over this for the time being and say something of Hrolleifr.)
Nú munum vér fyrst láta dveljask sǫguna of hríð ok segja heldr nakkvat frá þeim jartegnum háleitum. (Now we will let the saga [proper] rest for a while, and instead say something of those glorious miracles.)
Nú munum vér hvílask láta fyrst frásǫgn Þormóðar Kolbrúnarskálds ok segja nǫkkut af Þorgeiri. Nú er at segja frá Þorgeiri. (Now we shall let the account of Þormóðr Kolbrúnarskáld rest for a while and relate something of Þorgeirr. Now to tell of Þorgeirr.)

Terminating formulas include:

lýkr þar frá Geirmundi at segja (and there [the story] stops telling of Geirmundr)
er hann ór sǫgunni (he is out of the saga)
kemr hann ekki síðan við þessa sǫgu (he does not appear again in this saga)

The first point to be made about the language of stranding is that it is itself, or is immediately linked with, the most formulaic language of the sagas. Directly implicated are the narrator formulas ("Nú er þar til máls at taka [Now the story takes up at the point]," "Nú er at segja frá [Now it is to be told of]," and the like), which appear abundantly in connection with strand-shifting, particularly the resumption of suspended strands. Not all such junctures are marked by narrator formulas (the transition may also be accomplished silently or by means of such "neutral"

phrases as "svá er sagt (so it is said [that])," but the large majority of narrator formulas appear—at least in classical saga
narrative—most predictably and most conspicuously at retrieval
points. The mnemonic function of these phrases is confirmed by
the fact that their absence, presence, and form are to a large
extent determined by the length of elapsed time in question: the
longer the interval, the more likely there is to be a narrator formula (or formulas), the more elaborate it is likely to be, and the
more narrative information it is likely to embrace. An example of
a syntactically overloaded instruction is the one mentioned earlier
from *Grettis saga:* "Þar er nú til at taka, er áðr var frá horfit, at
Þorbjǫrn ǫxnamegin spurði víg Þorbjarnar ferðalangs, sem fyrr
var sagt" (Now to pick up a line of the story that was set aside
earlier, in which Þorbjǫrn ǫxnamegin learned of the slaying of
Þorbjǫrn ferðalangr, as was told before)—chap. 42. The line of
the story being retrieved was set aside some ten pages earlier
(roughly half an hour in oral performance).

The functional interrelation of narrator formulas and stranded
composition is nowhere more neatly demonstrated than in the
two versions of *Hallfreðar saga,* one in *Mǫðruvallabók (M)* and
the other in the *Longest Saga (O).* Derived from a common original, the *M* version is integral and the *O* version subdivided into
eight parts and stranded at intervals into its host narrative. An
examination of the sixteen narrative seams of the latter, and a
comparison of their wording with that of the corresponding passages in the integral version, reveal the compiler's method:

M:   Um várit sagði hann konungi, at hann lysti at sjá Ísland.

O:   <L>Jtlu siðaR vm varit en Olafr konungr hafði sent Leif Eiriks
     son til Grænlandz gekk Hallfreðr vandræða skalld fyrir konung
     einn dag ok bað ser orlofs at fara vt til Islandz vm sumarit.

(M:  In the spring he told the king that he wished to see Iceland.
     [chap. 9]

O:   A little later in the same spring that King Óláfr had sent Leif
     Eiriksson to Greenland, Hallfreðr went to the king one day
     and asked permission to journey to Iceland in the summer.)
     [chap. 232]

M:   Þat sumar fór Hallfreðr til Svíþjóðar ok kom á fund konungs
     ok kvaddi hann.

O: N<V> er þar til at taka er Hallfreyðr uandræða skalld var austr aa Gautlandi .ij. uetr. ok hafði gengit at eiga heiðna kono. hann for aa fund Olafs Suía konungs ok flutti honum drapu er hann hafði ort um hann.

(M: That summer Hallfi eði went to Sweden and went before the king and greeted him. [chap. 9]

O: Now [the story] takes up [at the point when] Hallfreðr had been east in Gautland for two years and had married a heathen woman. He went before Óláfr Svíakonungr and declaimed a *drápa* he had composed about him.) [chap. 219]

M: Ok um várit, er hann fór norðr, þá rak á fyrir þeim hríð.

O: N<V>skal þar til taka sem fyrr var fra horfit at Hallfreðr vandræða skalld sigldi ut til Islandz vm svmarit aðr en barðagiN varð aa Orminum. kom Hallfreðr vt fyrir norþan land ok reið suðr vm heiði sem aðr er sagt.

(M: And in the spring, when he went north, a storm broke over them. [chap. 10]

O: Now [we] shall take up where [we] left off before, when Hallfreðr sailed out to Iceland in the summer before the battle on the [ship] Ormr. Hallfreðr landed in the northern part of the country and rode south across the heath, as was told before.) [chap. 264]

Stranding generates formulas; and formulas, together with the summaries they accompany, explain the relation of the narrative parts.

The language of stranding, then, amounts to a set of narrative directions—formulas in which the narrator addresses the audience on the mechanics of composition. These instructions are authorial intrusions, even though their brevity, impersonality, and formulaic quality have tended to impede their identification as such. The phrase "Nú munum vér hvílask láta fyrst frásǫgn Þormóðar Kolbrúnarskálds ok segja nǫkkut af Þorgeiri (Now we shall let the account of Þormóðr Kolbrúnarskáld rest and relate something of Þorgeirr)" is an exact functional counterpart of "Now lat hire slepe, and we oure tales holde / Of Troilus, that is to paleis riden / Fro the scarmuch of the which I tolde" (*Troilus and Criseyde*, Book 2, vv. 932–34). But where Chaucer puts himself in the foreground and indulges the convention, the classical saga narrators normally remain in the background, with the result that their intrusions are not always obvious as such. The studied avoidance of first-person constructions appears, significantly, to be a late development in Norse prose—a point to be taken up in some detail in chapter 4.

## Material Art and Skaldic Poetry

The idea that viking art and skaldic poetry are manifestations of the same underlying sensibility is a commonplace of Scandinavian literary criticism. Axel Olrik drew the general comparison,[36] but it remained for Andreas Heusler to probe the analogy (despite his hesitations about a "germanisches Stilgefühl").[37] The classic statement is that of Hallvard Lie, who (well in advance of Vinaver and Leyerle) related the origin of *dróttkvætt* centrally to the "abstract, unorganic sense of form" of such material artifacts as the Oseberg carvings.[38] In his *"Natur" og "Unatur" in skaldekunsten* he writes:

> The characteristic syntax of the skalds is a form of literary interlace, and as such is closely associated with contemporary ornamental art. Recitation required a suppleness of voice, a method of shading and coloring the sounds, in order to bring out the logical line in the verbal braiding; a suppleness essentially like that on which the clear comprehension and enjoyment of ornamental art in the visual field is predicated; a suppleness, indeed, fundamental to the ancient conception of art as virtuoso performance.[39]

The sagas have not been subjected to such a comparison, but rather have been regarded as a thing apart: straightforward, natural, lucid, "classical" rather than baroque in impulse—the polar opposite of skaldic verse.[40] In light of this general view,

---

[36] Axel Olrik, *Nordisk aandsliv i vikingetid og tidlig middelalder* (Copenhagen: Gyldendal, 1907), p. 75.
[37] Andreas Heusler, *Die altgermanische Dichtung*, 2d ed. (Potsdam: Athenaion, 1941), pp. 140–43.
[38] Hallvard Lie, "Skaldestil-studier," *Maal og minne* (1952), p. 53.
[39] Lie, *"Natur" og "unatur,"* p. 28.
[40] See, for example, Dietrich Hofmann, "Vers und Prosa in der mündlich gepflegten mittelalterlichen Erzählkunst der germanischen Länder," *Frühmit-*

Hollander's brief analogy between the interbraided structure of *Eyrbyggja saga* and the contrived syntax of skaldic poetry stands out as all the more exceptional. Hollander perceived that style is one thing and composition another—an elementary distinction, but one that has proved curiously elusive in saga studies. The prose of the saga may be plain and natural, reflecting the patterns of an oral telling style; but the organization of the story is patently unnatural, closer in spirit to the sinuous patterns of skaldic diction, and in turn to the material art of early Scandinavia, than has generally been appreciated. The interlace aesthetic appears in fact to have been more tenacious in the verbal arts than in the visual ones, for viking ornament declined radically during the eleventh century, at least in its elite manifestations,[41] whereas its literary counterparts survived and even flourished well into the thirteenth. But to conclude, as Lie does, that skaldic poetry is "without doubt the most conservative artistic development in Europe's history"[42] is to ignore the prevalence of interlace forms in medieval art throughout Europe (notably in Romanesque ornamentation) and the corresponding development of labyrinthine structures in imaginative vernacular literature. It is less useful to regard viking art and skaldic poetry as retrograde and special developments than to see them as anticipatory ones—early northern expressions of what neoclassical detractors as well as modern scholars consider to be a characteristically medieval habit of mind. If saga composition is not the immediate inheritor of the northern patterns, it participates in the larger phenomenon.

## The European Context

The principle of interlace was first articulated by Ferdinand Lot with reference to the *Prose Lancelot*.[43] He observed that the

---

*telalterliche Studien,* 5 (1971), 135–75: "The highly developed prose art of the classical sagas and the similarly highly developed verse art of skaldic poetry are, in their form, as diametrically opposed as one can imagine; they are also clearly distinct with respect to their functions" (pp. 169–70).

[41]David M. Wilson and Ole Kindt-Jensen, *Viking Art* (Ithaca, N.Y.: Cornell University Press, 1966).

[42]Lie, "Skaldestil-studier," p. 92.

[43]Ferdinand Lot, *Etude sur le Lancelot en prose* (Paris: Champion, 1918), esp. the chapter "Le principe de l'entrelacement."

narrative was built up discontinuously in such a way that each episode appeared to be a digression from the previous one and a sequel to some earlier unfinished story: "The *Lancelot* is not a mosaic from which one can deftly remove the tiles in order to replace them with others, but a weaving or a tapestry; if one tries to make a cut in it, the whole thing unravels."[44] C. S. Lewis, working independently of Lot, came to the same conclusion about Spenser's poetry; he termed the structure "polyphonic" and saw it as a "quintessentially medieval characteristic."[45] He linked it with the impulse at work in much medieval architecture and decoration. "We may call it the love of the labyrinthine," he wrote, "the tendency to offer to the mind or the eye something that cannot be taken in at a glance, something that at first looks planless though all is planned. Everything leads to everything else, but by very intricate paths."[46]

It remained for Eugène Vinaver to examine the aesthetics of interlace narrative, to suggest its origin and trace its evolution. Vinaver related verbal interlace to the patterns of "multiplication and recurrence" in Romanesque churches and illuminated manuscripts from the ninth through the eleventh centuries, and he ascribed both the visual and the literary forms to a common "fascination of tracing a theme through all its phases, of waiting for its return while following other themes, of experiencing the constant sense of their simultaneous presence."[47] Interlace narrative thus arose as a technical solution to the idea of simultaneous action: "The next and possibly the decisive step towards a proper understanding of cyclic romance," he wrote, "is the realization that since it is always possible, and often even necessary, for several themes to be pursued simultaneously, they have to alternate like threads in a woven fabric, one theme interrupting another and

---

[44]Ibid., p. 28.

[45]C. S. Lewis, introduction to extracts from Spenser in George Bagshawe Harrison, ed., *Major British Writers*, 2 vols. (New York: Harcourt Brace, 1954), I, 97–98.

[46]C. S. Lewis, *The Discarded Image* (Cambridge: Cambridge University Press, 1964), pp. 193–94.

[47]Eugène Vinaver, *The Rise of Romance* (New York: Oxford University Press, 1971), p. 81. See also Cedric Edward Pickford, *L'evolution du roman arthurien en prose vers la fin du moyen âge d'après le manuscrit 112 du fonds français de la Bibliothèque Nationale* (Paris: Nizet, 1960), pp. 186–201 ("L'Entrelacement").

again another, and yet all remaining constantly present in the author's and the reader's mind."[48]

The idea of literature as word-weaving is an old one. It should be recalled that "text" and "textile" have a common etymon, *textus*, the past participle of *texere*, "to weave" (to which ON *þáttr* is also related). Jordanes, for example, concludes a digression by saying:

> quod [recte: quo?] nos interim praetermisso sic ut promisimus omnem Gothorum texamus originem.
>
> (Setting this aside, let us now weave the whole story of the origin of the Goths, as we promised.) [*Getica*, XLVII]

Aldhelm and Alcuin use such phrases as "fingere serta" and "texere serta" ("to fashion or weave intertwinings") to refer to their own poetry.[49] Old English poetry has the phrases "wordum wrixlan (to vary with words)" (as the scop's art is characterized in *Beowulf*, v. 874) and "ic . . . wordcræftum wæf (I wove word-art)" (Cynewulf, of his *Elene*).[50] A consonant image in Norse is evoked by the literary use of such words as "snúa," "snúna," and "snara" ("to twist, turn"). Even the standard phrase "setja saman" (literally "to set together") connotes composition as a process not only of linear creation but as the articulation of component parts. A crucial word, of course, is *þáttr*, which has the etymological meaning of "strand in a rope" and is used pervasively in connection with parts of a longer narrative, though precisely in what sense is unclear.[51]

If an earlier generation of scholars saw these phrases as nothing more than casual figures of speech, recent critics have begun to explore the possibility that they are semitechnical terms meant to denote specific aspects of style or composition. Peter Dale Scott argues that Alcuin's *fingere serta* signified a "sustained interlock-

---

[48]Vinaver, *Rise of Romance*, p. 76.
[49]Peter Dale Scott, "Alcuin as Poet: Rhetoric and Belief in His Latin Verse," *University of Toronto Quarterly*, 33 (1964), 233–57.
[50]See John Leyerle, "The Interlace Structure of *Beowulf*," *University of Toronto Quarterly*, 37 (1967), 1–17.
[51]John Lindow, "Old Icelandic *þáttr*: Early Usage and Semantic History," *Scripta Islandica*, 29 (1978), 3–44.

ing of figurative meanings, operating continuously as a single world of reference underneath the literal development of the poem."[52] Taking as a starting point the interlace designs common in Anglo-Saxon pictorial art of the seventh and eighth centuries, John Leyerle distinguished two types of interlace composition, stylistic and structural, present in and characteristic of Old English poetry, especially *Beowulf.*[53] His first category refers to a form of syntactic embedding that has no counterpart in Norse prose, though it is amply paralleled (indeed, drastically exceeded) in skaldic diction. As an example of structural interlace he offers the account of Hygelac's Frisian expedition, which is related in four segments (vv. 1202–14, 2354–68, 2501–9, and 2913–21) and which serves to add a historical-ethical dimension to the events at hand. To the extent that this expedition of Hygelac's is related nonconsecutively—unlike the Finn episode, which is a single unit—it resembles the techniques of stranding. But saga stranding, like interlace in the prose romances, has by definition to do with the primary or present story, not with past events invoked as contrasts or parallels to the immediate action. The Hygelac episode is, despite its subdivided form, more closely related to the traditional excursus or digression than to patterns in the sagas or later romances.[54]

Stranding per se in early Germanic vernacular epic, to the extent that it exists at all, is occasional and rudimentary.[55] In *Beowulf,* the stories of Grendel and his mother may be considered potential strands. More artful, and more reminiscent of saga practice, is the alternation of focus, in the passage describing Beowulf's offensive at the mere, between the hero underwater (A) and his waiting men on the shore (B). The passage is in this respect compositionally identical to its analogue in *Grettis saga* (chap. 66), in which Grettir undertakes an assault on a giant under a waterfall:

[52]Scott, "Alcuin as Poet," p. 251.
[53]Leyerle, "Interlace Structure," esp. pp. 4–7.
[54]For a critical comment on Leyerle's application of the interlace idea, see Howell D. Chickering, *Beowulf: A Dual-Language Edition* (Garden City, N.Y.: Doubleday, Anchor, 1977), pp. 19–20.
[55]See C. M. Bowra, *Heroic Poetry* (London: Macmillan, 1964), pp. 347–51.

A¹ + B¹   hero on shore with contingent
A²        hero descends, fights adversary; blood rises to the surface
B²        shore contingent sees blood, departs (the Danes in *Beowulf*,
          the priest in *Grettis saga*)
A³        hero completes task, ascends
A⁴ + B³   hero rejoins shore contingent

The blood rising to the surface is an example of what has been
called the "following technique," whereby focus is shifted from
one side of the story to another (here from A² to B²) by means of a
natural conduit (such as messengers, beggarwomen, and the
like).[56] In the *Chanson de Roland* the sound of the horn is the link
between Charlemagne's army and the rear guard:

> Li quens Rollant, par peine e par ahans,
> Par grant dulor sunet sun olifan.
> Par mi la buche en salt fors li cler sancs,
> De sun cervel le temple en est rumpant.
> Del corn qu'il tient l'oïe en est mult grant,
> Karles l'entent, ki est as porz passant.
> Naimes li duc l'oïd, si l'escultent li Franc.
> Ce dist li reis: "Jo oi le corn Rollant!
> Unc nel sunast se nu fust cumbatant."

> (Count Roland, with pain and suffering,
> With great agony sounds his oliphant.
> Bright blood comes gushing from his mouth,
> The temple of his brain has burst.
> The sound of the horn he is holding carries very far,
> Charles, who is going through the pass, hears it.
> Duke Naimes heard it, the Franks listen for it.
> The King says: "I hear Roland's horn!
> He'd never sound it if he weren't fighting.")
>                                   [*Chanson de Roland*, laisse 134]

The narrative of the *Roland* is notoriously episodic and the focus
ranges widely, lighting variously on different parts of the tab-

---

[56]Kenneth Sisam explains an apparent inconsistency in *Beowulf* vv. 837–927
(the return from the mere) as a primitive attempt to render parallel actions. See his
*The Structure of Beowulf* (Oxford: Clarendon, 1965), pp. 29–32.

leau.[57] Although the itinerant perspective gives the whole the appearance of a tapestry, it is quite a different sort from that of the sagas. The *Roland* "strands" are not logically interlocking stories, but static pictures that succeed and displace one another according to an aesthetic of parallelism, repetition, contrast, and balance. Only when the horn is blown and the interplay between the two parts of the army begins in earnest does the story fork briefly into two scenic lines.

Only in romance from the late eleventh and early twelfth centuries does interlace first emerge as a recurrent feature of composition. As was suggested in Chapter 1, there was a corresponding emphasis, in the rhetorical literature of the same period, on various forms of linear expansion or amplification, digression in particular. Geoffrey of Vinsauf, it will be recalled, distinguished two kinds of digression: *ad aliud extra materiam* (introducing outside matter—a digression proper) and *ad aliam partem materiae* (moving to another part of the same matter). The second, he explained, involves omitting the part of the matter that follows directly and jumping instead to a later part.[58] If the former type refers to the standard procedure of embedding a related but subordinate substory in the main story, the latter type indicates a system of coordinates, by which the main story itself is divided into parts and respliced in a new order. Geoffrey's digression *ad aliam partem materiae* is thus tantamount to a definition of interlace and as such appears to codify in theoretical terms a practice of such proportions and duration that it may be regarded as a defining characteristic of medieval narrative.

There is a sense in which the Tristan story is predicated on the technique of digression *ad aliam partem materiae*. Not one but several lines of action are developed separately, and the dramatic

---

[57]Erich Auerbach, *Mimesis: The Representation of Reality in Western Literature*, trans. W. R. Trask (Princeton: Princeton University Press, 1953), pp. 83–107; also Bowra, *Heroic Poetry*, pp. 348–49.

[58]"A materia ad aliam partem materiae, quando omittimus illam partem materiae quae proxima est et aliam quae sequitur primam assumimus (One goes to another part of the matter when one omits that part of the matter that follows directly and skips instead to a later part of the matter)". From Geoffrey of Vinsauf, "Documentum de modo et arte dictandi et versificandi," 2.2.18, in Edmond Faral, *Les arts poétiques du XIIᵉ et XIIIᵉ siècle* (Paris: Champion, 1958), p. 274.

interest of the story lies in their intersections. This is true of the versions of Béroul and Eilhart as well as that of Thomas, though their patterns of alternation are not identical. It would appear from a comparison of Thomas's fragments with *Tristrams saga* that the Norse redactor followed the original faithfully in this respect. At one major juncture, when narrative focus shifts from the ship carrying Ysolt and Caerdin from London to the wounded Tristan in Brittany, the Norse redactor supplies a retrieval formula: "Nú er at víkja sǫgunni til Tristrams... (Now the saga will turn to Tristram)"—(chap. 97). In the immensely popular *Prose Tristan,* which all but supplanted the poetic versions, the story is further fragmented and intertwined in the characteristic patterns of interlace.

Examples of interlace in the verse romances of Chrétien de Troyes are few and for the most part of the standard digressive type (*ad aliud extra materiam*).[59] But in the second half of *Li contes del graal,* when the story forks into a Gawain action and a Perceval action, the narrative accordingly strands *ad aliam partem materiae.* The same or a similar scheme recurs throughout the vast proliferations of the Grail story: in the Continuations, in Wolfram's *Parzival,* in the Norse *Parcevals saga* (which takes the story up to v. 6518) and *Valvers þáttr* (which corresponds to vv. 6519–9234), and above all in the monumental prose Vulgate Cycle of the thirteenth century. It is in this last suite of works that interlace finds its most characteristic form and saga composition its closest counterpart: story lines are interwoven, broken off, and then picked up again and knit together—not merely as a solution for a divided story, but for its own sake as a literary effect. The *Queste del saint graal,* for example, follows the peregrinations of Lancelot, Perceval, Bors, Gawain, and Galahad, stranding from one to another in succession and at unexpected junctures (sometimes mid-episode). These episodes are further interrupted with passages of a didactic nature, in the form of holy men's or hermits' speeches. As in saga narrative, fragmentation and discontinuity are not only tolerated but actively

---

[59]See Wilhelm Kellermann, *Aufbaustil und Weltbild Chrestiens von Troyes im Percevalroman* (Halle/Saale: Niemeyer, 1936), esp. pp. 50–51 and passim in chapter 3 ("Das kompositionelle Gefüge der Handlung").

pursued. In the *Prose Lancelot,* the "wounded knight" strand is
introduced; then suspended while the narrator tells of Lancelot
and Guinevere; retrieved as Lancelot aids him and swears to
avenge him; suspended while the narrator turns to several fresh
martial episodes involving Lancelot and Arthur; retrieved again
as Lancelot fights a battle on his behalf; then abandoned again;
and so on for some eight hundred pages.[60] The artificiality of the
exercise becomes apparent when, as in the case of Malory, there
is an effort to undo the process, to gather the constituent parts
into a normal or progressive order and thus to create a well-
circumscribed story. One of Malory's sources, the interlaced
*Suite du Merlin,* has three main themes: the doings of Merlin (A),
the wars of Arthur (B), and the machinations of Morgan le Fay
(C). In the middle portion of the story, they alternate in the order
$A^1 B^1 C^1 A^2 B^2 C^2 A^3 B^3 C^3$, and so on. But Malory, in reaction to
interlace composition and in an apparent effort to bring his material in line with the more straightforward English practice,[61]
changed the order to $A^1 A^2 A^3 B^1 B^2 B^3 C^1 C^2 C^3$, and so on. In
other words, Vinaver explains, the "three threads of the narrative
are unravelled and straightened out so as to form in each case a
consistent and self-contained set of adventures."[62] The interlace
procedure is nowhere more visible than in those cases where it is
reversed and the parts set together single file.

The composition of the Vulgate Cycle is also governed, as Lot
first perceived, by a principle of inseparability, whereby no single
part of the story is self-contained but is anticipated or recalled in
other parts of the story: "The web is uncuttable, the delayed
continuations necessary for enrichment of themes; the seeming
elaborations are essential parts."[63] The effect of the technique is
not only to chart what is to come, but to confer new meaning on
what has passed. From the *Prose Lancelot* comes an example in

---

[60]In Sommer's edition from III, 119, to IV, 96. See Vinaver, *Rise of Romance,*
pp. 81–83.

[61]Larry Benson stresses the difference in compositional practice between English romance (straightforward and simplex) and French romance (interlaced) in
his *Malory's Morte Darthur* (Cambridge, Mass.: Harvard University Press, 1976),
pp. 43–64.

[62]Eugène Vinaver, *The Works of Sir Thomas Malory,* 2d ed. (Oxford: Clarendon, 1967), p. lxx.

[63]Tuve, *Allegorical Imagery,* p. 369.

which Lancelot suddenly identifies the opponent he is facing in combat by means of his sword—Galehaut's sword, given by Lancelot to Bors over three hundred pages earlier:

This is the sword Lancelot has just taken from the tomb of Galehault. The death of this man, which occurred immediately before the cart episode, remains unknown to his friend for a long time (Baudemagu is careful to conceal it from him). It is only by chance, in going to the aid of Meléaguant's sister, that Lancelot encounters this tomb and that an epitaph reveals the truth to him. He arranges for the body of his companion to be transported to the Dolorous Gard and has it buried at the place where once, when he captured this castle, he had seen his name inscribed with these letters: "Here will lie the body of Lancelot of the Lake, son of King Ban of Benoyc." And in fact, on the last page of the work (the end of the *Mort Artu*), Lancelot's body lies in the very same tomb in which the body of his friend had been laid to rest.[64]

This, as Vinaver put it, "at once brings home, but only to those whose memory can retain it, a whole cluster of events in their subtle succession, culminating in the tragedy of Galehaut's death."[65] The same principle is put to excellent use in saga narrative.[66] Hallgerðr's refusal to donate her hair to the cause of Gunnarr's defense is a moment in which are crystallized the earlier references to its abundant beauty. Gísli's leaving the weapon Grásíða in Þorgrímr's body is, in light of that weapon's history and scheduled fate, a chilling act of hubris which marks the beginning of the end. Taken by itself, Óláfr Haraldsson's slip of the tongue as he faces the opposing force at Stiklastaðir has no particular point (*Legendary Saga*, chap. 89); but taken together with

[64]Lot, *Etude sur le Lancelot en prose*, p. 27.
[65]Vinaver, *Rise of Romance*, p. 83.
[66]Intertextural techniques have long been recognized in the sagas, but it remained for Anne Heinrichs to treat them categorically: "A feature . . . is 'intertextural' when it, as one part of a text, points directly to another part of the text that appears sooner or later (sometimes surprisingly late). The linking is usually indicated by the reappearance of the same or of similar phraseology. The text to come may be anticipated by the audience beforehand, or it may come as a revelation when it occurs, the author allowing a connection to appear only then. In this way a stylistic pattern is established that has, I think, certain similarities to that produced in the art of weaving or of embroidering tapestry . . . and also to the Germanic art of ornamental gold and metal work" ("'Intertexture,'" pp. 127–28).

the prophecy some sixty pages earlier that "skammt eigi hann þá
ólífat, er honum verðr mismæli á munni (he won't have long to
live once his tongue trips"—chap. 18) it becomes an announce-
ment that the fatal hour has arrived. In saga as in romance intertexture, as Vinaver put it, "no recapitulation or reminder is
needed; everything that happens remains present, firmly fixed in
the mind, as if the mind's eye could absorb simultaneously all the
scattered fragments of the theme, in the same way as our vision
can absorb the development of a motif along the entire length of
an interlaced ornament."[67]
     A work startlingly like *Flateyjarbók* in narrative conception is
*Les prophécies de Merlin*. A compilation made between 1272 and
1279, it incorporates in its otherwise didactic prophecies certain
stories, discontinuously told, of a more romantic nature. Lucy
Allen Paton distinguishes nineteen strands in the "rope" and outlines their order in a table of contents much like that of *Flateyjarbók*:[68]

Les prophécies de Merlin

| | |
|---|---|
| A[1] | Mador de la Porte |
| B[1] | The plots of Morgain la Fee and Claudas de la Deserte against the Dame du Lac |
| C[1] | Golistan le Fort |
| D[1] | Alisandre l'Orfelin |
| E[1] | The Tournament of Sorelois |
| F[1] | The Saxon Invasion |
| E[2] | The Tournament of Sorelois (continued) |
| G[1] | Perceval le Galois |
| E[3] | The Tournament of Sorelois (continued) |
| F[2] | The Saxon Invasion (continued) |
| G[2] | Perceval le Galois (continued) |
| H[1] | Morgain la Fee, Sebile l'Enchanteresse, and the Reine de Norgales |
| F[3] | The Saxon Invasion (continued) |
| G[3] | Perceval le Galois (continued) |
| I[1] | Segurant le Brun |
| F[4] | The Saxon Invasion (continued) |

---

[67]Vinaver, *Rise of Romance*, p. 83. See also the chapter "La création romanesque" in his *A la recherche d'une poétique médiévale* (Paris: Nizet, 1970), pp.
129–49.
[68]As in Paton's edition, I, xvii–xxi.

H²   Morgain la Fee, Sebile l'Enchanteresse, and the Reine de Norgales (continued)

I²   Segurant le Brun (continued)

F⁵   The Saxon Invasion (continued)

J¹   The War of Palamedes and Saphar with Karados de la Doulereuse Tour

F⁶   The Saxon Invasion (continued)

K¹   The Dame du Lac and Bohors

F⁷   The Saxon Invasion (continued)

J²   The War of Palamedes and Saphar with Karados de la Doulereuse Tour (continued)

F⁸   The Saxon Invasion (continued)

I³   Segurant le Brun (continued)

H³   Morgain la Fee, Sebile l'Enchanteresse, and the Reine de Norgales (continued)

F⁹   The Saxon Invasion (continued)

D²   Alisandre l'Orfelin (continued)

F¹⁰   The Saxon Invasion (continued)

L¹   Richard de Jerusalem

M¹   Arthur and the Knight of Carmelyde

K²   The Dame du Lac and Bohors (continued)

I⁴   Segurant le Brun (continued)

N¹   The Crusade of Archemais

D³   Alisandre l'Orfelin (continued)

O¹   The Plots of King Marc against Tristan

P¹   The Dame d'Avalon, the Reine de Norgales, Sebile l'Enchanteresse, and Morgain

O²   The Plots of King Marc against Tristan (continued)

C²   Golistan le Fort (continued)

Q¹   Lancelot and Gohenbert

R¹   The Plot of Claudas against Lancelot

D⁴   Alisandre l'Orfelin (continued)

S¹   The Tourney cried by Arthur for the Riche Roy Pescheor

The unusualness of the *Prophécies*—Paton calls it "a unique production even in an age of extraordinary compilations"[69]— makes all the more remarkable its similarity to *Flateyjarbók.* Just as the *Færeyinga saga, Orkneyinga saga, Jómsvíkinga saga, Kjartans þáttr, Fóstbrœðra saga,* and other narratives are inserted piecemeal into the two Óláfr sagas, so, in the *Prophécies,* the

[69]Lucy Allen Paton, "Notes on Manuscripts of the *Prophécies de Merlin*," *PMLA,* 8 (1913), 122.

history of the Saxon invasion (F) is related in ten parts, the story of Morgain la Fée (H) in three parts, the story of Perceval (G) in three parts, the story of Segurant le Brun (I) in four parts, the story of Alixandre l'Orphelin (D) in four parts, and so forth. Alixandre's story, also found in a late version of the *Prose Tristan,* thus stands in exactly the same relation to the *Prophécies* as the story of Hallfreðr does to the *Longest Saga.*[70] In each case, an independent story has been threaded nonconsecutively onto a host narrative (itself little more than a compilation of such strands), and in each case, the parts of this substory, removed from the larger text and set together single file, form a continuous and complete biographical history.

Just as interlace must originally have been related to certain rhetorical notions of digression and its classical antecedents, so may the verbal formulas of interlace be originally related to a figure Quintilian labeled an *aphodos:* a phrase by which an excursus is concluded and the theme resumed.[71] *Aphodoi* are regularly employed by certain medieval Latin historians. In his *Getica,* for example, Jordanes commonly begins or concludes chapters with such phrases as these:

> Nunc autem ad id, unde digressum fecimus, redeamus doceamusque, quomodo ordo gentis, unde agimus, cursus sui metam explevit.)
> (But now let us return to the point whence we made our digression

---

[70]On the Alixandre story, see Cedric Edward Pickford, "Miscellaneous French Prose Romances," in *Arthurian Literature in the Middle Ages: A Collaborative History,* ed. Roger Sherman Loomis (Oxford: Clarendon, 1959), esp. pp. 353–54; and also his *Alixandre l'Orphelin: A Prose Tale of the Fifteenth Century* (Manchester: Manchester University Press, 1951).

[71]Quintilian gives the example, "Longius evectus sum, sed redeo ad propositium (I have made a long digression, but now return to the point"—IX:3.87); see H. E. Butler, ed., *The Institutio Oratoria of Quintilian,* Loeb Classical Library (New York: Putnam's, 1921), III, 496–98. On the *aphodos,* see Heinrich Lausberg, *Handbuch der literarischen Rhetorik* (Munich: Max Hueber, 1960), p. 187. Ernst Robert Curtius noted: "The Middle Ages was far from demanding unity of subject and inner coherence of structure in a work of literature. Indeed, digression (*egressio, excessus*) was regarded as a special elegance.... Accordingly, the medieval conception of art does not attempt to conceal digressions by transitions—on the contrary, poets often point them out with a certain satisfaction" (*European Literature and the Latin Middle Ages,* trans. Willard R. Trask [New York: Harper & Row, 1963], pp. 501–2).

and tell how the stock of this people of whom I speak reached the end of its course.) [XIV]

Ceterum causa exegit, ad id, unde digressimus, ordine redeamus.
(But our subject requires us to return in due order to the point whence we digressed.) [XV]

Ad propositum vero, unde nos digressimus, iubante domino redeamus.
(But let us now with the Lord's help return to the subject from which we have digressed.) [XII]

Adam of Bremen employs the figure in a more general way to link and synchronize component parts of the same story:

Nunc ad cetera, unde incepimus, regrediamur.
(Now let us return to the other matters with which we began.) [I:17]

De cuius fortitudine vel potentia, quam super barbaros habuit, postea dicemus. Et haec quidem forinsecus dum varia sorte gesta sunt, in Bremis status rerum labefactari cepit.
(Of his valor and the power he had over the barbarians we shall speak presently. While, indeed, these things were with varying fortunes taking place abroad, the state of affairs in Bremen began to slip.) [II:79–80]

Nunc per hystoriae ordinem redeamus ad ecclesiae legationem.
(Now let us return in the order of our history to the mission of the church.) [II:50]

Likewise, Paul the Deacon in his *Historia Langobardorum*:

His cursim, quae omittenda non erant, narratis, ad nostrae seriem revertamur historiae.
(These things, which were not to be omitted, having been briefly told, let us return to the regular order of our history.) [I:26]

Exigit vero nunc locus, postposita generali historia, pauca etiam privatim de mea, qui haec scribo, genealogia retexere, et quia res ita postulat, paulo superius narrationis ordinem replicare.
(The topic now requires me to postpone my general history and relate also a few matters of a private character concerning the

genealogy of myself who write these things, and because the case so demands, I must go back a little earlier in the order of my narrative.) [IV:39]

Haec paucis de propriae genealogiae serie delibatis, nunc generalis historiae revertamur ad tramitem.
(These few things having been considered concerning the chain of my own genealogy, now let us return to the thread of the general history.) [IV:37]

Though infrequent, such phrases as these from the *Gesta Danorum* indicate Saxo's familiarity with the *aphodos* as a digressive device:

Sed ne peregrinis ulterius immorer, stilum ad propria referam.
(But let me not dwell further on foreign matters; I shall turn the discourse back to the subject proper.) [14:liv]

Et ne quis hunc bellis sexum insudasse miretur, quædam de talium feminarum condicione et moribus compendio modicæ digressionis expediam.
(And lest anyone wonder that this sex should exert itself at war, I shall communicate certain things about the circumstances and customs of such women in the form of a modest digression.) [7:vi]

Nunc a deverticulo propositum repetam.
(Now I shall return from this byway to my theme.) [7:vi]

The figure carried over into vernacular chronicle writing.[72] Such formulations as this one from the *Histoire de Saint Louis* are found occasionally in the histories of Villehardouin and repeatedly in those of Froissart and Joinville:

Or revenons à nostre matière, et disons ainsi, que tandis que li roys fermoit Cezaire, vint en l'ost messires Alenars de Senaingan, qui nous conta que il avoit fait sa nef ou réaume de Noroe, qui est en la fin dou monde devers Occident.

(Now we return to our main story and tell how, while the king was fortifying Caesarea, a certain Alenard of Senaingan came to the

[72]See Faral, *Les arts poétiques*, pp. 74–75; also Lewis, *Discarded Image*, p. 182.

army and told us that he had built his ship in the kingdom of Norway, which lies at the world's end, toward the west.) [XCVI]

The poetic romances use vernacular *aphodoi* less frequently, but in much the same way: in the first person and for digression in both of Geoffrey of Vinsauf's senses.

Or reviendrai al pedre et a la medre,
Et la 'spose que sole fut remese:
Quant il ço sovrent qued il fuiz s'en eret,
Ço fut granz dols qued il en demenerent,
Et granz deplainz par tote la contrede.

(Now I shall return to the father and the mother, and to the spouse who had remained alone; when they knew that he had fled, they mourned greatly, and great was the lamenting throughout the country.)[73] [*La vie de Saint Alexis*, st. 21]

Mes n'i vuel feire demorance
A parler de chascune chose.
A Thessala qui ni repose
de poisons feire et atanprer,
Vuel ma parole retorner.

(But I do not wish to stop to describe all this in detail. To Thessala, who does not pause in preparing and tempering her potions, my story wishes to return.) [*Cligès*, vv. 3245–50]

De monseignor Gavain se taist
Ichi li contes a estal,
Si commenche de Percheval.
Perchevax, ce nos dist l'estoire,
Ot si perdu la miemoire
Que de Dieu ni li sovient mais.[74]

(The story is silent about Sir Gawain at this point. Perceval, as the story tells us, had so lost his memory that he had forgotten God.) [*Perceval*, vv. 6214–16]

[73]Translation from William W. Ryding, *Structure in Medieval Narrative* (The Hague: Mouton, 1971), p. 70.
[74]The corresponding transition in *Parcevals saga* is: "En nú er at segja frá Parceval, at ... (And now it is to be told of Parceval, that..."—chap. 18).

Alle ir unmuoze    di lâzen wir nu sîn
und sagen, wie vrou Kriemhilt    unt ouch ir magedîn
gegen Rîne fuoren    von Nibelunge land.

(Let us leave their bustle and tell how Kriemhild and her maidens journeyed on towards the Rhine from the land of the Nibelungs.) [*Das Nibelungenlied*, st. 778]

Nu lâze wir daz belîben,    wie si gebâren hie.

(Now let us leave those of Hungary to their own devices.) [*Das Nibelungenlied*, st. 1506]

Middle English usage in the metrical romances appears for the most part to be a secondhand imitation of the French habit:

Lete we now þis fals knight    lyen in his care,
And talke we of Gamelyn    and loke how he fare. [*Gamelyn*, vv. 615–16]

But leue we of that lady here
And speake we more of that squyer. [*The Squire of Low Degree*, vv. 859–60]

Now let we of Blancheflour be
And speke of Florys in his countree. [*Floris and Blancheflour*, vv. 203–4]

Let him lye there stille,
He has nere that he soght.
And ye wil a while be stille
I shal telle yow how they wroght. [*Sir Gawain and the Green Knight*, vv. 1994–97]

Or from Chaucer:

But here I leve hire with hire fader dwelle,
And forth I wol of Troilus yow telle. [*Troilus and Criseyde*, V:28]

That the fictional use of *aphodoi* was not restricted to romance, but entered the epic sphere as well, is clear from examples in the thirteenth- and fourteenth-century *chansons de geste* (e.g., "Or le lairons ichi de Ogier ester" or "Or vos dirai de Ponchonet le fier" from *Ogier de Danemarche*, vv. 98 and 3946).

But it is, predictably, in the highly interlaced prose romances that *aphodoi* are used with great frequency—not to introduce the occasional digression, but in the service of a regular structural principle.[75] They are mostly of the intramural type, impersonal, and standard in form. Phrases such as the following from the *Mort Artu* occur with almost mechanical regularity throughout the Vulgate Cycle:

> Mais atant lesse ore li contes a parler del roi Artu et de sa compaignie et retorne a Lancelot por deviser l'achoison qui le detint d'aler a l'assemblee qui fut fete en la praerie de Kamaalot. Ci endroit dit li contes que quant Lancelos se fu partiz de Boort et d'Estor son frere, el chevaucha par mi la forest de Kamaalot une eure avant, autre eure arriere, et gisoit chascune nuit chiés un hermite a cui il s'estoit fez confés aucune foiz.

(But now the story stops telling of King Arthur and his company, and returns to Lancelot, to relate the event which prevented him from going to the tournament held in the meadow at Camelot. Here the story recounts that when Lancelot had left Bors and his brother Hector, he rode up and down in the forest of Camelot, and stayed each night with a hermit who had once confessed him.) [*Mort Artu*, 63–64]

The equivalent cliché, equally frequent, in *Amadís de Gaula* is "De los quales dexerá la hystoria de hablar, y contrará de don Galaor (The story will cease to talk of them, and tell of Don Galaor"—I:20). A similar phrase is employed by the compiler of *Les prophécies de Merlin* to connect the disparate parts of that work:

> Mes atant s'en test ore li contes et parole d'une autre aventure.

(But at this point the story is silent on this matter and speaks of another adventure.) [I:87]

---

[75]On the use of formulas in the prose Arthurian matter, see Pickford, *L'evolution du roman arthurien en prose*, pp. 156–58.

Mais je retornerai apres a vos pour conter de ce que j'ai comencie.
Ici fenest nostre matiere et retorne a l'autre.

(But I shall return to you later to tell what I have begun. Here our
material ends and returns to the other.) [I:116]

Four phases may thus be distinguished in the use of the
*aphodos*. The first phase is Latin history writing, in which the
figure occurs on a fairly regular basis in connection with digressions proper and digressions within the matter. At this stage,
the *aphodos* is emphatically personal and constitutes a conspicuous authorial intrusion. The same is true of the second phase,
which consists of the vernacular chronicles and the poetic romances. The frequency of the figure in the former indicates that it
is still associated primarily with history writing proper, but its
occasional use in the verse romances (and the chansons de geste)
indicates that it has also been adopted into the fictional sphere. In
both cases, the wording and function of the digressive phrases are
such that their Latin origins are obvious. It is in the third phase,
the prose romances, that the *aphodos* is first used on a grand
scale in fiction to effect digression within the matter (less often,
digression proper). The wording in the prose romances is stan-
dardized and impersonal and gives a strongly formulaic impression. Identical in tone and phrasing are the *aphodoi* of the fourth
"phase," the *Prophécies de Merlin;* here, however, they are used
not for moving about the lines of a coherent narrative, but for
gathering into a single frame, and thereby relating, a host of di-
verse and previously independent stories. As a concomitant of
narrative structure, the *aphodos* thus serves as an index to a
distinct and patterned change in literary taste during the medieval
period. In a strikingly similar way, the Norse stranding formulas
serve—as will be shown in chapter 4—as an index to the phases of
the evolving saga.

# CHAPTER 3

# Simultaneity

The phrase Axel Olrik chose to illustrate the literary habit of stranding in the sagas, "now the saga splits and the stories run along together," also illustrates something about their use of time.[1] It has been said that Homeric poetry does not render simultaneous actions,[2] and although this may be an overstatement, it points up, once again, a sharp distinction between classical and medieval practice—or, more precisely, between epic and romance practice. If a well-made, progressive narrative observes a roughly chronological order of events, interlace narrative involves a more fluid arrangement by which the unfolding of synchronous substories may be charted. By embracing narrative stranding and narrative simultaneity in a single "law," Olrik thus tacitly acknowledged their interdependence: a multi-ply story implies some degree of simultaneity, and simultaneous narration is predicated on a multi-ply story.

The reciprocal relation of interlace structure and the idea of things happening at the same time was stressed by Vinaver: "The next and possibly the decisive step towards a proper understanding of cyclic romance is the realization that since it is always possible, and often even necessary, for several themes to be pur-

---

[1]Axel Olrik, "Epische Gesetze der Volksdichtung," *Zeitschrift für deutsches Altertum*, 51 (1909), 8. See also his *Nogle grundsætninger for sagnforskning* (Copenhagen: Schønberg, 1921), chap. 3. See note 1 in chapter 2, above.

[2]Thaddaeus Zielinski, "Die Behandlung gleichzeitiger Ereignisse im antiken Epos," *Philologus: Supplementband*, 8 (1901), 418. Cf. Samuel Eliot Bassett, *The Poetry of Homer* (Berkeley: University of California Press, 1938), pp. 33–42.

sued simultaneously, they have to alternate like threads in a woven fabric, one theme interrupting another and again another, and yet all remaining constantly present in the author's and the reader's mind."[3] It goes without saying that narrative cannot apprehend events happening at the same time. Synchronic or simultaneous narration thus refers to those literary devices designed, as Rosemond Tuve writes, to "get around the fact that the medium of words cannot recount events happening simultaneously to different persons living through the same time; though we cannot play on several strings simultaneously, we accept the convention that we can show the polyphonic nature of what we have to tell by juxtaposing separable persons' stories."[4] Thaddaeus Zielinski, in a classic contribution on the subject, "Die Behandlung gleichzeitiger Ereignisse im antiken Epos,"[5] distinguished three such literary devices and found them to correspond to three stages of literary development. Although Zielinski's typology has met with criticism and attempts at revision, it remains, as the standard approach for older literature, the most useful point of departure for the sagas.[6] His scheme may be summarized as follows. (1) *Retrospective report.* The oldest and most primitive type is the "nachträgliche reproducirend-combinatorische" method, in which action A is described by the narrator and action B, understood to have happened at the same time, is reported by a character. The audience, listening to the character's story (B), mentally synchronizes it with the preceding

---

[3]Eugène Vinaver, *The Rise of Romance* (New York: Oxford University Press, 1971), p. 76.

[4]Rosemond Tuve, *Allegorical Imagery: Some Mediaeval Books and Their Posterity* (Princeton: Princeton University Press, 1966), pp. 362–63.

[5]Zielinski, "Behandlung," pp. 405–49.

[6]For a concise summary, together with bibliography, of scholarly treatments of narrative simultaneity in older literature (emphasis on medieval), see Hans-Hugo Steinhoff, *Die Darstellung gleichzeitiger Geschehnisse im mittelhochdeutschen Epos,* Medium Aevum, 4 (Munich: Eidos Verlag, 1964), esp. pp. 7–18. The main investigations of the role of time in saga composition are Maarten Z. van den Toorn, "Zur Struktur der Saga," *Arkiv för nordisk filologi,* 73 (1958), 140–68; the same author's "Zeit und Tempus in der Saga," *Arkiv för nordisk filologi,* 76 (1961), 134–52; and Hartmut Röhn, *Untersuchungen zur Zeitgestaltung und Komposition der Íslendingasögur: Analysen ausgewählter Texte,* Beiträge zur nordischen Philologie, 5 (Basel: Helbing/Lichtenhahn Verlag, 1976).

narrative covering the same time period. Classical epic offers some examples, but medieval narrators on the whole preferred the more sophisticated Types 2 and 3.[7] (2) *Discontinuous retrieval.* The second type is the "gleichzeitige analysirend-desultorische" method, in which the narrator follows action $A$ to a resting point and suspends it, turning to and following action $B$. There is no backward time jump, though simultaneity may be implied ($B$ is assumed to exist while $A$ is being described and vice versa). In diagram form:

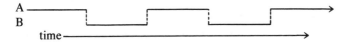

Discontinuous retrieval is used on occasion in *Beowulf,* the *Nibelungenlied,* the *Chanson de Roland,* and Chrétien's romances. It is also used alternately with Type 3 narration in the second phase of romance development. (3) *Continuous retrieval.* The "zurückgreifende" method involves an explicit backtracking in time. The narrator follows action A to a resting point and suspends it, picking up action B at some earlier point in time—while action A was still happening. In its complete form, the pattern yields two more or less continuous (but not consecutively told) story lines:

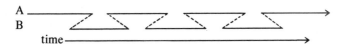

As the only procedure that actually contrives to give a full account of both (or all) actions, this type alone can lay a fair claim to simultaneity. It is regarded as patently literary. Together with Type 2 narration, it is a regular feature of composition in later romance tradition, particularly conspicuous in the Perceval continuations, the works of Wolfram von Eschenbach, and the prose romances (above all, the Vulgate Cycle).

[7]Steinhoff, *Die Darstellung gleichzeitiger Geschehnisse,* pp. 12–18.

## Simultaneous Narration in the Sagas

Type 1 narration is virtually nonexistent in the sagas.[8] The technique of discontinuous retrieval (Type 2), on the other hand, is a standard saga device. Three brief examples give an idea of its use. The first comes from *Þorsteins saga hvíta*. When Þorsteinn falls ill in Norway (chap. 4), the narrator leaves him, following instead his false friend Einarr's return to Iceland and marriage to Þorsteinn's fiancée under false circumstances (chaps. 4 and 5). Chapter 6 begins: "Þat er frá Þorsteini at segja, at honum batnaði. Bjó hann skip sitt til Íslands (It will now be told of Þorsteinn, that he recovered; he prepared his ship for the voyage to Iceland)." The time lapse is about a year. A second example comes from *Víga-Glúms saga*. In chapter 11 two sons are born to two families; in chapter 12 they reach the ages of four and six, and a sibyl predicts bad blood in their future dealings. The narrator then turns to other matters, reverting to the boys eight chapters and some years later: "Nú er þar til máls at taka, at þeir vaxa upp fóstbrœðr, Arngrímr ok Steinólfr (Now it is to be told that the foster brothers grow up, Arngrímr and Steinólfr)." It is mentioned that one marries and the other becomes a sailor merchant, but their story begins in dramatic earnest only when their friendship begins to deteriorate. The prophecy is fulfilled when, in the following chapter, Arngrímr sinks an ax in Steinólfr's head.

The third example is less typical than it is illustrative of the dramatic possibilities of the technique. It comes from *Gísla saga* in the passage following on the offer of Eyjólfr to provide Auðr

---

[8]This fact points up an interesting aspect of direct discourse in the sagas: it concerns present or future events, seldom past ones, and it does not itself bear factual plot information. *Yvain* opens with Calogrenant's telling the assembled company at Arthur's court a long tale of the humiliating adventures that had befallen him seven years earlier; this story prompts Yvain to set off in search of the place and persons involved in order to avenge the wrongs done to his cousin. To put, as Chrétien has done here, a crucial prehistory in the mouth of a character is at direct odds with classical saga practice. Maxwell's "principle of the integrity of episodes," whereby something worth telling is worth telling in scenic detail, may thus be qualified: something worth telling is worth telling by the narrator. No important item of plot information is entrusted solely to a character. A character's report of the situation is a complement to the narrator's account, not a substitute for it. The technique of retrospective report is, however, found in Scandinavian narrative outside of the classical sagas, for example in Reginn's account of his earlier dealings with Fáfnir in *Fáfnismál* and *Vǫlsunga saga*.

with sixty ounces of silver and a good second husband if she will reveal the whereabouts of Gísli:[9]

Hon svarar: "Þar þykki mér óvænst um," segir hon, "at vér verðim um þat sátt, at þú fáir mér þat gjaforð, at mér þykki jafnt við þetta. En þó er þat satt, sem mælt er, at fé er bezt eptir feigan, ok lát mik sjá, hvárt fé þetta er svá mikit ok frítt sem þú segir." Hann steypir nú fénu í kné henni, ok hefir hon hǫnd í, en hann telr ok tjár fyrir henni. Guðríðr, fóstra hennar, tekr at gráta. Síðan gengr hon út ok til móts við Gísla ok segir honum: "Fóstra mín er nú vitlaus orðin ok vill svíkja þik." Gísli mælti: "Ger þú þér gott í hug, því at eigi mun mér þat at fjǫrlesti verða, at Auðr blekki mik," ok kvað vísu.... Eptir þetta ferr mærin heim ok segir ekki, hvert hon hefir farit. Eyjólfr hefir þá talit silfrit.

(She answers: "It seems to me highly unlikely," she says, "that we could agree that any marriage you might arrange for me would seem to me as good as this one. On the other hand, as they say, 'cash is the widow's best comfort'; so let me see whether the silver is as much and as fair as you say." He now pours out the silver on her lap, and she fingers it, and he shows it off to her as he counts it. Guðríðr, her foster-daughter, starts to cry. Then she goes out and finds Gísli and tells him: "My foster-mother has lost her mind and wants to betray you." Gísli said: "Cheer up; the cause of my death will never be Auðr's betrayal" and he recited a stanza.... After this the girl goes back in and says nothing of where she has been. At that moment Eyjólfr has finished counting the silver.) [chaps. 31–32]

In the sagas, then, Type 2 narration is used when the events in the missing segment can be reconstructed from the information supplied before and after—and when, further, the action is neutral so far as the larger plot is concerned. The recuperation of Þorsteinn, the growing up of Arngrímr and Steinólfr, and the silver-counting of Eyjólfr are all actions that in themselves contribute nothing to the developing conflict and hence require no narrative elaboration. In Type 2 narration, in other words, two or more lines of action are understood to exist at the same time, but

[9]For a more complete analysis of this passage, see van den Toorn, "Zur Struktur," pp. 143–44. The phrase "Cash is the widow's best comfort" in the English translation of this passage is from *The Saga of Gisli*, trans. George Johnston (Toronto: University of Toronto Press, 1963), p. 50.

they are important to the main plot only in turns. It is when the lines are construed as simultaneously important that the narrator resorts to the temporal disjunctions of Type 3 narration. The fact that this narration is used alternately with Type 2 narration within the same saga suggests that in Icelandic practice, at least, there is no sharp conceptual difference between the two and no overriding aesthetic preference for one type over the other. Nevertheless, in their unusually complex and varied use of the techniques of continuous retrieval the sagas reveal not only the full extent of their art but their underlying conception of plot.

Simultaneous narration is, of course, a familiar feature in sequences leading up to battle. Here, as Andersson describes it, the shift of focus "is a camera technique familiar to any moviegoer accustomed to westerns or suspense films, where the camera focuses alternately on two groups as yet invisible to one another but bent on a clash."[10] Some of these shifts involve little or no temporal backtracking (they are Type 2), but others involve a full return to the initial moment. A simple but paradigmatic instance of continuous retrieval is found in chapter 11 of *Víga-Glúms saga*. After an ominous encounter one afternoon, Þorgrímr (strand A) and Glúmr's kinsman Arnórr (strand B) go their separate ways. That evening, on the suspicion that Glúmr might be mounting an attack, Þorgrímr gathers forces:

A

Þar var þá vað á ánni, er nú er ekki. Þeir sǫfnuðu nú at sér átta tigum vígra manna um nóttina ok bjuggusk við á hólinum framanverðum, því at þar var vaðit á ánni við hólinn sjálfan.

(At that time the river had a ford, which is no longer there. During the night Þorgrímr and his companions assembled eighty fighting men and they took up their position on the forward slope of the knoll because it faced directly on the river ford.)

[10]Theodore M. Andersson, *The Icelandic Family Saga: An Analytic Reading,* Harvard Studies in Comparative Literature, 28 (Cambridge, Mass.: Harvard University Press, 1967), p. 58.

B

En frá Arnóri er at segja, at hann finnr Glúm ok segir honum frá fǫrum sínum. Hann svarar: "Ekki kom mér þat at óvǫrum, at þeir léti eigi kyrrt, ok er nú á vandi nǫkkurr, svívirðing, ef kyrrt er, en allósýn virðing, ef við er leitat at rétta, en þó skal nú safna mǫnnum."

(And now it is to be told of Arnórr that he meets Glúmr and tells him of his journey. Glúmr answers: "It comes as no surprise to me that they would not let matters lie. And now we have a somewhat difficult choice: dishonor if we do nothing, but a dubious prospect of honor if we seek justice. But men shall be collected now.")

A + B

Ok er ljóst var um morgininn, þá kom Glúmr at ánni með sex tigu manna ok vildi ríða yfir ána. En þeir grýttu á þá, Esphœlingar, ok gekk eigi fram reiðin.

(And in the morning when it was light, Glúmr arrived at the river with sixty men with the intention of riding across. But the men from Espihóll stoned them, and they made no headway.) [chap. 11]

From the moment they part in the afternoon until the moment they collide the following morning, both sides are briefly but fully accounted for and in roughly equal detail.

The same technique is used in the account of Grettir's last stand. In chapter 81 Þorbjǫrn and his men prepare for and undertake a dangerous crossing to Drangey, where Grettir is lying at death's door with a festering leg wound. They arrive "late in the evening after dark" ("Kómu þeir um kveldit, er røkkvat var"). The narrator then reverts to Grettir in the morning of the same day:

Nú er frá því at segja, at Grettir var svá sjúkr, at hann mátti eigi á fœtr standa. Sat Illugi yfir honum, en Glaumr skyldi halda vǫrð. Hann hafði þá enn mǫrg orð í móti ok kvað þeim svá þykkja,

sem falla myndi fjǫr ór þeim, þó at ekki bæri til. Nú fór hann út ór
skálanum ok allnauðigr. Ok er hann kom til stiganna, mæltisk hann
við einn saman ok sagði nú, at hann skyldi eigi upp draga stigann;
tók hann nú at syfja mjǫk, ok lagðisk niðr ok svaf allan daginn ok allt
þar til, er Þorbjǫrn kom til eyjarinnar.

(It is now to be told of Grettir that he was so ill he was unable to
stand on his feet. Illugi stayed by him. Glaumr was supposed to stand
guard, but he kept objecting, saying that they seemed to think their
lives were in mortal danger even though there was no cause. It was
only under duress that he left the hut. And when he came to the
ladder, he started muttering to himself and said he was not going to
pull it up. Then he started getting very drowsy, and lay down and
slept all day—until the arrival of Þorbjǫrn on the island.)

[*Grettis saga*, chap. 82]

With this the game is up; Þorbjǫrn and his men break into the hut
and slay first Grettir and then the loyal Illugi. Similar but more
complex examples—sequences in which the number of shifts is
multiplied—are found in *Njáls saga* in the attacks on Gunnarr at
Hlíðarendi (chapters 76–77), Hǫskuldr at Ossabœr (chapters
110–12), and Njáll and his household at Bergþórshváll (chapters
127–31). Even more mannered in its use of time is *Laxdœla saga*,
especially in the attacks on Kjartan (chapters 48–49) and Bolli
(chapter 55). The existence of a particularly fine example in
*Heiðarvíga saga* (the attack on the sons of Þorgautr by Barði and
his men) suggests that the technique entered the Icelandic narrative repertoire at an early date.

Nor, as the following brief example from *Grettis saga* (chapter
11) indicates, were the saga authors deaf to the comic possibilities
of the device:

A

Maðr hét Þorfinnr; hann var húskarl Flosa í Árnesi.
Þenna mann sendi Flosi til hǫfuðs Þorgeiri; hann leyn-
disk í naustinu.

(There was a man named Þorfinnr, a servant of Flosi at
Árnes. This man was sent out by Flosi to kill Þorgeirr.
Þorfinnr hid in the boathouse.)

B

Þenna morgin bjósk Þorgeirr á sjá at róa ok tveir menn
með honum, ok hét annarr Hámundr, en annarr
Brandr. Þorgeirr gekk fyrst; hann hafði á baki sér
leðrflosku ok í drykk.

(That morning Þorgeirr got ready to row out to sea.
With him were two other men, one called Hámundr
and the other Brandr. Þorgeirr walked ahead of them,
on his back a leather flask full of drink.)

A + B

Myrkt var mjok, ok er hann gekk ofan frá naustinu, þá
hljóp Þorfinnr at honum ok hjó með øxi á milli herða
honum, ok sokk øxin ok skvakkaði við; hann lét lausa
øxina, því at hann ætlaði, at eigi myndi þurfa um at
binda, ok vildi forða sér sem skjótast.

(It was pitch dark, and when Þorgeirr was walking
down from the boathouse, Þorfinnr rushed at him and
struck him with an ax between the shoulders. There
was a squishy sound as the ax sank in. Þorfinnr let go
of it, figuring that this wound was beyond bandaging,
and aimed to escape as fast as he could.

A

Er þat af Þorfinni at segja, at hann hljóp norðr í Árnes
ok kom þar, áðr en alljóst var, ok sagði víg Þorgeirs ok
kvezk mundu þurfa ásjá Flosa; kvað þat ok eitt til, at
bjóða sættir,—"ok bœtir þat helzt várt mál, svá mikit
sem at er orðit." Flosi kvezk fyrst mundu hafa
fréttir,—"ok ætla ek, at þú sér allhræddr eptir stór-
virkin."

(It is to be told of Þorfinnr that he ran north to Árnes,
where he arrived just at daybreak. He announced the
slaying of Þorgeirr and declared himself in need of

Flosi's protection. He said that the only thing to do
was to offer a settlement—"and that's our best protection, given the gravity of the situation." Flosi said
he wanted to make his own inquiries first—"and I can
see your great feats have left you scared to
death.") [chap. 11]

However pointed the implication that the ax struck not the
victim's flesh but his flask, the fact itself is not stated until the
assailant's subsequent actions have been followed for the space
of some hours—from deepest darkness at the moment of the attack to shortly after dawn when he arrives at Flosi's. Only when
the story returns to the scene and the time of the crime (still pitch
dark) do we learn where Þorgeirr received the blow that was
delivered in the previous paragraph. It is a "consistent mode of
procedure" in the sagas, Ker was fond of pointing out, that "everything should present itself first of all as appearance, before it
becomes appearance with a meaning"—but here the narrative
technique itself has become accessory to the joke.[11]

Another plot situation that lends itself to synchronic treatment
is the story of the fiancé (husband) who fails to return within a
stipulated time and so forfeits his betrothed (wife) to another.[12]
Here, too, both sides of the story are of potentially equal interest,
and the skilled narrator plays them off against each other by
introducing chance delays, mistimings, and the like. An extended
example is found in *Gunnlaugs saga,* chapters 9–12. Gunnlaugr
and Hrafn, his soon-to-be rival for the hand of Helga, engage
in a poetic competition at the court of Óláfr Svíakonungr.
Gunnlaugr's poem (a *drápa*) wins over Hrafn's (a *flokkr*), and the
two part ways on something less than friendly terms. At this point
the story forks:

A

Hrafn sails to Trondheim in the spring and Iceland in
the summer. He enlists the aid of Skapti Þóroddsson

[11]W. P. Ker, *Epic and Romance: Essays on Medieval Literature,* 2d ed. (London: Macmillan, 1908; rpt. New York: Dover, 1957), p. 236.
[12]See, e.g., Margaret Schlauch, *Romance in Iceland* (Princeton: Princeton
University Press, and New York: American Scandinavian Foundation, 1934), pp.
37–41; Bjarni Einarsson, *Skáldasögur: Um uppruna og eðli ástaskáldasagnanna
fornu* (Reykjavík: Bókaútgáfa Menningarsjóðs, 1961).

in annulling the betrothal of Gunnlaugr and Helga and is himself conditionally betrothed to her—the condition being Gunnlaugr's continued absence during the coming summer. [chap. 9]

B

"Nú er at segja frá Gunnlaugi, at hann fór af Svíþjóðu þat sumar til Englands, er Hrafn fór til Íslands (Now it is to be told of Gunnlaugr that he left Sweden for England during the same summer that Hrafn went to Iceland)." Gunnlaugr enters Ethelred's service and stays in England that summer and winter. The following summer he sails to Trondheim and seeks passage to Iceland to claim Helga before the stipulated time, but he finds that all the Icelandic ships have left. He finally gets passage with the skald Hallfreðr, who passes on news of Helga's betrothal to Hrafn. Gunnlaugr and Hallfreðr arrive in Iceland two weeks before winter.

Gunnlaugr takes part in a wrestling match and injures his foot, thus causing yet a further delay in his arrival at Borg. He comes to Gilsbakki in Borgarfjǫrðr on the very Saturday evening when people are sitting at the wedding feast at Borg. He wants to continue on to Borg, but his injured foot prevents further travel. [chap. 10]

A

"Nú er at segja frá Hrafni, at hann sat at brúðlaupi sínu at Borg (Now it is to be told of Hrafn, that he sat at his wedding at Borg)." The mood is somewhat depressed, but the wedding takes place. Hrafn and Helga move to Mosfell. Hrafn has an ominous dream, which Helga interprets. A short time later the news of Gunnlaugr's presence in Iceland reaches them. Helga begins acting badly toward Hrafn. [chap. 11]

At this point the strands intersect. Another wedding takes place in the district, and Gunnlaugr, Helga, and Hrafn all attend. Helga and Gunnlaugr meet and converse in secret, and Gunnlaugr and Hrafn exchange angry words, bringing the feud and the saga to a new phase.

Events in such passages, as in the sagas in general, are temporally located not by reference to an external time scale (such as a calendar date or a king's reign), but by the popular form of timekeeping Ólafia Einarsdóttir has termed "intrinsic relative chronology."[13] In the usual case, this involves setting out in some chronological detail the fullest action first and then coordinating the events of any subsequent strand with those of the "lead" strand. *Kjalnesinga saga* offers a typical example. Upon Ólof's promise to wait three years for him, Búi goes abroad (summer 1). He arrives in the Orkneys late in the autumn (autumn 1) and spends the winter there with Earl Einarr Rǫgnvaldsson (winter 1). In the spring (spring 2) he goes to Trondheim and spends the summer there with the king (summer 2). At the beginning of winter (fall and winter 2) he goes to Dofrafjall and stays there with Dofri and his daughter Fríðr until the following summer (summer 3), when he returns first to Trondheim and then to Iceland. At the beginning of chapter 16, the narrative reverts to Ólof, jumping back three years to summarize her interim story:

*Þat sumar, er Búi fór útan,* gekk Ólof in væna með barni; fæddi hon um haustit mey, er hon kenndi Búa, ok var kölluð Þuríðr. Esja bauð meynni til fóstrs til sín, ok þat þágu þau Kolli. *En þat sumar er Búi var í Þrándheimi,* fóru til Íslands Helgi ok Vakr; sögðu þeir út þau tíðendi, at Búi væri látinn ok Haraldr konungr hefði sent hann forsending þá, er engi hefði aptr komit. En er þat spurðist, fór Kolfiðr til Kollafjarðar ok tók þaðan á brutt Ólofu ina vænu nauðga ok at óvilja föður hennar. Kolfiðr fór þá með Ólofu út til Vatns; var hon þar *sumar ok vetrinn eptir. En um sumarit eptir* kom skip suðr í Eyrarbakka, í höfn þá, er heitir í Einarshöfn; spurðist þat þar af, at þar var á Búi Andríðsson.

(That summer, when Búi went abroad, Ólof the Fair was pregnant; in the autumn she gave birth to a girl, who she said was Búi's and whom she called Þuríðr. Esja offered to foster the girl, and Ólof and her father Kolli accepted. And that summer when Búi was in Trondheim, Helgi and Vakr sailed to Iceland, where they let it be known that Búi, having been sent by King Haraldr on a mission so dangerous that no one had ever returned, was dead. And when that became

[13]Ólafia Einarsdóttir, *Studier i kronologisk metode i tidlig islandsk historieskrivning*, Bibliotheca Historica Lundensis, 13 (N.p.: Gleerup, 1964).

known, Kolfiðr went to Kollafjǫrðr and took Ólof the Fair away by
force and against her father's will. Kolfiðr then went to Vatn with
Ólof; she was there that summer and the following winter. But in the
following summer, a ship came south to Eyrarbakki, into the harbor
called Einarshǫfn; and it was learned that Búi Andríðsson was there.)
[chap. 16]

Einarsdóttir attributes to the force of Icelandic popular practice
the saga authors' preference for relative timekeeping over the
time-scale system employed by earlier Scandinavian writers and
medieval chroniclers in general.[14] However instructive this
analysis may be, its exclusive reliance on historical documents
makes its conclusions incomplete. The sagas' method of
timekeeping finds its fullest application and closest counterpart in
medieval fiction. ''Intrinsic relative chronology'' is a natural concomitant of interlace narrative: to date the events in strand B in
relation to events in strand A is to juxtapose the lines of action in
such a way as to invite mental comparison and to anticipate (as in
the case of Búi and Ólof) their next intersection—to suggest, in
short, that the drama and meaning of the work rest not in the
individual stories but in their relation to one another in a complex
whole.

*Víga-Glúms saga* offers an instructive example of simultaneous narration under somewhat different, though equally typical,
circumstances. When Glúmr is fifteen years old, he leaves his
mother Ástríðr in charge of the home farm and goes off to Norway to visit his kinsman Vigfúss (chapter 6). He gets a chilly
reception, but he succeeds in winning respect when, during the
winter feast, he batters an unpleasant berserk to death with a
firebrand. The following summer he is rewarded with a complement of valuable gifts, which he is enjoined never to relinquish if
he wishes to retain his authority, and he returns to Iceland to
rejoin his mother:

> Nú ferr Glúmr út til Íslands ok heim til Þverár. Ok móður sína hitti
> hann brátt, ok fagnaði hon honum vel ok sagði ójafnað þeira feðga ok
> bað hann þó hafa við þolinmœði, en kvazk til lítils um fœr at ganga
> þeim í móti. Síðan reið hann heim at garði. Þá sá hann, at fœrðr var

14Ibid., esp. pp. 276–92.

garðrinn ok gengit á hans hlut, ok þá kvað hann vísu. . . . En þat
hafði orðit til tíðenda út hér meðan.

(Now Glúmr returns to Iceland and goes home to Þverá. And he
immediately went to see his mother, and she greeted him warmly
and told of the injustice committed by the father and son [Þorkell
and Sigmundr], but she asked him to respond with patience, saying
that she was ill prepared to oppose them. After that he rode to the
home yard. He saw that the fence had been moved and his property
encroached on, and then he spoke a stanza. . . . And this is what had
happened here in Iceland in the interim.) [chap. 7]

At this point the narrator jumps back one year to tell the story of
Ástríðr's troubles during her son's absence. Her neighbors Þorkell and Sigmundr, who for some time have had designs on Þverá,
use an incident involving missing sheep as an excuse to appropriate the lands (they accuse her of having ordered her slaves to
steal, and they are awarded self-judgment in the matter). The
issue is dealt with at the summer assembly just prior to Glúmr's
return—which event, now that the second story has been up-
dated, is then stated a second time: "Ok litlu síðar sumars kom
Glúmr út ok er litla hríð við skip, ferr til bús síns með auð fjár (A
little later that summer, Glúmr arrived in Iceland, staying for a
short time at his ship and then going on to his farm with his
valuables"—chap. 7). The two strands are roughly equivalent in
length (about three pages) and degree of detail. The difference,
from the point of view of narrative unity, is that the mother's
story is an integral part of the ongoing conflict plot, whereas
Glúmr's story, a standard version of the Travel Pattern, is unnecessary and constitutes a digression.[15] One may speculate that
an older version of the saga might have consisted only of a main
action (that is, the story of Ástríðr's loss of land during her son's
absence) and that the Vigfúss strand was a later accretion, prompted
by the logic of entailment and modeled on the standard action
of the þáttr. In any case, the multiplication of the story during

[15]Vigfúss does not appear again in the saga, although Glúmr's dealings with him
are twice alluded to in the later plot. In chapter 9, Glúmr dreams of Vigfúss's
death and sees a woman he believes is his fetch. In chapter 25, Glúmr's enemies
remark that Glúmr is now doomed, for he has given away the gifts Vigfúss charged
him to keep forever.

this year is predicated on the idea and the techniques of simultaneous narration.

In *Hænsa-Þóris saga,* Þórðr gellir is tricked into taking over the prosecution of the case involving the burning of Blund-Ketill in his house by Hœnsa-Þórir and his cohorts. As soon as Hœnsa-Þórir learns of the summons, he disappears. His supporters gather their forces, however, and go to the assembly site, where they engage the forces of the prosecution in an armed battle and so block their entry. The case is rescheduled for the Althing; still Hœnsa-Þórir is missing. In the summer, Þórðr goes about collecting his supporters for a second round. But Hersteinn, the son of Blund-Ketill, falls ill and must stay behind. The narrative then follows Þórðr as he proceeds to the assembly. This time they arrive early and engage the forces of the defendants in a major battle. But there is an intervention, and the two parties are separated and forced to enter into arbitration. Hœnsa-Þórir is still missing.

Leaving the ongoing action at the Althing, the narrator returns to Hersteinn: "En nú skal segja nǫkkut af Hersteini, at honum létti brátt sóttarinnar, er þeir riðu til þingsins; ferr hann þá í Ǫrnólfsdal (And now it will be told of Hersteinn, that as soon as the others rode to the Thing, his health improved, and he rode to Ǫrnólfsdalr)"—chap. 15). One day, during his stay with Ǫrnólfr, the farmer comes to him and prevails upon him to look after a sick cow. As Hersteinn accompanies him out into the back hills, he sees the glint of a shield in the trees and realizes that he is being led into an ambush. He has the farmer lie down, rushes back to gather his men, then returns and has the farmer signal the ambushers as he had been instructed. Hœnsa-Þórir rushes out of the woods with a dozen man, but they are soundly defeated by Hersteinn's group. Hersteinn himself has the satisfaction of removing Hœnsa-Þórir's head, and he takes it with him directly to the Althing, which is still in session when they arrive, and he is publicly commended for his deed.

Ari Þorgilsson's *Íslendingabók* offers a somewhat different version.

En þeir váru sóttir á þingi því es vas í Borgarfirði í þeim stað, es síðan es kallat Þingnes.... En þeir bǫrðusk þar, ok mátti þingit eigi

heyjask at lǫgum. . . . En síðan fóru sakarnar til alþingis, ok bǫrðusk
þeir þar þá enn. Þá fellu menn úr liði Odds, enda varð sekr hann
Hœnsa-Þórir ok drepinn síðan ok fleiri þeir es at brennunni váru.

And they were prosecuted at the Borgarfjǫrðr Thing, which was held
in that place afterward known as Þingnes. . . . But they fought there,
and the assembly could not be legally convened. . . . And later the
cases went to the Althing, and there too was a battle. Men in Oddr's
force fell, and Hœnsa-Þórir was outlawed and later killed along with
others who had been at the burning. [chap. 5]

Here Þórir is apparently present at the Althing; he is in any case
outlawed and killed in consequence of it. In the saga, he is killed
during the time the assembly is being held, but at a great distance
away and independently of it; the arbitration is still in session
when Hersteinn arrives with the news and, presumably, the head
to prove it.

Sigurður Nordal argued that this and other discrepancies indicated that the saga author knew Ari's version in *Íslendingabók*
but chose to alter it in the interest of fictional effect.[16] Andersson
argued that the author may or may not have known Ari's account
but based his version on an oral variant of the tradition.[17] In
either case, the discrepancy points up the modus operandi of the
classical saga. Ari's account is simplex; the saga's is duplex. Ari
has Hœnsa-Þórir's death follow logically from his outlawry; the
saga develops the dimension of surprise and coincidence. Ari is
sequential; the saga is simultaneous. The fascination, once again,
is with the "synchronic idea" that at the exact moment when
Blund-Ketill's burning is under tense consideration by a large cast
of supporting characters at the Althing, the principals—the hero's
son and the villain—are colliding in an ambush off in the home
district.

A particularly complex example of simultaneous narration is
the Atlantic Interlude of *Njáls saga*. Here it is a question not of
two but of five intertwined stories, all temporally complete and all
potentially freestanding. In other words, the author goes over

---

[16]Sigurður Nordal, introduction to the Fornrit edition, pp. vii–xxx.
[17]Theodore M. Andersson, *The Problem of Icelandic Saga Origins: A Historical Survey* (New Haven: Yale University Press, 1964), pp. 104–8.

one two-year period five different times (see chart on page 30 above). The stranding begins in chapter 75, when the narrator dispatches first Þráinn, then Grímr and Helgi, and then, after his fraternal dispute with Gunnarr, Kolskeggr. The narrative then follows Gunnarr's strand for something over a year, checking time by seasons: "Gunnarr sitr nú heima þetta haust ok vetrinn (Gunnarr now stays home this fall and winter)," "líðr nú vetr ór garði (winter now passes)," "en á þingi um sumarit (but at the Thing, in the summer)," and "um haustit sendi MQrðr Valgarðsson orð, at Gunnarr myndi [vera] einn heima (in the autumn, MQrðr Valgarðsson sent word that Gunnarr would be alone at his home)"—this last being the autumn of his death. When Gunnarr's story is fully told, the narrator retrieves Kolskeggr's story, suspended some pages earlier:

Nú er at segja frá Kolskeggi, at hann kemr til Nóregs ok er í Vík austr of vetrinn, en um sumarit eptir ferr hann austr til Danmerkr.

(Now it is to be said of Kolskeggr that he arrives in Norway and spends the winter east in Vík; and the following summer he travels east to Denmark.) [chap. 81]

Kolskeggr was baptized in Denmark but, finding no happiness there, he moved on to Russia "ok var þar einn vetr (and was there for one winter)." From there he moved to Constantinople, where he stayed "til dauðadags, ok er hann ór sQgunni (until he died, and now he is out of the saga)." The latter part of Kolskeggr's career is perfunctorily told, but the earlier part—the time period up to and shortly after Gunnarr's death—is systematically accounted for.

The narrative then retrieves a strand left to rest seventeen pages and many years earlier: "Nú er þar til máls at taka, at Þráinn Sigfússon kom til Nóregs (Now the story picks up at the point where Þráinn Sigfússon came to Norway)." But if Gunnarr's and Kolskeggr's stories were told consecutively to the end, Þráinn's is pursued for only two years, the seasons methodically marked: "Var Þráinn þar um vetrinn ok virðisk vel (Þráinn spent the winter there in great esteem)," "fór Þráinn með honum um sumarit (Þráinn accompanied him during the summer)," "var

Þráinn með jarli allan þann vetr (Þráinn spent that whole winter with the earl)," "um várit spurði jarl Þráin, hvat hann vildi þar vera eða fara til Íslands (in the spring, the earl asked Þráinn whether he wanted to stay there or go to Iceland)," and, when the news of Gunnarr's death reaches the court, "var hann með honum eptir (he stayed there with him)." At this point the strand is suspended and the narrator once again makes a two-year backtrack to the initial summer:

> Nú er þar til máls at taka, at þeir Grímr ok Helgi Njálssynir fóru af Íslandi þat sumar, sem þeir Þráinn fóru utan.

Now the story picks up at the point where the Njálssons, Grímr and Helgi, left Iceland during the same summer that Þráinn went abroad with his companions. [chap. 83]

Like Þráinn's, the Njálssons' itinerary is carefully charted: "Þeir váru þá með jarli um vetrinn ok váru vel virðir (They spent the winter with the earl in great esteem)," "þeir váru með jarli þann vetr ok um sumarit, þar til er Kári fór í hernað (they were with the earl that winter and in the summer until Kári set out on a raiding expedition)," "þeir herjuðu víða um sumarit (they raided far and wide during the summer)," "váru þeir með jarli um vetrinn (they stayed with the earl that winter)," "um várit beiddusk þeir Njálssynir at fara til Nóregs (in the spring the Njálssons asked leave to sail to Norway)." This strand, too, is prematurely interrupted, for the narrator brings the Njálssons to Norway and abandons them in order to pick up a fifth and final strand:

> Kolbeinn hét maðr ok var Arnljótarson; hann var þrœnzkr maðr. Hann sigldi þat sumar út til Íslands, er þeir Kolskeggr ok Njálssynir fóru heðan; hann var þann vetr í Breiðdal austr. En um sumarit eptir bjó hann skip sitt í Gautavík.

(Kolbeinn Arnljótarson was the name of a man from Trondheim. He sailed out to Iceland during the same summer that Kolskeggr and the Njálssons had gone abroad. He stayed east in Breiðdalr that winter, and in the following summer he made ready to sail from Gautavík.) [chap. 87]

Kolbeinn's story is eclipsed by that of his passenger Hrappr, whose misadventures are followed for a space of about a year. The climax of the Atlantic Interlude is in chapter 88, where, in the spring of the second year, the three strands converge:

Nú er þat at segja, at um sumarit fóru Njálssynir af Orkneyjum til Nóregs ok váru þar í kaupstefnu um sumarit. Þráinn Sigfússon bjó þá skip sitt til Íslands ok var þá mjǫk albúinn. Þá fór Hákon jarl á veizlu til Guðbrands. Um nóttina fór Víga-Hrappr til goðahúss þeira jarls ok Guðbrands ok gekk inn í húsit.

(It is now to be told that in the summer the Njálssons left the Orkneys for Norway, where they spent the summer trading. Þráinn Sigfússon was preparing his ship for a voyage to Iceland at the time and was almost ready to sail. Earl Hákon, meanwhile, was attending a feast at Guðbrandr's estate. During the night, Víga-Hrappr came to the earl's and Guðbrandr's temple and went inside.) [chap. 88]

Hrappr burns the temple, flees to the harbor, is rebuffed by the Njálssons, and makes a narrow escape with Þráinn, on whose farm in Iceland he spends the next year:

Hrappr fór með honum ok var með honum þau misseri, en annat sumar fekk Þráinn honum bú á Hrappstǫðum, ok bjó Hrappr þar.

(Hrappr went with him and then stayed with him that year; and the following summer Þráinn got him a farm at Hrappstaðir, and Hrappr settled down there.) [chap. 88]

Having thus lodged Þráinn and Hrappr in a domestic routine of sorts in Iceland, the narrator jumps back to Norway to the harbor fray of the previous year:

Nú er þar til at taka, er Hákon jarl missti Þráins, at hann rœddi við Svein, son sinn: "Tǫku vit nú langskip fjǫgur ok róum eptir þeim Njálssonum ok drepum þá, því at þeir munu vitat hafa með Þrána."

(Now to take up [the story] at the point where Þráinn slipped away from Earl Hákon. Hákon said to Sveinn, his son: "Let us take four longships and row after the Njálssons and kill them, since they must have been in on this with Þráinn.") [chap. 89]

The Njálssons are pursued and captured, but they escape and, through Kári's intervention, are pardoned. They go with Kári to the Orkneys and "váru með jarli um vetrinn (stayed with the earl that winter)." "En um várit bað Kári Njálssonu at fara í hernað með honum (And in the spring Kári asked the Njálssons to join him on a raiding expedition)." They do so on the condition that Kári return with them to Iceland afterward. This he does: "Þat sumar bjoggusk þeir Kári ok Njálssynir til Íslands (That summer, Kári and the Njálssons make ready to go to Iceland)." Their return completes the Atlantic Interlude.

Of all the features in the Atlantic Interlude which conspire against the idea of natural narrative, the treatment of time in the synchronizing of stories does so most completely. The time scheme is not labored, but it is almost pedantically observed. The question is whether these chapters could have been written "naively" from beginning to end, or whether the author was not in fact working with a prearranged time scheme. The latter possibility has important implications, for if this passage was diagramed in advance, so might other passages, indeed other sagas, have been. The interweaving of five temporally complete story lines over a period of years, with a coincidental intersection of three of them in the third year, is not, of course, normal saga procedure. But a tour de force is a matter of degree, not kind. *Njála* is by no means the first or the only example of simultaneous narration; it simply exploits the techniques more completely—to the point where, in these chapters, the effect is clearly studied.

The dimensions of the two Óláfr sagas in *Flateyjarbók* are such that they are best seen not as biographies but as anecdotal surveys of the western Scandinavian arena during their two reigns. No other biography, royal or skaldic, is so saturated with peripheral matter as these. The means of compilation are derived from the compositional techniques of the family sagas: the classical process of stranding is extended, in *Flateyjarbók*, to entire *þættir* and sagas, and their inclusion is justified by the fact that they are taken to be historically contemporaneous with the king's career and at some point impinge on it, however briefly. The incorporation of the short tale of Stefnir Þorgilsson is paradigmatic. A *þáttr* of only three pages in all, it is broken into three parts, and inserted at long intervals into the *Óláfs saga Tryggvasonar*.

The first part tells how the Icelander traveled to Norway and after some royal urging agreed to return to Iceland as a missionary. His efforts are met with opposition, and he decides to return to Norway. In the spring he sets sail, and after a perilous journey (which the Icelandic heathens attribute to the gods' wrath) he makes land. At this point the narrator abandons Stefnir to tell of other things. He is retrieved seventy-five pages later in this brief entry:

> Nv er þar til at taka er fyrr uar fra horfit at Olafr konungr hafde verit .ij. uetr j Noregi ok kristnat vm uetrinn allan Þrandhæim. þa gerde konungr ordsendingar vt til Færeyia til Sigmundar Brestissonar ok bodade honum a sinn fund. let hann ok þat fylgia ordsendingu at Sigmundr skyllde fa sæmdir ok uerda mestr madr j Færeyium ef hann uillde geraz hans madr. þat sumar kom a fund konungs vtan af Jslande Stefnir Þorgilsson er konungr hafde sent vt þangat hit fyrra sumarit sem adr er getit. tok hann uit honum med hinne mestu blidu ok var Stefnir med hird konungs ok sagde honum allt hit sanna vm sinar ferdir ok huersu þungliga hans mali var tekit a Jslande. kuetzst þat ætla at sæigt munde væita at kristna Jsland.

(Now the story resumes where it left off earlier, at the point where King Óláfr had spent two years in Norway and had converted all of Trondheim during the winter. The king sent messages to the Faeroes to Sigmundr Brestisson summoning him to a meeting. He included in the message that Sigmundr would receive honors and become the most powerful man in the Faeroes if he would become his vassal. That summer there came to the court Stefnir Þorgilsson, whom the king had sent out to Iceland the previous summer, as was related earlier. He received him most graciously, and Stefnir joined the king's following; he told him the true account of his travels and how negatively his mission had been received in Iceland. He said he thought it would be a hard task to convert Iceland.) [*Flateyjarbók* I:294]

He then drops out of sight again, to reappear 137 pages later:

> Stefnir Þorgilsson hafde verit med Olafi konungi Trygguasyni sidan konungr hafde sent hann til Jslandz sem fyrr er ritat.

(Stefnir Þorgilsson had been with King Óláfr Tryggvason ever since the king had sent him to Iceland, as was written before.) [I:392]

The rest of his story is dispatched in a few sentences: en route to Rome he stops in Denmark, where, as the result of an impolitic stanza he recites before the earl, he is immediately killed. The narrator then reverts to King Óláfr:

> Nv skal uikea rędunne til þeirra frasagna er þat sanna er Olafr konungr hafi a brott komizt ór bardaganum a þeirre somu snekkiu sem fyrr var getith.

(Now [we] shall turn the discourse to those accounts alleging that King Óláfr escaped from the battle on the same ship that was mentioned before.) [I:393]

The reference is to the famous sea battle at Svǫldr, related some five pages earlier.

As with the story of Stefnir, so with those of Hallfreðr, Kjartan, the Jómsvíkings, and the colonial histories of the Faeroes, Orkneys, Iceland, and Vinland, all of which are entered piecemeal into the saga of Óláfr Tryggvason. Together with the twenty-three *þættir* that are entered wholesale, they show just how far the unrolling of simultaneous themes can go: all thirty-one subplots, some of which are themselves full-length and internally stranded sagas, are understood to be contemporaneous with all or part of the king's own life-span and, in varying degrees, each other. If the chronology is not always convincing, and if certain elements have a suspiciously unhistorical ring (e.g., *Nornagests þáttr*), the general effect of synchrony holds. Through the techniques of discontinuous and especially of continuous retrieval, and what is by classical standards an excessive use of interlace formulas, the author marshals the mass forward, keeping it roughly abreast of the present. Missing in *Flateyjarbók*, however, is the dramatic dimension. The parts of a given story are at such a distance from one another that the tension slackens. Nor does one find the same playful use of coincidence and delay; despite the narrator's repeated verbal reminders that events are to be understood as happening at the same time, there is no evidence of the "simultaneous idea." The technique is intact, if in bloated form, but it is fictionally empty.

## The Language of Simultaneity

The language of stranding is to a certain degree a language of simultaneity.[18] Clear concomitants of "zurückgreifende" narrative are such retrieval phrases as:

Nú er at segja frá Snorra goða, at hann fór til féránsdóms í Bitru norðr, sem fyrr var ritat.

(Now it is to be told of Snorri goði that he went to the court of confiscations north in Bitra, as was written before.) [*Eyrbyggja saga*, chap. 60]

Even more pointed are phrases that put the stories in a "meanwhile" relation:

Nú er at segja frá Þormóði, hvat hann hafðisk at, meðan Þorgeirr var í fǫrum.

(Now to tell of Þormóðr and what he was doing while Þorgeirr was abroad.) [*Fóstbrœðra saga*, chap. 9]

Þessu næst skal segia huat Æirekr jall hafðizt at medan konungarnir bǫrduzst vid Noregs konung.

(Next shall be told what Earl Eiríkr was doing while the kings were fighting against the king of Norway.) [*Flateyjarbók*, I:379]

Nú er at segja frá Ingjaldi, at hann snýr heim á Goddastaði, þá er þeir Þórólfr hǫfðu skilizk.

(Now it is to be told of Ingjaldr, that he heads home to Goddastaðir when he and Þórólfr had parted company.) [*Laxdœla saga*, chap. 15]

But the narrators also had at their disposal a rich variety of formulations indicating more explicitly that things were to be under-

[18]For some early remarks on the unnatural chronology of saga narrative, see Richard Heinzel, *Beschreibung der isländischen Saga*, Sitzungsberichte der Kaiserlichen Akademie der Wissenschaften (Wien), phil.-hist. cl., 97 (1880), 197–203 and 280–84. Transitional techniques have also been treated by van den Toorn, "Zur Struktur der Saga."

stood as happening at the same time. Words and phrases such as *jafnskjótt, mjǫk jafnskjótt, jafnsnimma, jafnfram, senn, í því bili,* and *í þeirri sǫmu stundu* are common elements of quick action sequences, all meaning roughly "at that very moment" or "simultaneously." A dramatic evocation of three concurrent actions is found in *Eyrbyggja saga:*

> Steinþórr hljóp til ok brá skildi yfir Þórð, er Þorleifr vildi hǫggva hann, en annarri hendi hjó hann til Þorleifs kimba ok undan honum fótinn fyrir neðan kné. En er þetta var tíðenda, þá lagði Freysteinn bófi til Steinþórs ok stefndi á hann miðjan. En er hann sá þat, þá hljóp hann í lopt upp, ok kom lagit milli fóta honum; ok þessa þrjá hluti lék hann senn, sem nú váru taldir.

> (Steinþórr rushed toward them and thrust his shield over Þórðr just as Þorleifr was about to strike him; and with his other arm he swung at Þorleifr kimbi, taking his leg off at the knee. And at the same time this was happening, Freysteinn bófi turned on Steinþórr, aiming a spear at his middle; but when Steinþórr saw that, he jumped up in the air, and the thrust went between his legs. And these three things, which have just been told, Steinþórr did all at once.) [chap. 45]

The actions are recorded sequentially and only then explained as having happened simultaneously. Similarly, Snorri notes that Hákon had been with Knútr "alla stund til þess er hér er komit sǫgunni (the whole time, up to the point where the saga is now)." "Váru þessir atburðir jafnsnimma eða sumir litlu fyrr eða síðar (These events were simultaneous, or some a little earlier or later)," concludes the description of the concatenation of battlefield events surrounding the death of Saint Óláfr at Stiklastaðir.[19] But it is in the verbal anticipations that the idea of simultaneity finds its most graphic expression—not least in the phrase singled out by Olrik as an impossibility in folk narration, "nú ferr tvennum sǫgum fram" (roughly, "now the saga splits and runs along in two stories" or "now the saga 'twins' "). It is found in a variety of contexts:

---

[19] These two examples come from *Óláfs saga helga* in *Heimskringla,* chapters 130 and 227 respectively.

Nú ferr tvennum sǫgum fram, ok skal þar nú til taka, sem frá var horfit, er frá því var sagt, er Óláfr Haraldsson hafði frið gǫrt við Óláf Svíakonung.

(Now the saga "twins," and [we] shall now pick up the [story line] that was set aside before, when Óláfr Haraldsson had made peace with Óláfr Svíakonungr.) [*Hkr, Óláfs saga helga*, chap. 104]

Nú því, at tvennum ferr sögunum fram, ritar fyrst Hrafn til Árna byskups, at honum þykkir rofit sáttmál.

(Now, because [we] are proceeding with a divided story: Hrafn first writes to Bishop Árni that the agreement seemed to him to have collapsed.) [*Árna saga biskups*, chap. 55]

Both of these "split saga" formulations are genuine; they refer, that is, to passages in which the authors pursue parallel stories at some length and (particularly in the case of Snorri) some degree of elaborateness. The same phrase is used in *Gautreks saga* for another purpose:

Nú ferr tveim fram sögunum. Skal nú segja fyrst frá því, er áðr var horfit, at Gautrekr konungr....

(Now the saga proceeds in two stories. First that one will be told which was put aside before, in which King Gautrekr....) [chap. 8]

In this case it is not a question of two sides of one story, but of two logically unconnected stories brought into apparent alignment by use of a synchronizing formula. The role of interlace techniques in the process of agglomeration is nowhere more patent than in *Gautreks saga*, which as a whole work owes its very existence to the concept and mechanics of stranding.

Especially intriguing are the remarks that expressly note the inability of narrative to apprehend simultaneous actions. The point is made several times in *Sturlunga saga*. "Margar sögur verða hér samtíða, og má þó eigi allar senn rita (Many of these sagas happened at the same time, and yet [one] can't write them simultaneously)" states the preface to *Prestssaga Guðmundar góða*. Likewise in *Guðmundar saga dýra*: "Nú hefir fleira orðit senn en einn hlutr, ok verðr þó frá einum senn at segja (Now more things than one happened simultaneously, but they will be told one at a time"—chap. 9). The account of the Flugumýri burning is similarly prefaced:

> Nú urðu margir atburðir senn, ok má þó frá einum senn segja.

> (Now many events occurred simultaneously, though one can relate them only one at a time.) [*Íslendinga saga,* chap. 172]

From the *fornaldarsǫgur* (legendary sagas) come several striking examples, including:

> Nú af því, at eigi má í senn segja meir en eitt, þá verðr nú at skýra, sem fyrr hefir til borit í sögunni, ok er þar nú til at taka fyrst, at Hleiðr. . . .

> (Now, because not more than one thing can be told at a time, [we] shall now elucidate [a matter] which happened before in the saga, picking it up at the point where Hleiðr. . . .) [*Bósa saga ok Herrauðs,* chap. 10]

> Víkr nú aftr sögunni þangat, er fyrr var frá horfit, því at eigi verðr af tveimr hlutum sagt í senn, þótt báðir hafi jafnfram orðit. Nú er frá því at segja, at þau fóru ór Garðaríki.

> (Now the saga turns back to where it left off earlier, for double stories cannot be told at the same time, even though both may have happened simultaneously. It is now to be told that they departed from Garðaríki.) [*Göngu-Hrólfs saga,* chaps. 23–24]

Finally, from *Jómsvíkinga saga:*

> Nú hefst upp annar þáttur sögunnar, sá er fyrr hefir verið en þetta væri fram komið, ok má eigi einum munni allt senn segja.

> (Now begins the second strand of the saga, which belongs before what has just been told—one cannot tell everything at the same time with one mouth.) [chap. 8]

True enough; but in the context of an art that consistently conceives of its "story" as a multisided proposition and consistently

renders "simultaneous" passages with the full variety of literary
devices, such remarks as those quoted above strike a rude note.
One has the impression that these narrators have inherited the
mechanics of simultaneous narration without having quite
grasped the underlying artistic conception. The value of their
verbal asides is that they remind us just how artificial the procedure is and how deliberate its use even in passages where it is
accomplished fluently.

## The European Context

Although narrative time is not given separate consideration in
the rhetorical treatises, it is broached in the discussions of natural
and artificial order (*ordo naturalis* and *ordo artificialis*). In narrative, says Hugh of St. Victor, order is natural "when deeds are
recounted in the order of their occurrence" and artificial "when a
subsequent event is related first and a prior event is told after
it."[20] The chief classical sources of the doctrine are the *Rhetorica
ad Herennium* (attributed in the Middle Ages to Cicero) and
Horace's *Ars poetica*.[21] One passage in the latter had a particular
impact on the medieval discussions:

> Ordinis haec virtus erit et venus, aut ego fallor,
> ut iam nunc dicat iam nunc debentia dici,

[20]"Ordo . . . attenditur . . . in narratione secundum dispositionem, quae duplex
est; naturalis, videlicet quando res eo refertur ordine quo gesta est, et artificialis,
id est, quando id quod postea gestum est prius narratur, et quod prius, postmodum
dicitur" (Hugh of St. Victor, *Didascalion*, III, 8). For a general discussion of
medieval statements on order, with examples, see Faral, *Les arts poétiques*,
pp. 55–60.
[21]The chief classical discussions of order are those in Horace, *Satires, Epistles,
and Ars Poetica*, ed. H. Rushton Fairclough, Loeb Classical Library (Cambridge,
Mass.: Harvard University Press, 1955), vv. 42–45 (pp. 453–54); Martianus
Capella, "De rhetorica," chap. 30 in *Rhetores latini minores*, ed. Karl Halm
(Leipzig: Teubner, 1863), pp. 471–72; Sulpitius Victor, "Institutiones oratoriae,"
chap. 14, ibid., p. 320; and *Ad Herennium*, ed. Harry Caplan, Loeb Classical
Library (Cambridge, Mass.: Harvard University Press, 1968), esp. p. 186. The
chief medieval discussions are those in the *Scholia vindobonensia ad Horatii
artem poeticam*, ed. Joseph Zechmeister (Vienna: Apud C. Geroldum Filium
Bibliopolam, 1877). pp. 4–5; Geoffrey of Vinsauf, "Poetria nova," vv. 101–25, in
Faral, *Les arts poétiques*, pp. 200–201; and Matthew of Vendôme, "Ars versificatoria," ibid., pp. 3–13. See also Charles Sears Baldwin, *Medieval Rhetoric
and Poetic* (New York: Macmillan, 1928; rpt. Gloucester, Mass.: Peter Smith,
1959), pp. 195–96; and Faral, *Les arts poétiques*, pp. 55–60, for a general discussion and list of references.

pleraque differat et praesens in tempus omittat
hoc amet, hoc spernat promissi carminis auctor.

(Of order, this, if I mistake not, will be the excellence and charm that
the author of the long-promised poem shall say at the moment what
at that moment should be said, reserving and omitting much for the
present, loving this point and scorning that.) [*Ars poetica*, vv.
42–45]

After a labored effort to parse Horace's sentence,[22] the unknown
author of the eighth-century *Scholia vindobonensia* offered this
paraphrase:

> nam sententia talis est: quicunque promittit se facturum bonum car-
> men et lucidum habere ordinem, amet artificialem ordinem et sper-
> nat naturalem. omnis ordo aut naturalis aut artificialis est. naturalis
> ordo est, si quis narret rem ordine quo gesta est; artificialis ordo est,
> si quis non incipit a principio rei gestae, sed a medio, ut Virgilius in
> Aeneide quaedam in futuro dicenda anticipat et quaedam in
> praesenti dicenda in posterum differt.

(For the meaning is as follows: whoever undertakes to make a good
poem with a clear order should love artificial order and scorn natural
order. Every order is either natural or artificial. Natural order is
when one narrates the deeds in the order in which they happened;
artificial order is when one does not begin from the beginning of an
exploit but in the middle, as when Virgil in the *Aeneid* anticipates
some things which should have been told in the future and puts off
until later some things which should have been told in the present.)
[*Scholia vindobonensia*, p. 5]

The *Scholia vindobonensia* may be regarded as a harbinger of the
medieval interest in artificial order and approval of the Virgilian
example in particular.

The author of the *Scholia vindobonensia* may have been Al-

---

[22]"*Hoc*, id est, ut nunc dicat iam debentia dici quantum ad naturalem ordinem:
*amet auctor promissi carminis*, id est, amet artificialem ordinem; *hoc*, id est,
contrarium ordinis artificialis, id est, ordinem naturalem *spernat auctor promissi
carminis;* hoc breviter dicit. (*Hoc*, that is, he should say now what ought to have
been said before according to natural order; *amet auctor promissi carminis*, that
is, should love artificial order. *Hoc*, that is, the opposite of artificial order, that is,
*spernat auctor promissi carminis* natural order; Horace says this briefly)." From
the *Scholia vindobonensia*, pp. 4–5. See John Leyerle, "The Interlace Structure of
*Beowulf*," *University of Toronto Quarterly*, 37 (1967), 6.

cuin.[23] Certainly his two lives of St. Willibrord seem intended to illustrate the distinction between natural and artificial arrangement as it is outlined in that treatise.[24] The prose version[25] uses natural order, beginning with an account of the saint's parents and proceeding chronologically through his *vita, mors,* and *miracula.* The version in hexameter verse, however, puts the early life of the saint at the end, beginning *in medias res* with a dramatic event from his adult life (his visit to Pippin).[26] Of particular interest is Alcuin's statement, in his preface to the latter version, that he wrote the different versions for different audiences: the prose one (that is, the naturally ordered one) for oral delivery at a public worship, and the poetic one (that is, the artificially ordered one) for private study in the monastic schools.[27]

The idea that *ordo naturalis* was more appropriate to oratory and sermon, whereas *ordo artificialis* was for the edification of the reader, is expressed in a variety of forms in both classical and medieval sources. It should be remembered that the *Aeneid,* the medieval benchmark of *ordo artificialis,* was intended primarily for private reading. Alcuin made the point again in his *Rhetoric:* in a speech, he said, "Clarity in narration is achieved if what happened first is explained first, and if the order of the episodes in the story is determined by the order of real events and time. ... Care should be taken to exclude intricacy and confusion from the story, and to avoid digression."[28] The issue is memory, wrote Robert of Basevorn in his *Forma praedicandi.* Of the ornament "circuitous development" he writes that it "is more dec-

---

[23]See Zechmeister's introduction to his edition of the *Scholia vindobonensia,* p. iii; also Faral, *Les arts poétiques,* p. 57, note 1.

[24]Leyerle, "The Interlace Structure of *Beowulf,*" (1967), pp. 1–17.

[25]Bruno Krusch and Wilhelm Levison, eds., *De vita sancti Willibrordi,* Monumenta Germaniae historica, Scriptores rerum merovingicarum (Hannover: Hahn, 1919), VII, 113–41.

[26]Ernst Dümmler, ed., *De vita Willibrordi episcopi,* Monumenta Germaniae historica, Poetae latini medii aevi (Berlin: Weidmann, 1881), I, 207–20.

[27]Ibid., preface.

[28]"Aperta autem narratio poterit esse, si ut quidque primum gestum erit, ita primum exponetur, et rerum ac temporum ordo servabitur. ... Hic erit considerandum, ne quid perturbate, ne quid contorte dicatur, ne quam in aliam rem transeatur" (Wilbur Samuel Howell, *The Rhetoric of Alcuin and Charlemagne: A Translation, with an Introduction, the Latin Text, and Notes* [Princeton: Princeton University Press, 1941], pp. 100–101).

orative than useful; I generally do not use it even when it presents itself, because it dulls the mind of the listener by making an unsolvable labyrinth, unless the reader is very subtle.''[29] It is probably no accident that enthusiasm for artificial order in narrative poetry coincided with the rise of a literary public, so that an author could envision publication not only in the form of oral delivery, but by multiplication of manuscripts intended for private reading. Indeed, the very distinction between "natural" and "artificial" may be an indirect reflection of oral and literary narrative patterns. For Geoffrey of Vinsauf, *ordo naturalis* was the "main street of nature" and *ordo artificialis* was the "footpath of art.''[30]

> Civilior ordine recto
> Et longe prior est, quamvis praeposterus ordo.
> Ordinis est primus sterilis, ramusque secundus
> Fertilis et mira succrescit origine ramus
> In ramos, solus in plures, unus in octo.

(More sophisticated than natural order is artistic order, and far preferable, however much permuted the arrangement be. The first sort of order is barren, but the second branch is fertile; and from that origin one branch miraculously grows up into many, the single into several, one into eight.)[31] [*Poetria nova,* vv. 99–103]

---

[29]"Utrum autem isto ornamento [circulatio] utile fuerit uti, dubium est nonnullis. Hoc scio, quod est magis curiosum quam utile. Ego communiter illo non utor, etiamsi se offert, quia quasi inexplicabile labyrinthum faciens, ingenia auditorum, nisi fuerint valde sub tiles, obtundit'' (Robert of Basevorn, *Forma praedicandi,* p. 302). Other remarks of Robert's along the same lines: "Sed hoc [i.e., digressio] succinte faciendum est in sermone—p. 297 (But in a sermon, a Digression must be brief"—p. 186); "Tertii, super haec vanissimi, addunt confirmare particulas convolutionis auctoritatibus Scripturae. Sed, ut credo, hoc secundum aliquas partes potest fieri, nunquam secundum omnes. Ideo semper vitium erit in tali convolutione. Ideo non consulo quod aliquis illo modo utatur, quia simpliciter inutilis est et secundum totum, ut reputo, impossibilis"—p. 306 ("Other third groups, most vain, add a confirmation of the parts of the interlacing with authorities of Scripture. But, as I believe, this can happen for some parts, never for all. Therefore, there would be error in such Convolution. Therefore, I counsel that no one use this method, because it is simply useless, and in the whole, as I think, impossible"). Translation by Leopold Krul O.S.B. in James J. Murphy, ed., *Three Medieval Rhetorical Arts* (Berkeley: University of California Press, 1971), p. 191.

[30]"Ordo bifurcat iter: tum limite nititur artis,/Tum sequitur stratam naturae" (Geoffrey of Vinsauf, *Poetria nova,* vv. 87–88, in Faral, *Les arts poétiques*).

[31]Translation by Jane Baltzell Kopp in James J. Murphy, ed., *Three Medieval Rhetorical Arts,* p. 36.

The desired result of artificial order, he continues, is a dark and tangled forest which the reader penetrates only by the careful exercise of intelligence (vv. 104–11):

Circiter hanc artem fortasse videtur et aer
Nubilus, et limes salebrosus, et ostia clausa,
Et res nodosa. Quocirca sequentia verba
Sunt hujus morbi medici: speculeris in illis;
Invenietur ibi qua purges luce tenebras,
Quo pede transcurras salebras, qua clave recludas
Ostia, quo digito solvas nodosa. Patentem
Ecce viam! Ratione viae rege mentis habenas.

(Now in the area of this technique the air may seem to be dark, the path rugged, the doors closed, and the problem knotty. The following words, then, are doctors of this malady: ponder them. There will be found the means by which you may cleanse the shadows from the light, the foot on which you may traverse the rugged ground, the key with which you may open the doors, and the finger with which you may loose the knots. Look, a road lies open! Guide the reins of your mind by the law of this road.) [vv. 104–11]

These statements perhaps more than any others in the treatises capture the nature of much medieval narrative: artificial order is not only a question of rearranging segments of a linear story, but of multiplying the parts of the story into brachial forms whose meaning is not immediately apparent but must be pondered. The artistic text is a knot to be untied, a door to be unlocked, darkness to be dispelled, rugged terrain to be traversed—the list is Geoffrey's—by means of study.

By this measure, interlace narrative is, in its organization of the matter, both natural (within the strand) and artificial (in the larger work). Within the strand narrators are punctiliously sequential, tolerating neither flashbacks, flash forwards, nor any other kind of *ordo artificialis* mentioned in the treatises. Things are told in the order in which they happen. But if one stands back and looks at the larger narrative, the picture is quite different. Here the natural chronological flow is repeatedly disrupted by backward jumps, and the whole takes on a peculiarly artificial zigzag design. Chronology is observed in the individual line; but the moment the narrator shifts attention to another line of action, the order becomes artificial. It is hard to know whether the medieval rhetoricians had in mind the sort of interlace narrative that began to enjoy a certain popularity in the early thirteenth century. But we may assume that their concern with the question of order and their enthusiasm for artificialities involving major temporal disjunctions are symptomatic of the emerging sensibility. If *ordo artificialis* is not per se an adumbration of simultaneous narration, it certainly sets the scene.

The shift from nonsimultaneous to simultaneous narration is dramatically evident, in literary practice, in a comparison of Chrétien's *Conte del graal* with its later reworkings and continuations. The second half of Chrétien's poem divides into a Gawain action and a Perceval action. The narrator first follows Gawain for three days, telling of his tournament at Tintagel and his stay at Escavalon; then returns to Perceval, telling of his three-day stay with the hermit; then picks up the Gawain strand where it was left off earlier (Escavalon) and tells of his adventures with l'Orgueilleuse, the Magic Castle, and Guiromelant—and at this point the poem breaks off. But if the Gawain strand is temporally complete (by use of continuous retrieval), the Perceval story is entirely out of the time frame, taking place five years later. This incongruity, together with a general vagueness and implausibility with regard to time sequence in the poem as a whole, led Hermann Weigand to argue that "Chrétien had only a rudimentary understanding of the narrator's problem of interweaving the strands of his story. He had no idea of setting his two heroes on a simultaneous course or of having them meet on a common ground."[32] Wolfram von Eschenbach, on the other hand, fitted the entire poem into an exact, closely reasoned calendar and, more important, synchronized the two strands of the latter half in such a way as to

---

[32]Hermann Weigand, "Narrative Time in the Grail Poems of Chrétien de Troyes and Wolfram von Eschenbach," in *Wolfram's* Parzival: *Five Essays with an Introduction,* ed. Ursula Hoffman (Ithaca, N.Y.: Cornell University Press, 1969); originally "Die epischen Zeitverhältnisse in den Graldichtungen Crestiens und Wolframs," *PMLA,* 53 (1938), 917–50. For a discussion of incipient interlace in Chrétien's romances see also William W. Ryding, *Structure in Medieval Narrative* (The Hague: Mouton, 1971), pp. 139–45; Wilhelm Kellermann, "Aufbaustil und Weltbild Chrestiens von Troyes im Percevalroman," *Beihefte zur Zeitschrift für romanische Philologie,* 88 (Halle: Niemeyer, 1936), 5–6 and 11–16; and Jean Frappier, "La composition du *Conte du graal,*" *Le moyen âge,* 64 (1958), 67–102.

bring all of their phases into one continuous scheme.<sup>33</sup> Wolfram
also, by way of explaining an especially dramatic interruption in
his tale, offered a comparison of his narrative technique with the
operation of a bow:

> wer der selbe wære,
> des vreischet her nâch mære.
> dar zuo der wirt, sîn burc, sîn lant,
> diu werden iu von mir genant
> her nâch sô des wirdet zît,
> bescheidenlîchen âne strît
> unde âne allez für zogen.
> ich sage die senewen âne bogen.
> diu senewe ist ein bîspel.
> nû dunket iuch der boge snel:
> doch ist sneller daz diu senew jaget.
> ob ich iu rehte hân gesaget,
> diu senewe gelîchet mæren sleht:
> diu dunkent ouch die liute reht.
> swer iu saget von der krümbe,
> der wil iuch leiten ümbe.
> swer den bogen gespannen siht,
> der senewen er der slehte giht,
> man welle si zer biuge erdenen
> sô si den shuz muoz menen.
> swer aber dem sîn mære schiuzet,
> des in durch nôt verdriuzet:
> (wan daz hât dâ ninder stat
> und vil gerûmeclîchen phat
> zeinem ôren în, zem andern vür),
> mîn arbeit ich gar verlür,
> ob den mîn mære drünge:
> ich sagete oder sünge,
> daz ez noch baz vernæme ein boc
> oder ein ulmeger stoc.

(Who he was you shall learn later. And you shall hear from me,
when the proper time has come, clearly and without any protest or

<sup>33</sup>Weigand, "Narrative Time," p. 73. See also Joachim Bumke, *Wolframs
Willehalm: Studien zur Epenstruktur und zum Heiligkeitsbegriff der ausgehenden
Blütezeit* (Heidelberg: Winter, 1959), p. 98, note 76: "Wolfram is, as far as I can
see, the first to make conscious use of such simultaneity."

delay, the name of the host, his castle, and his land. I tell my story
like the bowstring and not like the bow. The string here is a figure of
speech. Now *you* think the bow is fast, but faster is the arrow sped
by the string. If what I have said is right, the string is like the simple,
straightforward tales that people like. Whoever tells you a story like
the curve of a bow wants to lead you a roundabout way. If you see
the bow and it is strung, you must admit the string is straight—unless
it be bent to an arc to speed the shot. Of course if I shoot my tale at a
listener who is sure to be bored, it finds no resting place, but travels
a roomy path, namely, in one ear and out the other. It would be labor
lost if I annoyed such a one with my tale. A goat would understand it
better, or a rotten tree trunk.)   [*Parzival*, 241:1–30]

A commonplace of medieval biblical exegesis ("the rigidity of the
Old Testament letter is bent by the spiritual understanding of the
New Testament"[34]), the bow metaphor entered the secular
sphere in the early thirteenth century and is used by Wolfram,
accused by his contemporaries of being overly digressive,[35] to
"defend and elucidate the artistic disposition of his narrative."[36]
One is reminded of the different but equivalent metaphor, making
much the same point, in the *Longest Saga:* "Just as running
water flows from various sources yet all comes together in a
single place, so, in like wise, do all these stories from various
sources have a single goal" (see page 36 above).

Wolfram's improvements are very much in the spirit of the
thirteenth-century reworkings of the romances. If simultaneous
narration is an occasional feature in, for example, *La vie de Saint
Alexis*, the *Roman de Troie*, and the *Guillaume d'Angleterre* (attributed by some critics to Chrétien),[37] it is a compositional fact in
the prose romances. Vinaver, it will be recalled, considered that

[34]A paraphrase of St. Gregory the Great by Arthur B. Groos, Jr., "Wolfram von
Eschenbach's 'Bow Metaphor' and the Narrative Technique of Parzival,"
*Modern Language Notes*, 87 (1972), 396. Groos examines the connection between
exegetical tradition and the medieval rhetorical writings on natural and artificial
order.

[35]See, in particular, Gottfried's attack in his *Tristan*, vv. 4638–90 (Friedrich
Ranke, ed., *Gottfried von Strassburg: Tristan und Isolde*, 9th ed. [Zurich: Weidmann, 1965]).

[36]Groos, " 'Bow Metaphor,' " p. 397.

[37]See esp. Jean Frappier, *Chrétien de Troyes: L'homme et l'œuvre*, Connaissance des lettres, 50 (Paris: Hatier-Boivin, 1957), pp. 75–84.

the idea of synchrony "caused" interlace narrative: if themes were to be pursued simultaneously, they had to "alternate like threads in a woven fabric, one theme interrupting another and again another, and yet all remaining constantly present in the author's and the reader's mind."[38] In the Vulgate Cycle the threads are Arthur's knights, who undertake errands and then part ways to wander about the landscape, now encountering each other unexpectedly, now diverging again. "We are in an age," wrote Vinaver, "when character has no existence outside destiny, and destiny means the convergence of simultaneously developed themes, now separated, now coming together, varied, yet synchronized, so that every movement of this carefully planned design remains charged with echoes of the past and premonitions of the future."[39] As Lot pointed out, the time scheme of days and hours in the *Prose Lancelot* is such that at any given moment one can gauge exactly where the several wandering knights stand in relation to one another[40]—indeed, the corresponding emphasis on spatial detail seems to invite the audience to visualize the crisscrossings in the mind's eye.[41] *La queste del saint graal* is constructed on the same principle, but its time scheme is, as Frappier writes, "loose rather than strict," thus relaxing the interlace in such a way as to "permit longer stretches of continuous narrative."[42]

But it is in the final section of the Vulgate Cycle, the *Mort Artu,* that we see simultaneous interlace in its finest form. Particularly in the first part, according to Frappier, the interlace is "combined with a firm and precise chronology.... No other prose romance of the Middle Ages offers a texture so tightly woven."[43] One

[38]Vinaver, *Rise of Romance,* p. 76.
[39]Ibid., p. 92.
[40]Ferdinand Lot, *Etude sur le Lancelot en prose* (Paris: Champion, 1918), pp. 17–64.
[41]The visual dimension of interlace is brought out by Susanna Greer Fein, "Thomas Malory and La queste del saint graal," *University of Toronto Quarterly,* 46 (1977), 215–40.
[42]Jean Frappier, "The Vulgate Cycle," in *Arthurian Literature in the Middle Ages: A Collaborative History,* ed. Roger Sherman Loomis (Oxford: Clarendon, 1959), p. 303.
[43]Ibid., p. 308. On the temporal arrangement of the parts, see also Jean Rychner, *L'articulation des phrases narratives dans la* Mort Artu, Université de Neuchâtel: Recueil de travaux de la Faculté des lettres, 32 (Geneva: Droz, 1970).

example illustrates the author's method. The adultery of Lancelot and Guinevere comes to the attention of King Arthur, and a plot is devised to catch them in the act: the king will invite Lancelot to go hunting with him, knowing that he will decline in order to use the opportunity to visit the queen; once he is in her chamber, the king's men will attack and capture him. All goes according to plan: observed by spies, Lancelot steals in through a private garden and lodges himself in the queen's bed. The king's men break down the locked door and come at Lancelot, but when he manages to kill one knight on the spot, they retreat briefly. Arming himself with the dead knight's equipment, Lancelot manages to fight his way through the courtyard and so escapes to his lodging. There he confers at some length with Bors on what has happened. Hector arrives during this scene, and together the three lay plans to save the queen from what they suspect will be capital punishment. They gather men, thirty-eight in all, and assemble on the edge of a forest outside town. A squire is sent to Camelot to ascertain whether the queen has in fact been sentenced to death.

> Lors se part li vallez de Lancelot et s'en va seur son roncin la plus droite voie qu'il pot vers Kamaalot, et fet tant qu'il vient a la cort le roi Artu. Mes atant lesse ore li contes a parler de lui et retorne as trois freres monseigneur Gauvain, si comme Lancelos se parti d'eus quant il l'orent trouvé en la chambre la reïne. Or dit li contes que, a celi point que Lancelos se fu partiz de la reïne et fu eschapez de ceus qui le cuidierent prendre, cil qui furent a l'uis de la chambre, maintenant que il virent qu'il s'en fu alez, entrerent en la chambre et pristrent la reïne et li firent honte et laidure assez plus qu'il ne deüssent et distrent que ore estoit la chose prouvee et qu'ele n'en puet eschaper sanz mort. Assez li firent honte, et ele escoutoit tant dolente que trop et pleure tant durement que bien en deüssent avoir pitié li felon chevalier. A eure de none vint li rois del bois.

(Then the boy left Lancelot, mounted his horse, went by the quickest route to Camelot, and arrived at King Arthur's court. But now the story stops telling of him, and returns to Sir Gawain's three brothers at the moment when Lancelot escaped from them after they had found him in the queen's room. Now the story relates that, when Lancelot had left the queen and fled from those who were hoping to catch him, the men at the door of the room, seeing that he had gone, went in and caught the queen. They insulted and taunted her more than they should have done, saying that now they had proof and that she would not escape with her life. They treated her with a total lack of respect, and she heard them as distressed as could be, weeping so bitterly that the wicked knights should have pity on her. At None the king returned from the hunt.) [*Mort Artu,* 91–92]

Arthur dispatches men to intercept Lancelot in his lodge, but they arrive there to find him already gone. Arthur vents his anger on Guinevere and sentences her to death by burning. She is led through the streets, dressed in red, to a field outside of town where the pyre is blazing. When this news is brought to Lancelot, he mounts an attack and saves the queen. The passage might be represented as in Figure 1.

It is in this zigzag logic, characteristic both of the *Mort Artu* as a whole and the prose romances in general, that the Icelandic saga finds its closest structural counterpart. However unfamiliar the moral sentiments of the Vulgate Cycle might have seemed to a thirteenth-century Icelandic audience, the principles of composition would have been immediately transparent. The author alternates between actions by means of the techniques of discontinuous and continuous retrieval in free variation. Certain fixed

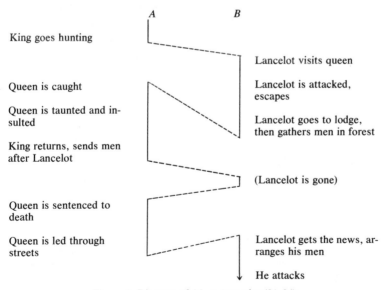

*Figure 1.* Diagram of *Mort Artu* plot (91–94)

phrases are used to effect the narrative shifts and to relocate the action in time and place. The lines are played off against one another for purposes of suspense, delay, forecast: the audience knows before Lancelot that he and Guinevere will be discovered, before the king that his men will not find Lancelot at home, and before Guinevere that she will be saved from the blaze. Despite the complexity and the sheer bulk of the material, one has the sense that there is behind it a skilled narrator in full control. As Frappier said, "These are no mechanical repetitions, the sign of an impoverished imagination, but rather organic themes which are articulated as they develop. This manner of composition is not the result of mere chance; it follows from the author's real intention and is a rule of his art."[44]

The same "rule of art" governs the narrative of the sagas. Their precise concern with timekeeping is traditionally regarded as a reflection of the strong chronicle impulse in medieval Iceland. But as Ólafia Einarsdóttir points out, although some of the fixed dates that serve as points of departure for the elaborate system of "intrinsic relative chronology" are historical, others are not, but are rather "ascribable to the authors' own constructions."[45] The reason is that where there is interlace narration, there is necessarily a manifest time scheme; the greater the degree of simultaneity, the more detailed that time scheme must be. If the necessary calendar can be derived from or made to match a historical sequence, as in the case of much classical saga narrative, so much the better. But as the prose romances document, the same procedure can be worked out on a purely fictional plane. The fact that saga authors had recourse to fictional dates in time of narrative need would seem to indicate that their first loyalty was not, after all, to historical accuracy, but to the art of "fine-fabling." The real value of the grand chronology Vigfússon deduced from the Icelandic sagas lies not so much in its historical dimension but in the fact that, like the "temporal blueprints" that

[44]Jean Frappier, *Etude sur La mort le roi Artu: Roman du XIII^e siècle* (Paris: Droz, 1936), p. 368; 2d rev. ed. (Geneva: Droz, 1961).

[45]Einarsdóttir, *Studier i kronologisk metode*, p. 249. See also Walter Baetke, *Über die Entstehung der Isländersagas*, Berichte über der Verhandlungen der Sächsischen Akademie der Wissenschaften zu Leipzig, phil.-hist. Kl., 102, pt. 5 (1956), pp. 32–34.

Lot, Frappier, and Pauphilet deduced from the Vulgate Cycle, it lays bare the authors' artistic calculations.[46] Walter Morris Hart said the simple ballad plot consists of a single narrative stream: "Synchronistic events are exceptional, and synchronism is never necessary for the working out of the plot."[47] In interlace narrative, the synchronic events *are* the plot. The question is not one of complicating a simple story, but of imagining a complex story, a coherence of interlocking and simultaneous stories. The distinction is crucial, for it points up two fundamentally different attitudes toward time. For the audience of the simple or well-made story, what is being told at any given moment represents the whole story and so the present. When an event is complete, the present moment is complete and the story looks to the future. The pace may vary, but the direction is only forward; such a tale is "true to nature because its current of life flows onward."[48] Interlace narrative, on the other hand, rests on the understanding that the immediate story is not necessarily the whole story, but only half or a smaller fraction of it. For behind the immediate story are other equally important stories, happening at the same time, and waiting their narrative turn. Each retrieval of a story line represents a renegotiation of the present, and one is left with the sense that time, like the plot itself, is never quite "finished and done with"[49] but subject to infinite multiplications. The narrator who chooses, at the end of every episode, either to advance the plot or to turn it back on itself, and the audience whose enjoyment depends on being repeatedly confronted with that set of opposite possibilities, have together conspired against the notion of the linear story to a degree unprecedented in earlier European literature and paralleled only in our own day. The idea that things happen at the same time may not be a new one, but its central role as a structural device in literature belongs to the Middle Ages.

[46]Guðbrandur Vigfússon, "Um Tímatal í Íslendinga-Sögum," *Safn til sögu Íslands,* I (1856), 185–502.
[47]Walter Morris Hart, *Ballad and Epic: A Study in the Development of the Narrative Art* (Boston: Ginn, 1907), p. 39.
[48]Bassett, *Poetry of Homer,* p. 42.
[49]Ker, *Epic and Romance,* p. 237.

# CHAPTER 4

# Toward the Classical Saga

## The Preclassical Texts

"The origins of the classical prose," wrote E. O. G. Turville-Petre, "can perhaps be discerned best if Icelandic literature of pre-classical ages is considered."[1] This proposition is hardly a fresh one—scholars have long wondered about the extent to which thirteenth-century literary developments may have been prefigured in the twelfth century—but the fact that it could be the point of departure for a major work as recently as 1953 suggests just how inconclusive earlier treatments have been. The task of establishing continuities is not as straightforward as it may seem. One problem is the paucity of extant texts from the early period. A second problem is that those texts that do survive are not entirely apposite, consisting of translations of foreign works, history writing (partly in Latin) of a fairly standard sort, and royal biographies of a strongly clerical stamp. A third problem has to do with the fact that these texts appear in rapid succession, and although we have some idea of their relative chronology, we get little sense of literary phases displacing one another and evolving toward the vernacular and secular masterpieces of the thirteenth century. Still, if these early documents do not offer a neat prehistory of the saga phenomenon as a whole, they provide an insight into certain of its aspects, not the least of which is the category of composition, mentioned only in passing in Turville-Petre's study.

[1] E. O. G. Turville-Petre, *Origins of Icelandic Literature* (Oxford: Clarendon, 1953), p. v.

With the classical patterns of composition in mind, therefore, we may review some early texts in the historical tradition which may have a bearing on the rise of the saga.

*Sæmundr and Ari.* The first history of the Norwegian kings of which we have record is that of the Icelander Sæmundr the Wise (died 1133). Nothing survives of Sæmundr's work save the two sentences cited in Oddr's saga of Óláfr Tryggvason.[2] Sæmundr's work was an important source for Ari and other early writers, however, and their references to it indicate something of its scope and content (it appears to have ranged rather widely, even into Icelandic matter), but next to nothing is known of its style and composition. Snorri (in his prologues to *Heimskringla* and the *Separate Saga of Saint Óláfr*) names Ari as the first person to write learned works in the vernacular, from which it may be inferred that Sæmundr's history was in Latin. Tradition holds that Sæmundr studied in France.

The only surviving work by Ari (died 1148) is the ten-page *Íslendingabók (Libellus Islandorum),* written in the early twelfth century.[3] Purporting to be a summary history of Iceland from the time of its settlement down through the life of Bishop Gizurr, the *Íslendingabók* may seem to the modern eye somewhat arbitrary in its selection and coverage of events.[4] Although Ari makes a point of synchronizing events in Iceland with those in Europe,[5] there is no hint, in this very spare and synoptic treatment of local matters, of double lines of action. Certain stylistic traits are reminiscent of later saga prose, but there is no discernible point of

---

[2]On Sæmundr's authorship, see Svend Ellehøj, *Studier over den ældste norrǿne historieskrivning,* Bibliotheca Arnamagnæana, 26 (Copenhagen: Munksgaard, 1965), pp. 15–25.

[3]On Ari's authorship, ibid., pp. 26–84.

[4]Andreas Heusler, "Are's Íslendingabók und Libellus Islandorum," *Arkiv för nordisk filologi,* 23 (1907), 319–37.

[5]For example, "Á því ári enu sama obiit Paschalis secundus páfi fyrr en Gizurr byskup ok Baldvini Jórsalakonungr ok Arnaldus patriarcha í Híerúsalem ok Philippus Svíakonungr, en síðarr et sama sumar Alexíus Grikkjakonungr; þá hafði hann átta vetr ens fjórða tegar setit at stóli í Miklagarði (In that same year Pope Paschal the Second died, before Bishop Gizurr; Baldwin, King of Jerusalem; Arnulf, Patriarch of Jerusalem; Philip, King of the Swedes; and, later the same summer, Alexius, Emperor of the Greeks—at that time he had occupied the throne at Constantinople for 38 years"—chap. 10).

contact on the level of composition. There are no transitional formulas.

*Landnámabók.* There are five extant versions of *Landnámabók,* three medieval and two seventeenth-century, all thought to derive from a now-lost version by Styrmir Kárason (died 1245).[6] Styrmir was probably operating within an established tradition; it is thought that some kind of settlement book existed at least a century earlier—perhaps, as some references suggest, authored by Ari. The second chapter of Ari's *Íslendingabók* consists of an abbreviated list of settlers and their progeny, and it is possible that an older version, the *Liber Islandorum,* also contained similar settlement records. In the form we now have it, *Landnámabók* names about 400 original settlers of Iceland and specifies what land they took. The organization is geographic, moving clockwise around the island. The genealogies are typically made to extend backward into previous generations in Norway and forward into the life and times of their Icelandic progeny; two of the redactions boast some 3,500 personal names and 1,500 place names.[7] The factual lists are occasionally supplemented with narrative anecdotes, the importance of which, in the evolution of the Icelandic family saga, is generally acknowledged.[8] It would appear that the earlier versions were shorter and the later ones longer, the result in part of the provision of fuller genealogical information and in part of the accretion of anecdotes. Of some interest from the point of view of open composition is the theory that Ari did not author a settlement book per se, but wrote numerous short notices or *schedae* that remained for his inheritors to gather into manuscript form.[9]

[6]For a summary of the textual problems, see the introduction to the Fornrit edition, pp. 1–cvi.

[7]Jakob Benediktsson, "Landnámabók" in *Kulturhistorisk leksikon for nordisk middelalder* (Oslo: Gyldendal, 1965).

[8]Of some interest from the point of view of composition is Walther Heinrich Vogt's contention that the combination of *Erzählungen* and *Berichte* in *Landnámabók* evolved into classical saga style. See his "Die Frásagnir der Landnámabók," *Zeitschrift für deutsches Altertum und deutsche Literatur,* 58 (1920), 161–204.

[9]Halldór Hermannsson, *The Book of the Icelanders (Íslendingabók),* Islandica, 20 (Ithaca, N.Y.: Cornell University Library, 1930), pp. 40–42, and his article "Ari Þorgilsson fróði," *Skírnir,* 122 (1948), 20–22; also Einar Ólafur Sveinsson's introduction to the Fornrit edition of *Laxdœla saga,* esp. p. xxxvi.

From the purely descriptive point of view, *Landnámabók* is a polycentric work, a sequence of family clusters susceptible (as a comparison of versions shows clearly) of lateral amplification either in the form of further genealogical matter or anecdotes. Simultaneity in the broad sense is inherent in the format. The narrator's problem is how, on one hand, to be chronological within the cluster and, on the other, to correlate certain events in that cluster with events in other clusters; for the family chronicles do not exist in isolation, but interact and overlap with one another to the point where, in some cases, they are for all practical purposes inextricable. The solution is a rudimentary form of stranding. Persons are necessarily mentioned in connection with stories other than their own (e.g., the stories of the families into which they marry, or events in which they participate as minor figures). The cross-referencing formulas in the *Sturlubók* and *Hauksbók* redactions point either backward (*er fyrr var getit*, "as was mentioned before") or forward (*sem enn mun sagt verða*, "as is still to be told") to the "main" entry.

One of the longest and most colorful narrative passages in the *Sturlubók* redaction is the story of Auðr in djúpúðga (known in fuller form from *Laxdœla saga*). Mentioned first in the list of Ketill flatnefr's children (*S* 13), she is put aside for some pages until her marriage to Óleifr inn hvíti brings her back onto center stage (*S* 95). After the deaths of her husband and son, Auðr has a ship built in secret which she then sails to Iceland, taking with her twenty freedmen—*dux femina facti*. The narrator devotes a paragraph to the members of her retinue (*S* 96), chiefly Kollr (later to become Dala-Kollr), and Erpr, son of the Scottish earl Meldún, who together with his mother Myrgjol, a declassed Irish princess, continues to serve Auðr faithfully even after manumission. After her arrival in Iceland and settlement at Hvammr, Auðr parcels out land to her retainers (*S* 93) and arranges marriages for her children; in each case the person in question heads a descending genealogy. Finally, the narrator returns to Auðr and tells the story of her death-feast and burial. Auðr's "story" may be outlined thus:

A¹ Auðr introduced as one of Ketill flatnefr's children.
   (Other portions of *Landnámabók*.)
A² Auðr marries Óleifr inn hvíti. He dies, leaving Auðr with a son,

Þorsteinn, and a grandson, Óláfr feilan. Þorsteinn is killed. Auðr
has a ship made in secret and escapes with a large retinue.
B¹  Kollr is mentioned.
C¹  Erpr and his mother Myrgjol are mentioned.
A³  Auðr goes first to the Faeroes, then to Iceland. Spends the winter
with her brother, then takes her own land and settles at Hvammr.
She gives land to her retinue:
D¹  Ketill (land claim, genealogy)
E¹  Hǫrðr (land claim, genealogy)
F¹  Vífill (brief anecdote, land claim, genealogy)
G¹  Hundi (land claim)
H¹  Sǫkkólfr (land claim, genealogical note)
C²  Erpr (land claim, genealogy)
    (Inserted genealogy)
B²  Kollr (land claim, genealogy)
I¹  Herjólfr (genealogy)
J¹  Þórhildr (married by Auðr, genealogy)
K¹  Ósk (married by Auðr, genealogy)
L¹  Óláfr feilan (reared by Auðr, genealogy)
A⁴  Auðr hosts a large feast, during which she dies.

There is no question of plot braiding here because all the
"strands" are of a nonnarrative nature—mere lists of facts which
take as a starting point Auðr's generosity or matriarchal acts. The
exception is the miniature entailed subplot concerning Erpr and
Myrgjol:

Erpr hét leysingi Auðar; hann var son Meldúns jarls af Skotlandi,
þess er fell fyrir Sigurði jarli enum ríka; móðir Erps var Myrgjol,
dóttir Gljómals Írakonungs. Sigurðr jarl tók þau at herfangi ok þjáði.
Myrgjol var ambátt konu jarls ok þjónaði henni trúliga; hon var
margkunnandi. Hon varðveitti barn drottningar óborit, meðan hon
var í laugu. Síðan keypti Auðr hana dýrt ok hét henni frelsi, ef hon
þjónaði svá Þuríði konu Þorsteins rauðs sem drottningu. Þau
Myrgjol ok Erpr son hennar fóru til Íslands með Auði.

(Erpr was the name of a freedman of Auðr. He was the son of Earl
Meldún of Scotland, who was defeated by Earl Sigurðr inn ríki.
Erpr's mother was Myrgjol, the daughter of the Irish king Gljómall.
Earl Sigurðr took the two of them, mother and son, as war captives
and enslaved them. Myrgjol was the servant of the Earl's wife, and
she served her faithfully; she was clever in many things. She cared

for the queen's unlegitimated child while she was at the baths. After that Auðr bought her for a high price and promised her freedom if she would serve Þuríðr, the wife of Þorsteinn the Red, as well as she had the queen. Myrgjol and her son Erpr went to Iceland with Auðr.) [*Landnámabók, S* 96, *H* 83]

The result of such insertions, whether they are narrative or report, is that Auðr's story is not told consecutively but broken into parts. The dramatic account of her flight and settlement is separated from the equally dramatic story of her self-arranged funeral by several pages of nondramatic matter, just as the notice of her birth is separated from the story of her marriage by a long span of other settlement information. The patterns of interruption and suspension which lie at the center of the classical saga aesthetic are, in other words, implicit in *Landnámabók*, prompted by a concern with correct chronology and conditioned by the pluralistic nature of the subject matter.

*Ágrip.* Probably written by a Norwegian cleric toward the end of the twelfth century, *Ágrip* is a summary in about thirty pages of some 250 years of Norwegian history.[10] The Latin training of its author is apparent in the syntax and certain verbal mannerisms. The pace is too brisk to allow for the pursuit of any length of different sides of the action, but the scope and complexity give the broad impression of synchronic events:

> En þá var Sveinn frá fallinn í Danmǫrko ok svá Knútr faþir hans í Englandi, ok réþ þá fyrir Danmǫrko bróþir Sveins, Hǫrþaknútr at nafni, ok helt her á móti Magnúsi ok fundosk í Brenneyiom.

> (At that time Sveinn had died in Denmark and likewise his father in England; and Sveinn's brother, whose name was Hǫrðaknútr, was ruling in Denmark, and he launched a campaign against Magnús [of Norway] and they met on the Brenneyjar.) [chap. 36]

Unremarkable in themselves, such notices become, in later kings' saga tradition, dramatically fleshed out into fully simultaneous

[10]On *Ágrip*, see Ellehøj, *Studier*, pp. 197–304; and Bjarni Aðalbjarnarson, *Om de norske kongers sagaer*, Skrifter utgitt av Det Norske Videnskaps-Akademi i Oslo, II, hist.-fil. kl., no. 2 (1936), pp. 1–54.

narration. There is also a hint of open composition in such lateral extensions as the folktale-derived story of Snæfríðr (chaps. 3–4).[11] There exist a few verbal tags such as *svá er sagt* and cross-referencing phrases such as *sem fyrr var sagt*, but no actual transitional formulas.

*Historia de antiquitate regum Norwagiensium.* In the introduction to his history of the Norwegian kings (written ca. 1177–80),[12] Theodoricus, a Norwegian monk possibly trained abroad, outlines his narrative procedure:

> Digressiones etiam more antiquorum chronographorum non inutiles, ut arbitramur, ad delectandum animum lectoris locis competentibus adjunximus.

(We have also added digressions in the appropriate places according to the custom of ancient writers, not ill-suited, as we think, to delight the mind of the reader.) [Prologue]

The form of digression Theodoricus uses is much like that of Jordanes (to whom he refers in chapter 17) and Paul the Deacon, whose use of the device is singled out for approval:

> Paulus quoque Diaconus, monachus Cassinensis coenobii, qui conscripsit historiam pulcherrimam de Pannonia provincia, in qua multas utiles et non minus delectabiles fecit digressiones, pæne idem loquitur de Charybdis natura.

---

[11]The folktale origins of the Snæfríðr episode are restated by Bjarni Aðalbjarnarson in his introduction to the Fornrit edition of *Heimskringla*, p. lix and note 3. Jan de Vries, following Finnur Jónsson's observation of a Latinate phrase, argues for a Latin original; see his "Harald Schönhaar in Sage und Geschichte," *Beiträge zur Geschichte der deutschen Sprache und Literatur*, 66 (1942), 55–117 (esp. pp. 85–86). De Vries agrees with Finnur Jónsson and disagrees with Anne Holtsmark about the Latin original; see her "Om de norske kongers sagaer," *Edda*, 38 (1938), 145–64.

[12]On Theodoricus's *Historia*, see Ellehøj, *Studier*, pp. 175–96; Arne Odd Johnsen, *Om Theodoricus og hans Historia de antiquitate regum Norwagiensium*, Avhandlinger utgitt av Det Norske Videnskaps-Akademi i Oslo, II, hist.-fil. kl., no. 3 (1939), pp. 1–112; Jens Th. Hanssen, "Theodoricus Monachus and European Literature," *Symbolae Osloenses*, 27 (1949), 70–127; and Bjarni Guðnason, "Theodoricus og íslenskir sagnaritarar" in Einar G. Pétursson and Jónas Kristjánsson, eds., *Sjötíu ritgerðir helgaðar Jakobi Benediktssyni*, 2 vols. (Reykjavík: Stofnun Árna Magnússonar, 1977), II, 107–20.

(Paul the Deacon, monk in Monte Cassino, who wrote the excellent history of the province of Pannonia, in which he made many useful and no less delightful digressions, gave nearly the same account of the nature of Charybdis.) [chap. 17]

Theodoricus's own digressions are for the most part of the stan dard "philosophical" sort. The event of Hákon's drowning occasions a long description of Charybdis, which shades into a passage on the Huns and ends with a pious quotation from Psalms (chap. 17). The narrative returns to local matters when, in chapter 18, news of Hákon's death reaches his uncle Knútr in England. Other digressions involve learned speculations on the age of the world, Charlemagne, ill-fated ambition, the progressive diminution in the size of men, and so forth—all effected by a conventional array of *aphodoi* clearly imitative of those used by Paul the Deacon, Adam of Bremen, or some similar practitioner of this "highly favored rhetorical figure":[13]

Sed ad nostra redeamus. (But we should return to our topic.) [chap. 5]

Sed revertamur ad nostra. (But let us return to our topic.) [chap. 8]

Sed regrediamur in Norwagiam. (But let us return to Norway.) [chap. 23]

Nos ista in medio relinquimus. (We leave these things in the middle.) [chap. 33]

But not every such phrase in Theodoricus's *Historia* involves a *digressio ad aliud extra materiam* (to refer again to the distinction drawn by Geoffrey of Vinsauf). At least two cases are sufficiently local to be classified as *digressiones ad aliam partem materiae.* The phrase "Hæc de his dicta sufficiant (But enough has been said about this)" concludes a short chapter on the activities of Þangbrandr in Iceland (chapter 12) and brings the narrative back

[13]Thorkil Damsgaard Olsen, "Kongekrøniker og kongesagaer," *Norrøn fortællekunst: Kapitler af den norsk-islandske middelalderlitteraturs historie,* ed. Hans Bekker-Nielsen, Thorkil Damsgaard Olsen, and Ole Widding ([Copenhagen]: Akademisk forlag, 1965), p. 49.

to Óláfr's continuing conversion effort in Norway. More strikingly intramural is the following example:

> Variis deinde conflictationibus inter se agentes Magnus et Sveino
> plura proelia gesserunt in diversis locis, quorum maxima ista fuer-
> unt: apud Helganes unum, aliud apud Aros et non multa præterea.
> Sed quia longum est singulis immorari, transeamus ad cætera.
> Videns itaque Sueino, se non posse resistere viribus Magni, discessit
> a patria; quem insecutus rex cum classe applicuit in loco, qui dicitur
> Ourarsund.

(Then taxing each other with various conflicts, Magnus and Sven
waged several battles in various places, of which the greatest were
the following: one at Helgenes, the second at Aarhus, and not many
besides these. But because it is tedious to dwell on particular events,
let us pass on to other things. Thus Sven, seeing that he could not
resist the power of Magnus, departed his homeland; the king, pursuing him with his fleet, hove into that place called Øresund.) [chaps.
24–25]

Evidently, Theodoricus was not bound by a strict definition of
digression, but like his Latin-writing contemporaries could use it
simply to mark a time dislocation within the matter. His history
therefore documents not only an enthusiasm for the device in
both the narrow and the broad sense, but also a nonconsecutive
approach to narrative.

*Historia de profectione Danorum in Hierosolymam.* Preserved in the same manuscript as Theodoricus's *Historia* is the
*Profectio Danorum,* a short chronicle, written some time before
the death of Sverrir in 1202, about a Scandinavian crusade to the
Holy Land.[14] It is generally held to be of marginal literary or
historical concern, but it is of some interest from the point of view
of composition because of its fuller use of intramural digressions
and *aphodoi* involving clear temporal dislocations and a concern
with proper order. For example, after citing a long, impassioned

---

[14]On the *Profectio,* see Vegard Skånlund, "Profectio Danorum in
Hierosolymam," in *Kulturhistorisk leksikon for nordisk middelalder;* and Eirik
Vandvik, *Om skriftet De profectione Danorum,* Avhandlinger utgitt av Det
Norske Videnskaps-Akademi i Oslo, II, hist.-fil. kl., no. 4 (1954), pp. 3–35.

papal letter calling for the liberation of Jerusalem, the chronicler
turns to matters in Denmark:

> Hec et alia quamplurima pagina continebat apostolica, exhortans
> singulos, confuitans uniuersos. Nunc autem ad ea, que in Dacia
> super hoc lachrymabili negotio gesta nouimus, uertamus articulum.

(This and many more things the pope's letter contained, exhorting
the individual, encouraging all. But now let us turn the "article"
[portion of the narrative] to those matters that we know transpired in
Denmark concerning this lamentable business.)[15] [chap. 3]

Somewhat later, a digression on the term "land of milk and
honey" concludes with these words:

> Non est tamen presentis occupationis mysteria perscrutari; sed ad
> narranda, que restant, reuocetur oratio. Porro uiri pretaxati ad sua
> peragenda negotia perseueranter insistunt, armamenta nauium col-
> ligentes.

(It is not, however, our present task to probe mysteries; let our
discourse rather return to the telling of those matters which remain.
The men already mentioned diligently pursue the business at hand,
gathering the ships' gear.) [chaps. 6–7]

A description of an encounter between Sverrir and the Danes is
similarly concluded:

> Vt enim ea, que narrare gestio, luculentiori stilo ualeam indagare,
> superiori reincipiendium est exordio.

(So that I may be able to explore more clearly those matters I desire
to relate, it is necessary to return to my previous point of departure.)
[chap. 13]

The promised explanation has to do with the political state of
affairs Sverrir inherited in Norway.

The first two-thirds of the *Profectio* are in effect a prelude in

---

[15]For a comparison of transitional formulas in Theodoricus's *Historia* and the
*Profectio*, see Vandvik, *Om skriftet De profectione Danorum*, p. 16.

which the would-be pilgrims travel about Scandinavia making preparations and gathering support for their cause. The crusade proper begins in chapter 15, when they embark from Bergen in three groups: first the Danes, then Sven, then Ulf. At exactly its most dramatic phase, in other words, the account splits into three stories. The narrator's solution closely resembles classical saga stranding both in its composition and its use of verbal transitions. The passage may be outlined as follows:

A + B    The Danes and Sven leave Bergen and go to an island, where they wait for Ulf. Dissension breaks out; the Danes depart, leaving Sven and his men in wait.

B + C    Ulf arrives; he and Sven trade speeches; Sven and his men depart.

C    After some time, Ulf departs and is carried to his destination by the same wind that drove the others off course. "Ad narrandum denique, quamquam rudi stilo et incomposita uerborum serie, quod cepimus, reuertamur (Let us then return to the narration which we began, though it be in rough style and disorderly sequence"— chap. 18).

B    Sven, having been abandoned by the Danes and no longer in company with the Norwegians "ut supra diximus (as we stated above)," foolhardily attempts an ocean crossing by himself. He sails night and day and encounters a long and violent storm that seems to spell doom; but at last it clears and they are saved. The following day, however, the storm breaks out again and causes a shipwreck. Many men are drowned, but some, by God's grace, are saved. (The narrator devotes an emotive chapter to the miraculous rescue of these crew members, and no more is heard of them.)

A    "Ad illos iterum reuertamur, quorum mentionem supra factam lector inueniet (Let us return again to those whom the reader will find mentioned above"—chap. 22). The Danes encounter the same storm, but they jettison all their goods and reach Frisia, where they sell their ships and travel the rest of the way, via Venice, by land.

The braiding, such as it is, could easily be undone. Just as Ulf's story was told all in a piece, so could those of the Danes and Sven have been told consecutively. But by dividing and interspersing them, the narrator has dramatized (if rather lamely) a certain simultaneous idea: the north wind that spurred the Danes on their way is the same north wind that drove Ulf's ship the "straight way" down the coast and the same wind that develops into the storm that shipwrecked Sven and brought the Danes to near ruin off the coast of Frisia. All this action occurs over the same Wednesday, Thursday, and Friday. To the extent that it has been treated at all by critics, the *Profectio Danorum* has not fared well. Eirik Vandvik judged it to be a pupil's exercise: "The execution itself points in this direction: it is in a number of respects an immature work—bumbling in its composition, not infrequently deaf to the nuances of Latin words and phrases, and sprinkled with random learning."[16] The question is whether the "pupil" invented this piece of parallel narration or drew on a model, and if the latter, whether the model was foreign or native. Whatever its other shortcomings, the *Profectio Danorum* contains a full-fledged example, complete with verbal apparatus, of simultaneous narration.

*Historia Norwegiæ*. The introduction of the *Historia Norwegiæ* concludes with the following words:[17]

> Huc usque situm et circumstantias Norwegiæ ostendimus, nunc autem trifariam ejus habitationem exsequamur.

(Up to this point we have shown the setting and conditions of Norway, but let us now describe her three habitable regions.) [p. 76]

First comes a description of the coastal regions, ending with the formula:

> Revertentes a maritimis transferamur ad montana.

(Turning from the maritime regions, let us pass on to the mountains.) [p. 80]

A brief paragraph on the highlands ends similarly:

[16]Ibid., p. 34.
[17]On the *Historia Norwegiæ*, see Ellehøj, *Studier*, pp. 142–74; Aðalbjarnarson, *Om de norske kongers sagaer*, pp. 1–55; and Jens Th. Hanssen, *Omkring Historia Norwegiae*, Avhandlinger utgitt av Det Norske Videnskaps-Akademi i Oslo, II, hist.-fil. kl., no. 2 (1949), pp. 70–127.

Peragratis montanis silvas Finnorum ingrediamur perscrutatum.

(Having explored the mountains, let us now enter the forests of the Finns to investigate them.) [p. 82]

From the Finnish forests the narrator looks west to the insular colonies:

Circumscriptis utcunque Norwegiæ finibus tendamus ad tributarias insulas, nam insulas, quæ adjacent Norwegiæ, præ multitudine nemo numerare potest.

(Having described the borders of Norway, however, let us turn to the tributary islands, for no one can count the islands which flank Norway because of their great number.) [p. 87]

This survey in turn is concluded:

Hactenus tributarias insulas carptim descripsimus; nunc vero qui reges Norwegiam rexerunt vel unde processerunt ad exponendum stilum vertamus.

(Thus far we have described the tributary islands one by one; but now let us turn our pen to relate what kings ruled Norway and whence they descended.) [p. 97]

At this point the narrator turns to the succession of kings, ending (apparently prematurely) with the arrival of Saint Óláfr in Norway.

One of the immediate sources for the *Historia Norwegiæ* was Adam of Bremen's church history.[18] But if Adam used *aphodoi* both to mark off sections of the narrative and as devices for internal digressions within the matter, the *Historia Norwegiæ* uses them only in the former sense.[19] The royal history proper

---

[18]See Ellehøj, *Studier,* esp. pp. 146–61.

[19]Cf. the *aphodos* (clearly of learned origins) used by the First Grammarian to mark off the sections of that treatise: "Nú lýk ek hér umrœðu raddarstafanna, en ek leita viðr, ef guð lofar, at rœða nǫkkut um samhljóðendr (Here I close my consideration of the vowels, and, God willing, I shall try to say something about the consonants)." From Einar Haugen, ed., *The First Grammatical Treatise,* Language Monograph No. 25 of the Linguistic Society of America, 2d ed. (London: Longman, 1972), pp. 22–23.

(the last twelve pages) contains no such phrases and is in general linear, nondramatic, and nondigressive.

*Hryggjarstykki.* The special importance of Eiríkr Oddsson's Norwegian history (ca. 1150 or 1170) lies in the fact that unlike such works as *Ágrip* and the *Historia* of Theodoricus it relied not on older sources but on the reports of contemporary witnesses.[20] *Hryggjarstykki* is not extant as a separate work, but it is possible, by examining those portions of *Morkinskinna, Fagrskinna,* and *Heimskringla* which incorporated it, to make at least a rough assessment of its content and form. In general, *Hryggjarstykki* appears to display the brachial composition characteristic of early kings' saga tradition. The royal biography is not conceived as a static portrait, but as a dynamic sequence of interactions. Thus not only the king but also those with whom he interacts— supporters and competitors—necessarily receive a measure of narrative attention. Many threads are advanced together with the main thread, and though they are seldom pursued long enough to be considered subplots, the larger pattern—the nervous alternation among focal points—suggests an incipient form of stranding. It would appear, for example, that Eiríkr Oddsson wove together at some length the stories of Sigurðr slembir, Magnús inn blindi, and the Danish king Eiríkr with at least a rough degree of understood simultaneity as they converge and part.[21] But there are no transitional formulas (nor are there elsewhere in *Fagrskinna,* although they appear with some frequency in *Heimskringla* and *Morkinskinna*), and one is left with an overall impression not of deliberate or artful plot weaving, but of a haphazard exposition, presumably conditioned by the nature of the sources and, of course, the events themselves.

*Oldest Saga, Legendary Saga,* and *Styrmir's Saga of Saint Óláfr.* Brief as they are, the six fragments of the *Oldest Saga*

[20]The most recent contribution on *Hryggjarstykki* is that of Bjarni Guðnason, *Fyrsta sagan,* Studia Islandica, 37 (Reykjavík: Bókaútgáfa Menningarsjóðs, 1978). See also Aðalbjarnarson, *Om de norske kongers sagaer,* pp. 156–69; Sigurður Nordal, "Sagalitteraturen," *Nordisk kultur,* 8, pt. B (1953), 195–97; and Jan de Vries, *Altnordische Literaturgeschichte,* II, Grundriss der germanischen Philologie, 16, 2d ed. rev. (Berlin: de Gruyter, 1967), 233–35.

[21]See especially pp. 304–9 in *Heimskringla;* 345–49 in *Fagrskinna;* and 409–19 in *Morkinskinna.*

(ca. 1200) permit certain conclusions about the form of the now-lost whole.[22] The paratactic and scenic quality of the text reflects an established mode of anecdotal storytelling. The capacity for plot proliferation by means of entailment is documented in Fragment I with the story of Ásbjǫrn selsbani. Ásbjǫrn breaks a royal prohibition on the transfer of grain and is caught and humiliated by the king's steward Þórir selr; he seeks revenge by dropping in on a royal progress feast and decapitating Þórir before the king's eyes. The king calls out for Ásbjǫrn to be captured and killed, but Skjálgr intervenes—here the fragment breaks off. Similarly, the anecdotes in Fragments II and III indicate a strong interest in the lives of the skalds—another rudimentary form of lateral expansion. Finally, there is a full-fledged stranding formula:

> Nú skal þar til taka, sem fyrr var frá horfit. Þá er Óláfr inn sænski var frá fallinn, þá tók Önundr Svíþjóð ok allt ríki eftir föður sinn.

> (Now to take up what was left off earlier: After Óláfr inn sænski had fallen, Önundr took over Sweden and all his father's realm.) [p. 413]

The reference is missing, but the phrase itself indicates some degree of simultaneity.

If the *Oldest Saga* was once thought to be a predecessor of the *Legendary Saga,* they may now be regarded as variants.[23] The latter is somewhat more compendious than the former, but they otherwise appear to conform to more or less the same scheme of composition. The *Legendary Saga* author's narrative fixation on the figure of the king betrays a hagiographic orientation (one of the chief differences between the *Legendary Saga* and the *Separate Saga,* and in turn between the *Separate Saga* and the *Heimskringla* versions of the Óláfr biography, is the proportion of

---

[22]Jonna Louis-Jensen, " 'Syvende og ottende brudstykke': Fragmentet AM 325 IV α 4to" in *Opuscula,* IV, Bibliotheca Arnamagnæana, 30 (Copenhagen: Munksgaard, 1970), pp. 31–60.

[23]See Jónas Kristjánsson, *Um Fóstbræðrasögu* (Reykjavík: Stofnun Árna Magnússonar, 1972), p. 167: "The texts of the fragments and the *Legendary Saga* are so closely related that the most obvious solution is to consider them one and the same saga." See also Louis-Jensen, " 'Syvende og ottende brudstykke,' " pp. 59–60.

narrative devoted to the "other side").[24] Yet despite its generally
unilateral quality, the *Legendary Saga* makes occasional excur-
sions, by a process of entailment, into other matter—subplots
that intersect, at some point, with the life of the king. Again, the
story of Ásbjǫrn selsbani serves as an example. After his slaying
of Þórir selr (to continue where the *Oldest Saga* left off), Ásbjǫrn
is made to await sentence; Skjálgr and Þórarinn intervene on his
behalf, and their efforts, together with a display of force on the
part of Erlingr Skjálgsson, bring the king around. Ásbjǫrn is himself appointed steward, but shortly thereafter he breaks the terms
and is sought out and killed. This last phase is told briefly in a
coda paragraph:

> Ferr nú Ásbjǫrn norðr heim fyrst ok segir Þóri, frænda sínum, hver
> lykt er á varð. Hann segir svá, at ill var in fyrra fǫr hans, en sjá var
> hálfu verri, er hann skyldi vera konungs þræll alla ævi sína. Svá talar
> hann um fyrir honum, at hann ferr nú ekki norðan ok dvaldist nú
> heima. Konungrinn fréttir nú þetta, at hann helt ekki þat, sem mælt
> var, sendir til menn at drepa hann.

> (Ásbjǫrn now goes north to his home and tells Þórir, his kinsman,
> how things have turned out. He says that bad as his first journey had
> been, it was not half as bad as this one, for he was now destined to
> be the king's thrall for the rest of his life. He declared to Þórir that he
> would not go south, and so he stayed at home. The king now learns
> that Ásbjǫrn was not keeping to the agreement they made, and he
> dispatches men to kill him.) [*Legendary Saga*, chap. 49]

Ásbjǫrn's story hardly forms a self-contained subplot. Yet the
very fact that it has been pursued to a certain extent for its own

[24]The shift from the unilateral account of Óláfr's political downfall to a more
balanced one is traced in Wolfgang Fleischhauer, *Kalf Arnason: Die Berührungen
zwischen Heldenlied und Königssaga* (Cologne: Orthen, 1938); also, with special
reference to hagiographic traditions, in my "*Runzivals þáttr, Njáls saga*, and
*Legendary Saga*: A Structural Comparison" (Ph.D. dissertation, University of
California at Berkeley, 1972), esp. pp. 77–169. If the *Oldest Saga* was similarly
king-focused (as the fragments suggest it was), it, too, may be considered affected
by hagiographic conventions. Cf. Louis-Jensen ("'Syvende og ottende
brudstykke,'" p. 60): "In the NRA 52 fragments themselves there is nothing to
suggest that the *Oldest Saga* contained any matter whatever of a legendary nature, and the burden of proof rests on those who see the *Oldest Saga* as a clumsy
attempt to combine a model borrowed from foreign hagiography with Ari's his-
toriographic principles." See also Kristjánsson, *Um Fóstbræðrasögu*, pp. 151–72.

sake, above and beyond its immediate relevance to the royal
biography, is a significant harbinger of future developments in the
evolving tradition. Like the skaldic subplots, Ásbjǫrn's will eventually assume the proportions of a self-contained *þáttr*. The tendency toward plot proliferation is thus documented in this work
from what Nordal called "the infancy of saga-writing."[25]

At no point does the narrator of the *Legendary Saga* lapse, in
prebattle or battle sequences, into full parallel narration, but
rather alternates rapidly among the focal points in the manner of
*Hryggjarstykki*—far from artful, but nonetheless indicating the
inclination toward fragmentation and interruption. The aesthetic
of suspense and delay is further suggested by the fact that of the
two items added to his biography by the *Legendary Saga* author,
one, the *Kristni þáttr*, is divided and inserted in two parts (the
other, a list of miracles, is attached as a sequel). There are numerous verbal tags throughout the saga (e.g., *svá er sagt*), and on
those few occasions when the narrative actually divides (e.g.,
between the king and Dala-Guðbrandr in chapters 32–33) there
are found phrases of the type *Nú er frá því at segja*. But there are
otherwise no simultaneous formulas (the above-cited formula in
the *Oldest Saga* does not appear in the *Legendary Saga*).

Styrmir's version of the Óláfr biography was widely used by
later redactors, but, like Styrmir's other literary production, it no
longer survives as a separate work. The only extant texts that can
be ascribed to Styrmir with a fair degree of certainty are the
"articles" preserved in *Flateyjarbók*.[26] These give no evidence
whatsoever of multi-ply composition or transitional formulas; on
the contrary, they appear to be even more monothematic than the
*Legendary Saga* or the *Oldest Saga*. It may, of course, be that
the "articles" are not representative of Styrmir's other production (that being one reason they were segregated as "articles").
But the assimilated state of his other production (e.g., in the
*Great Saga*) defeats any effort to arrive at conclusions about
Styrmir's compositional habits.[27]

[25]Nordal, "Sagalitteraturen," p. 201.
[26]*Flateyjarbók*, III, 237–48; *Great Saga*, II, 683–95.
[27]See esp. Sigurður Nordal, *Om Olaf den helliges saga: En kritisk undersøgelse* (Copenhagen: Gad, 1914).

*Sverris saga.* The first full-length biography of a contemporary king, *Sverris saga* is thought to have been at least begun by the Icelandic abbot Karl Jónsson (died ca. 1212), perhaps in consultation with the king himself. Just how much of the existing work can be ascribed to Karl (the so-called *Grýla* portion) is not known.[28] What is clear, however, is that the middle part of the saga (ca. chapters 32–100) differs emphatically, in both its style and its composition, from the preceding part (the *Grýla?*) and, to a somewhat lesser extent, from the one following. The earlier part is almost wholly monothematic, whereas the following portion is thoroughly and richly stranded. Ludvig Holm-Olsen's description of the narrative technique between chapters 33 and 38 is worth quoting at length:

> The narrative in these chapters is superbly composed. We are prepared for the coming battle and held in mounting suspense by being plunged alternately into Sverrir's camp and that of the enemy. We follow Sverrir, during the course of the evening, across the river Nið and then the Gaular, ostensibly in a direction away from Niðaróss. In the next chapter (34) we are in the town, among Erlingr's and Magnús's men, where a mood of insecurity and nervousness prevails because no one knows what Sverrir's plans are. "Now it is to be told of the Birkibeinar [Nú er at segja frá Birkibeinum]," says the author (chap. 35). They have arrived in the vicinity of the town in the first light of dawn. Sverrir dismounts at Feginsbrekka and delivers a speech to his men. It turns out that he wants to try an attack on Niðaróss. We leave them on their way down from Steinbjörg, and the scene shifts again. Once more we find ourselves among Magnús's men (chap. 36), this time out on Eyrar, just as they catch sight of the Birkibeinar. We follow the hectic preparations right up to the point when Earl Erlingr marches out, at the head of his men, against the enemy. But the battle does not begin until the author has brought his readers back to Sverrir's army. Only after relating an episode involving a priest Özurr, whom we shall soon meet again, does our author turn to the description of the battle. It is this method of unfolding the narrative—by revealing the events alternately from the point of view of one party and then the other—that is also employed

[28]See Ludvig Holm-Olsen, *Studier i Sverres saga,* Avhandlinger utgitt av Det Norske Videnskaps-Akademi i Oslo, II, hist.-fil. kl., no. 3 (1952), pp. 7–104.

so brilliantly in the account of the battle in Nórafjǫrðr from chapter
81 on.[29]

Differences in form are reflected in the use of formulas. There are
none up to chapter 36, but many, including several elaborate
ones, after that. Holm-Olsen, reviewing the occurrence of such
phrases as *Nú er at segja frá* ("Now it is to be told of") and *Nú er
at segja nǫkkura atburði* ("Now certain events are to be related"), concludes: "If it is so that [AM 327 4°] represents the
original form here, the text from chapter 36 to chapter 156 is set
off by a characteristic set of introductory formulas."[30] There is,
moreover, a slight but significant tendency for AM 327 4°, presumably the most conservative of the manuscripts, to use first-
person-plural formulations where *Flateyjarbók* and *Eirspennill*
give impersonal equivalents (or avoid them altogether.)[31] A striking example is the following:

Nu munum ver segia noccora parta þa er gerðuz i fundi þeira .ii.
konunga er nu hefir aðr verit noccot af sagt verþr nu þar til at taca er
aþr var fra horfit. at Birkibeinar reru ut fra landi.

(Now we will tell certain parts [of the events] which occurred in the
encounter between the two kings, of which something has been said
before. The story picks up at the point where it left off earlier, when
the Birkibeinar rowed out from the shore.) [AM 327 4°, chap. 91]

Nu er at segia nokcura atburði þa er gerduz i fundi þessa .ij.
konunga. er þar til at taka at Birkibeinar reyru vt a mot Heklungum.

(Now are to be told certain events which occurred in the encounter
between the two kings. The story picks up where the Birkibeinar
row out toward the Heklungar.) [*Eirspennill*, chap. 81]

Not only does *Eirspennill* show a preference for an impersonal
construction (as opposed to the *munum vér* of AM 327 4°), it uses
the standard word *atburðr* instead of the bookish *partr*.

Of *Sverris saga* we may therefore say, first, that its middle

[29]Ibid., pp. 71–72.
[30]Ibid., p. 70.
[31]Ibid., pp. 68–71.

portion is emphatically stranded and simultaneous in all the manuscripts and, second, that the version regarded as oldest is also the one in which the phrasing of the transitional formulas is so like the Latin *aphodoi* that they may be considered vernacular derivatives. The receptiveness of the *Sverris saga* author or authors to foreign influence, including Latin chronicles, is well known. That this receptiveness extended to composition seems clear from the phrasing of the transitions, among other reasons. One of the most sagalike narratives of the preclassical period, in other words, is also one of the most manifestly Latin-influenced.

*Oddr's Saga of Óláfr Tryggvason.* The first independent biography of Óláfr Tryggvason was written about 1190 by Oddr Snorrason, a monk of Þingeyrar. The Latin original is lost, but the surviving vernacular manuscripts are thought to be fairly accurate reflections of the translation made about 1200.[32] On the basis of the manuscripts it may be determined that the translation was a standard, serviceable combination of single-ply and multi-ply narration, depending on whether the focus is on the king or the political matrix, and that this must reflect, in turn, the formal organization of the matter in the Latin original. Some question may be raised about the originality of the many transitional formulas in AM 310 4°, however, for they are often missing or seriously altered in Stockholm 18 4°, as shown by the following examples:

| AM 310 4° | Stockholm 18 4° |
| --- | --- |
| Nu er þar til at taca at Hakon j. heyrir micla fregð af morgum orrostum. (Now to pick up where Earl Hákon hears of the great fame [Óláfr won] in many battles.) [chap. 19] | Hakon iarl heyrðe mikla fregð at Olafi ok orrostvm hans. (Earl Hákon heard of Óláfr's great fame and of his battles.) [chap. 13] |
| Þar er til at taca at iþann tima reð Noregi Hakon j. Sigurþar s. er fyrr var fra sagt. | Ok i þann tima reð Hakon iarl Sigurðar s. Noregi er fyʀ var fra sagt. |

---

[32]See Aðalbjarnarson, *Om de norske kongers sagaer*, esp. pp. 55–85; also Ólafur Halldórsson, "Óláfs saga Tryggvasonar," in *Kulturhistorisk leksikon for nordisk middelalder.*

([The story] is to be taken up at that time when Earl Hákon Sigurð-arson was ruling Norway, as was said before.) [chap. 18]

(And at that time Earl Hákon Sigurðarson was ruling Norway, as was said before.) [chap. 12]

Nu er þat þessu næst at segia. at þa er aleið æfi Hakonar j. . . .
(Now the next thing to tell is that when Hákon's life was drawing to a close. . . .) [chap. 20]

En er a leið æfi Hakonar iarls. . . .
(And when Earl Hákon's life was drawing to a close. . . .) [chap. 14]

Þat viliom ver oc rita, at a þeim v. arum er Olafr konungr reð Noregi. . .
(We want also to write that during the five years when King Óláfr was ruling Norway . . .) [chap. 63]

Þat er sagt meðan O. konungr Tryggva s. var konungr at Norege. . .
(It is said that while King Óláfr Tryggvason was king in Norway . . .) [chap. 51]

In light of these differences, it is hard to know whether the first translation had transitional formulas, much less whether the Latin original had *aphodoi,* at the corresponding junctures. (If Oddr, as is supposed, had a copy of Theodoricus at hand, he was well acquainted with the techniques of digression and the figure of the *aphodos.*)[33] The versions do agree, however, in their use of parallel stories; and whether accompanied by formulas or not, this proliferation may be assumed to derive from the original *vita.*

*Gunnlaugr's Óláfs saga Tryggvasonar.*   The case of Gunnlaugr Leifsson is more difficult than that of his monastic brother Oddr but at the same time potentially more rewarding. Shortly after Oddr, Gunnlaugr wrote another, expanded version, also in Latin, of the life of Óláfr Tryggvason. The saga no longer exists in the original, though portions of the Icelandic translations were incorporated in the *Longest Saga of Óláfr Tryggvason.* If we rely on Bjarni Aðalbjarnarson's identification of these portions, restricting our attention to passages on which the redactions agree, we may make the following observations.[34] First, the wide-ranging

---

[33]See Aðalbjarnarson, *Om de norske kongers sagaer,* pp. 69–80.
[34]Ibid., pp. 85–135, esp. pp. 92–96.

focus, the narrative detail devoted to minor figures, and the inclusion of long *þættir* leave little doubt as to Gunnlaugr's inclination toward copiousness and digressiveness. Second, the frequent use of such transitional phrases as the following suggests simultaneous narration:[35]

| AM 61 fol. | Flateyjarbók |
|---|---|
| <A>þeim sama tíma sem nv var aðr fra sagt. var þat dæmt æ sam kvamu af heraðs mònnum at fyrir sakir sultar ok sva mikils hallæris... | A þeim sama tima sem nu uar adr fra sagt uar þat dæmt a samkuomu af heradsmonnum ok firir saker hallæris ok suo mikils sulltar... |
| (At the same time, as was told earlier, it was determined at a meeting of the men of the district that on account of hunger and such great famine...) | (At the same time, as was told earlier, it was determined at a meeting of the men of the district that on account of famine and such great hunger...) |
| N<V>skal vikia ræðunni til þeira frasagna er þat sanna at Olafr konungr hafi lifs æ brott komiz or bardaghanum þa er OrmriN var vnninn. | Nv skal uikea rędunne til þeirra frasagna er þat sanna er Olafr konungr hafi a brott komizst ór bardaganum a þeirre somu snekkiu sem fyrr var getith. |
| (Now [we] shall turn the discourse to those accounts alleging that King Óláfr has escaped with his life from the battle in which the [ship] Ormr was captured.) | (Now [we] shall turn the discourse to those accounts alleging that King Óláfr escaped from the battle on the same ship that was mentioned before.) |

The originality of at least a few such formulas would seem to be guaranteed by the fact that they appear not at the beginning or end but embedded in the middle of passages attributed to Gunnlaugr and, moreover, that they play a functional role in the composition. If this is so, they may be vernacular renditions of Latin *aphodoi*. A third point is that also embedded within passages ascribed to Gunnlaugr are numerous cross-referencing

---

[35] AM 61 fol passages from chapters 226 and 267; *Flateyjarbók* passages from chapters 346 and 393.

phrases (*sem sagt mun verða* "as will be told [later]," *sem áðr er getit* "as was mentioned before," *sem fyrr var sagt* "as was told earlier"). These too may be the compiler's insertions; but if they are Gunnlaugr's own, they confirm the impression that his saga was richly stranded. There is, finally, the authorial reflection ascribed to Gunnlaugr (see p. 36 above):

> Now it is not to be wondered at that many of the tales and stories written here seem not to belong to the saga of Óláfr Tryggvason. For just as running water flows from various sources yet all comes together in a single place, so, in like wise, do all these stories from various sources have a common goal—to clear the way for those events which concern Óláfr Tryggvason and his men, as will become apparent in what follows.

The existence of a comparable metaphor in a different connection in the *Jóns saga helga* ascribed to Gunnlaugr would seem to confirm the attribution to him of the "network of streams" image and also to suggest that it may be a religious conceit.[36] But of more concern than the metaphor, in this context, is the first sentence, the tone and inclusion of which must be taken to indicate that the composition of Gunnlaugr's Latin biography of Óláfr Tryggvason was more copious and fragmented than was considered customary by the aesthetic standards for religious biography in the late twelfth century. Moreover, by retaining the note in the *Longest Saga*, the compiler has generalized the sense of the original to the larger encyclopedia and so maintained the continuity of the stylistic tradition.

*Fagrskinna.* Like its predecessors in the kings' saga tradition, *Fagrskinna* (Norwegian, 1220s) casts its net broadly, taking in political developments not only in Norway and Denmark, but also in the North Atlantic colonies, including England.[37] The composition is undistinguished, consisting in the main of synoptically told events laid end to end in time (*litlu síðarr* "a little later," *eptir*

---

[36]Aðalbjarnarson, *Om de norske kongers sagaer,* esp. p. 104.
[37]On *Fagrskinna,* see ibid., pp. 173–87; de Vries, *Altnordische Literaturgeschichte,* II, 282–85; and Gustav Indrebø, *Fagrskinna,* Avhandlinger fra Universitetets Historiske Seminar, 4 (Oslo: Grøndahl, 1917).

*þetta* "after that," *um haustit eptir* "the following autumn,"
*þessu næst* "thereupon"). As Gustav Indrebø said, "The author's strength lies in holding firmly to certain main themes—a
single thread. He follows straight lines, as it were, without digressions.... The artful biaiding of many threads is not his
style."[38] The rare efforts to apprehend parallel events are, like
the following one, wooden:

Eiʀikr lagðe þa undir sec Noregh sva sem aðr var sagt. oc þæir.ii.
brœðr varo iarlar oc var Eirikr rikare. han atte Gyðu dottor Svæins
Dana konongs. þæira sunr var Hacon. Eirikr var hærmaðr mikill
mikla æfe oc langa. oc allra manna sigrsælastr. hann gerðe frægðar
værk þat at hann drap Tiðenda-Skofta er fyrr var ritat.

(Eiríkr conquered all of Norway, as was told before. And of the two
brothers who were earls, Eiríkr was the more powerful. He was
married to Gyða, daughter of the Danish king Sveinn; their son was
Hákon. Eiríkr was for a very long period of time a great warrior, and
of all men he was the most successful in battle. He accomplished the
famous deed of killing Tíðenda-Skopti, as was written before.) [chap.
24]

What stranding there is conforms to this pattern: nonscenic
notices correlated by means of cross-referencing formulas. Apart
from these phrases, the only noteworthy formula is

Þa urðu þau tiðendi er aðr var til visat. at þeir funnuz Magnus
konongr oc Haralldr faðr broðer hans.

(Then those events occurred which were referred to earlier, in which
King Magnús and Haraldr, his uncle, met.) [chap. 44]

In fact, this retrieval phrase is gratuitous, because the meeting in
question is immediately adjacent (it comes at the end of the preceding chapter). We may suppose that there was such a formula
in *Fagrskinna*'s immediate source, an earlier version of
*Morkinskinna*. The extant version of *Morkinskinna*, however, indicates the transition with this switch:

[38]Indrebø, *Fagrskinna*, p. 237.

Nv er þar til sogo at taca er fyʀ var fra horfit er þeir fiɴaz iDanmorc
M. konvngr oc Haralldr foþorbroþir hans.

(Now there will be taken up in the saga what was put aside earlier,
when King Magnús and Haraldr his uncle meet in Denmark.) [chap.
5]

This, of course, is standard saga phrasing, whereas the
*Fagrskinna* formulation is Latinate in tone (cf. "Ad illos iterum
reuertamur, quorum mentionem supra factam lector inueniet (Let
us return again to those whom the reader will find mentioned
above"—*Profectio Danorum*). It is hard to know whether the
*Fagrskinna* author has retained or substituted a bookish phrase to
mark this new story phase, but in either case it is symptomatic of
the conservatism of the work as a whole. Despite its length,
*Fagrskinna* is very much in the synoptic tradition, having much
more in common with *Ágrip* and *Hryggjarstykki* than with
*Morkinskinna, Sverris saga,* or the *Legendary Saga.*

*Morkinskinna.*    In its present form, *Morkinskinna* (Icelandic,
ca. 1220) marks a sharp departure in the kings' saga tradition. If
*Fagrskinna,* as Ker comments, attempts to "restrict and select
and give form to the material of tradition," *Morkinskinna* tends
outward, making "large circuits and sweeping in all sorts of rem-
iniscences and tales."[39] To the bare bones of Norwegian history have been added numerous anecdotes and whole *þættir:
Þorsteins þáttr Hallssonar, Hreiðars þáttr heimska, Halldórs
þáttr Snorrasonar, Auðunar þáttr vestfirzka,* among others—
several of which bring Icelandic matter into the Norwegian
sphere. Certain unevennesses of style, composition, and authorial attitude have led to the speculation that at least some of these
subplots were not original but added at a later stage.[40] Yet the
lively presentation and the scenic quality both in the "digressions" and the "main topic" point to an accomplished narrator who, in Turville-Petre's words, "could tell many secrets
about the history of Icelandic literature."[41]

---

[39]W. P. Ker, "The Early Historians of Norway," *Collected Essays,* II (London: Macmillan, 1925), 150.
[40]Aðalbjarnarson, *Om de norske kongers sagaer,* pp. 135–73.
[41]Turville-Petre, *Origins,* p. 217. See also de Vries, *Altnordische Literaturgeschichte,* II, 280–81.

All this matter is, or appears to be, knotted to the larger structure by the verbal apparatus of stranding: such phrases as "Nv er þar til sogo at taca er fyr var fra horfit (Now to pick up a line of the saga that was set aside earlier)," "Nu er þar enn til ath taka (Now to take up [this matter] once again)," "nv er at nefna mann er het Ivar huíti (now to name [i.e., bring into the saga] that man called Ívarr hvíti)," and "oc lycr nv her at sinni fra Haconi i. oc Haralldi konungi (And now [let us] stop telling here of Earl Hákon and King Haraldr for the time being)." But there is a certain disparity between these verbal promises, as it were, and the actual composition of the matter. The formula "nv er þar til sogo at taca er fyr var fra horfit (Now to pick up a line of the saga that was set aside earlier)" refers (as does its counterpart in *Fagrskinna*) not to a long-suspended action, but to the immediately preceding paragraph. The matter is conceived in lines, but the lines are not pursued at length, are not subject to a systematic alternation, and are not synchronized to the point where it is possible to speak of simultaneous narration. The sense of concurrence is clear enough, but the haziness of the short-term chronology defeats any effort to uncover an underlying time scheme.

Despite its shortcomings, *Morkinskinna* stands on the threshold of classical saga narrative. The delight in multiplicity, the unrolling of subthemes which then come back to and connect with the main topic, and the abundant use of conventional transitional phrases in the process—all these prefigure the aesthetic, if not the precise form, of the Icelandic family sagas.

*The Great Saga of Saint Óláfr (Stockholm 2 4°).* Stockholm 2 4° is the oldest preserved manuscript of the so-called *Great Saga* (or *Separate Saga*), a work in a later and shorter version included in *Heimskringla*. The *Great Saga*, then, belongs properly to the classical kings' saga tradition. But because it marks the culmination of a long development and because it relies heavily on earlier versions of the Óláfr biography (particularly that of Styrmir), it will be briefly considered in its preclassical context.

The greater length of this version of the Óláfr biography is largely accounted for not by significant additions to matter actually concerning the king, but by the inclusion of greater numbers of longer and more elaborate extensions into "other" matter. It departs in this respect from the *Oldest* and *Legendary* sagas, which, despite their occasional outward branchings, remain strongly king-focused in a manner reminiscent of traditional hagiography. The *Great Saga* is compositionally more akin to *Morkinskinna*, the middle portion of *Sverris saga*, and even the monkish sagas of Óláfr (Oddr's certainly and Gunnlaugr's probably) than it is to its immediate predecessors. Focus is not exclusively on the king, but distributed among the many minor figures, both at home and abroad. It straddles, in other words, the border between biography and social or political narrative.

The processes of expansion and assimilation of this lateral matter are best seen in that venerable element of the Óláfr tradition, the story of Ásbjǫrn selsbani. Ásbjǫrn's story was incompletely told in the *Oldest Saga*, but we may gauge by the narrative pace in the existing portion that it might have occupied two pages. In the *Legendary Saga* it occupies six pages and is told all of a piece. In the *Great Saga* it assumes the proportions of a miniature saga, occupying some eighteen pages, of which the last three consist of a full, dramatic account of the bloody death of Ásbjǫrn at the hands of the king's henchmen—an event related only cryptically in *Legendary Saga*.[42] But more significant than the dilation of the matter per se is the fact that it is divided into two parts. Chapters 102–8 relate the conflict part of the story (how Ásbjǫrn violated the grain ban, was caught and humiliated by the king's steward, killed the steward in retribution, was captured and released and, upon appointment to the vacant stewardship, sent home), and chapter 112 tells the outcome (how he was sought out and killed).

[42]For a recent discussion of the evolution of the Ásbjǫrn story—in particular its political dimension as it relates to the story of Þórir hundr—see Ingebjørg Sogge, *Vegar til eit bilete: Snorre Sturlason og Tore hund* (Trondheim: Nordisk Institut, 1975), esp. pp. 31–37. There is an extensive literature on the evolution of the kings' sagas. Works that have some bearing on narrative developments include Sigurður Nordal, *Om Olaf den helliges saga;* the same author's *Snorri Sturluson* (Reykjavík: B. Þorláksson, 1920; Toralf Berntsen, *Fra sagn til saga. Studier i kongesagaen* (Oslo: Gyldendal, 1923); Siegfried Beyschlag, *Konungasögur. Untersuchungen zur Königssaga bis Snorri. Die älteren Übersichtswerke samt Ynglingasaga*, Bibliotheca Arnamagnæana, 8 (Copenhagen: Munksgaard, 1950); Gustav Storm, *Snorre Sturlassöns historieskrivning. En kritisk undersøgelse* (Copenhagen: B. Lunos bogtrykkeri, 1873); and Hallvard Lie, *Studier i Heimskringlas stil*, Avhandlinger utgitt av Det Norske Videnskaps-Akademi i Oslo, II. hist.-fil. kl., no. 5 (1936), pp. 7–136.

But between the conflict and the outcome are inserted three quite different themes: one telling of Óláfr's ongoing conversion efforts (chap. 109), one telling how Óláfr settles in for the winter at Trondheim and how Einarr þambarskelfir goes to England and then to Rome (chap. 110), and one telling how Álfhildr, the king's mistress, becomes pregnant and gives birth to Magnús inn góði (chap. 111). What is told, in the *Legendary Saga,* as a single lateral digression is thus in the *Great Saga* a full *þáttr* that has been inserted in two parts, the intervening matter consisting of ongoing themes to be resumed at a later point. The particular value of the Ásbjǫrn story is that it documents the developmental stages between narrative digression and full narrative stranding. The *Great Saga* uses discontinuous and continuous retrieval with equal ease, the choice depending on the nature of the matter. The switch between chapters 111 and 112 is discontinuous (there is about a year's lapse), probably for the reason that Ásbjǫrn's life between the moment he returns home and the time he faces the king's henchmen is of no particular narrative interest. Where both actions are of interest, the narrator renders them both, using the full array of verbal devices to do so. The beginning of chapter 62 ("Nv er þar til mals at taca er þeir menn como til Raugnvallz iarls er Ingigerðr konungs dottir oc þau Hialti haufðv sent austan [Now the story picks up at the point where those men whom Ingigerðr, the king's daughter, and Hjalti had sent from the east came before Earl Rǫgnvaldr]") retrieves a line suspended, with no gap in time, some seven pages earlier (chap. 55).[43] The beginning of chapter 71 ("Nv er þar til mals at taca er aðr var fra horfit at Olafr konungr enn digri for brvðferð [Now to pick up a line of the story set aside earlier, in which King Óláfr inn digri went on his bridal journey]") retrieves a line suspended, with no gap in time, about twelve pages earlier (chap. 65). There is even simultaneous alternation within the *þáttr* of Ásbjǫrn selsbani: the first line of chapter 108, "Nv er þar til mals at taka er fyʀ var fra horfit er þeir Erlingr oc Scialgr son hans gerðv rað sin vm þetta vannkveði (Now to take up a line of the story suspended earlier, in which Erlingr and his son Skjálgr made their plans regarding this diffi-

[43]Other manuscripts add to this phrase the words "er fyrr var frá horfit" ("which was set aside before"). See *Great Saga,* p. 160, note.

culty)," refers back to the end of chapter 106 ("Síðan hafaz þeir feðgar orð við; segir þa Scialgr Erlingi allan atburð vm vig Selþoris [After that the father and son discussed this; Skjálgr then told Erlingr the whole story of Selþórir's slaying]"). In other words, the story splitting incipient or latent at this point in the *Oldest* and the *Legendary* sagas is fully realized in the *Great Saga*.

It is in the *Great Saga* that the formula by which Olrik set so much literary stock is first attested:

Nv feʀ tvennvm savgvnom fram oc scal þar nv til taca sem fra var horfit. oc fra þvi var sagt er Olafr konungr Harallz son hafði frið gørt við Olaf Svia konung. oc þat at Olafr konungr for þat svmar norðr til Þrandheims.

(Now the two stories proceed together, and [we] shall pick up where [we] left off before, where it was said that King Óláfr Haraldsson had concluded a peace with King Óláfr Svíakonungr, and that King Óláfr went north that summer to Trondheim.) [chap. 90]

The two stories in question are the so-called *Orkneyinga saga* and the ongoing history of Óláfr's Norwegian regency. In chapters 79–80 Óláfr concludes a peace with Óláfr Svíakonungr and goes to Trondheim (strand 1). The narrator then shifts to the Orkneys (strand 2), giving first a thumbnail historical orientation and then an account, itself stranded, of the political strife among the earls there. Only when this strand is advanced to the present moment of the other strand—that is, at the point when Óláfr went to Trondheim after the settlement with Óláfr Svíakonungr—does the narrator shift the focus back and knot the two stories together with the "split saga" formula. The synchrony is both full and sweeping, involving a period of some twenty-five years (ca. 995–1019). With this plot braiding we have arrived at complete narrative stranding or interlace. The "brilliantly gifted and autonomous narrator" of the *Great Saga* may fairly be considered the first "classical" narrator in the kings' saga tradition.[44]

---

[44]Damsgaard Olsen, "Kongekrøniker og kongesagaer," p. 67.

## Literary Features

If stranded composition is an old feature in Norse tradition, we might expect to see some evidence of it in the earliest vernacular histories (*Íslendingabók, Ágrip, Hryggjarstykki*). But we do not find it there, even at those junctures where it would seem a likely and appropriate solution. Even though these early texts embrace an intrinsically complex subject matter, they stay for the most part close to the main theme and avoid or give only cursory treatment to minor themes—themes that in later works (e.g., *Morkinskinna*) are developed into fully dramatic subplots. The reluctance of the early historians to include historical marginalia in their accounts (we may assume that they knew considerably more than they wrote down) is a comment on their idea of what constituted a proper history—an idea that appears not to include lateral expansion or the scenic realization of the matter. Both narrative tendencies exist, to be sure (in *Hryggjarstykki* in particular), but when they occur they stand out as exceptions or lapses, not as normal procedure. Even *Landnámabók*, which as a formal construction lacks a main theme altogether but consists exclusively of minor themes, is oddly strict about keeping its family histories separate, telling consecutively stories that are understood as happening at the same time and depicted as interlocking in later versions. Again there are exceptions: stories are sometimes cross-referenced or on rare occasions interspersed. But such examples are too few and too rudimentary to qualify as stranded narration in the classical sense. The first vernacular histories document a concept of narrative that is brief, synoptically told, monocentric (with the exception of *Landnámabók*), and straightforwardly ordered. Insofar as the "lapses" tend in the direction of plot complication and the scenic mode, they seem to indicate an impatience with these restrictions. But the fact that they are exceptional, together with the fact that they in no sense constitute a consistent artistic solution, leads to the conclusion that the classical notion of composition is at most nascent at this early stage.

Latin prose is another matter. Like the European historians who stood as their models, the unknown authors of the *Historia Norwegiæ* and the *Historia de profectione Danorum in*

*Hierosolymam,* and, above all, Theodoricus in his *Historia de antiquitate regum Norwagiensium* make abundant use of digression, not only in the strict sense (to bring in external matter) but also in the broader sense (to move about within the matter), using, in both cases, the figure of the *aphodos* to effect the transition. The first example in Norse tradition of the explicit and sustained use of simultaneous narration for dramatic effect, complete with transitional formulas, comes from the *Profectio Danorum.* The fact that *aphodoi* are used interchangeably for digressions proper and lateral digressions is of fundamental importance, for it indicates that the two were equated in the minds of the early historians. This obvious point has been missed by modern scholars, whose narrow definition of the device may correspond with classical notions but is out of tune with actual medieval practice as it is represented both in the rhetorical treatises and in the texts themselves. To single out the philosophical sort of digression and declare that its rarity in the classical sagas proves that their authors repudiated the Latin model is to misunderstand what digression meant and how it was used by the medieval Latin chroniclers. For them, the unrolling of side themes was no less a form of digression than the insertion of abstract speculations or far-fetched analogies. From the point of view of literary history, the former category is much the more significant, for as a specifically medieval "improvement" it points up a larger drift in the literary taste of that period, the clear direction of which in Norse tradition is toward the entailed narrative of the Icelandic sagas.

Fortunately, the link between Latin writings and classical saga practice is documented. It consists of two groups of hybrid texts: the translations into Norse of the royal biographies written originally in Latin and the early biographies written in the vernacular under the immediate influence of Latin models. The first category includes Oddr's and Gunnlaugr's lives of Óláfr Tryggvason, written first in Latin and composed, as nearly as we can tell, along Latin lines (Gunnlaugr's probably to a greater degree). The translation of such works as these involved more than a shift of language; it gave vernacular form to Latin digressiveness, and it invented or adapted from native stock a set of transitional phrases answering to the Latin *aphodoi* (the oldest wordings of the Norse phrases point firmly toward a Latin derivation). The second cate-

gory includes the *Legendary Saga* and *Sverris saga* (especially
its highly digressive middle portion, the transitional phrases of
which, once again, have a distinctly Latin flavor). The depen-
dence in varying degrees of these works on learned style and
subject matter has long been recognized. What has not been sufficiently appreciated, however, is the extent to which their specific
patterns of composition were also influenced by Latin practice.
Like their Continental counterparts, these authors were quick to
use the digression *ad aliam partem materiae* as a means of entail-
ing the lives and activities of lesser characters onto the main
theme and so to develop the social and political dimensions of the
biography. That this type of composition was still in the formative
stages at this point is suggested by the unevenness of its use from
text to text (in sharp contrast with the relative uniformity of classical practice). That it is associated with foreign literary practice
is suggested by the residue of Latin phrasings.

These two groups of texts may thus be said to form a "Latin
connection"—a transitional phase in which the naturalization of a
foreign narrative mode is under way but not yet complete. Once
appropriated into the vernacular, the digressive mode established
itself and evolved quickly on its own terms. *Morkinskinna* is
digressive to an unprecedented degree, extending the device beyond the single biography to a succession of reigns and so realiz-
ing, in a way that the earlier synoptic histories did not, the dramatic potential of political history. With the *Great Saga,* the
"vernacularization" is for all practical purposes complete: narrative digression has become narrative stranding, and *aphodoi* have
become the ubiquitous and standard verbal formulas of classical
saga prose. As in the Icelandic sagas, the procedure is so fluently
handled that its foreign origins are no longer identifiable—
although even in the family sagas one encounters occasional uses
of digression proper (e.g., in *Njáls saga*), which serve to remind
us that Latin composition was still a viable model for Icelandic
writers even at this late stage.[45]

[45]The often-mentioned digressions of *Fóstbrœðra saga* may be considered
stylistic rather than structural, though equally associated with Latin practice.
Jónas Kristjánsson dates the saga to the late thirteenth century and views the
"digressive" versions as more original (*Um Fóstbrœðrasögu,* esp. pp. 55–96 and
292–307).

This model of development permits us to distinguish more precisely the oral from the literary layer of saga narrative—the former being those features that, because they have no immediate counterpart in early Latin sources but are on the contrary associated with folktelling patterns, may be safely assumed to represent "native" narrative tradition. As oral features may be counted, in addition to the language itself, the smaller denominations of plot: scenes, episodes, and *þættir*. Scene is the smallest particle of story and may be defined in strictly formal terms as a tripartite "paragraph" consisting of a dramatic encounter preceded by a narrative preface and followed by a narrative conclusion.[46] The following scene from *Grettis saga* (chapter 41) is a typical example. The preface establishes time, place, characters, and situation; the dramatic encounter consists of an exchange of dialogue (here a rather long conversation between Grettir and his brother Þorsteinn); and the conclusion tells how the encounter comes to an end and the participants part ways.

[*Preface:*] Nú var Grettir með Þorsteini, þat sem eptir var vetrarins ok fram á várit. Þat var einn morgin, er þeir brœðr, Þorsteinn ok Grettir, lágu í svefnlopti sínu, at Grettir hafði lagit hendr sínar undan klæðunum. Þorsteinn vakði ok sá þat. Grettir vaknaði litlu síðar. [*Dramatic Encounter*] Þá mælti Þorsteinn: "Sét hefi ek handleggi þína, frændi," sagði hann, "ok þykki mér eigi undarligt, þó at mǫrgum verði þung hǫgg þín, því at einskis manns handleggi hefi ek slíka sét." "Vita máttir þú þat," sagði Grettir, "at ek mynda ekki slíku til leiðar koma, sem ek hefi unnit, ef ek væra eigi allknár." "Betr þœtti mér," segir Þorsteinn, "þó at væri mjórri ok nǫkkuru gæfusamligri." Grettir segir: "Satt er þat, sem mælt er, at engi maðr skapar sik sjálfr. Láttu mik nú sjá þína handleggi," segir hann. Þorsteinn gerði svá; hann var manna lengstr ok grannvaxinn. Grettir brosti at ok mælti: "Eigi þarf at horfa á þetta lengr; krœkt er saman rifjum í þér, ok eigi þykkjumk ek slíkar tengr sét hafa, sem þú berr eptir, ok varla ætla ek þik kvenstyrkvan." "Vera má þat," sagði Þorsteinn, "en þó skaltu þat vita, at þessir inir mjóvu handleggir munu þín hefna, ella mun þín aldri hefnt verða." "Hvat má vita,

[46]See Carol J. Clover, "Scene in Saga Composition," *Arkiv för nordisk filologi,* 89 (1974), 57–83; Lars Lönnroth, *Njáls Saga: A Critical Introduction* (Berkeley: University of California Press, 1976), esp. pp. 42–101; Richard F. Allen, *Fire and Iron: Critical Approaches to* Njáls saga (Pittsburgh: University of Pittsburgh Press, 1971), esp. pp. 57–75.

hversu verðr um þat, er lýkr?'' segir Grettir, ''en allólíkligt þykki mér þat vera.'' Eigi er þá getit fleira um viðrtal þeira. [*Conclusion:*] Leið nú á várit; kom Grettir sér í skip ok fór út til Íslands um sumarit. Skilðu þeir brœðr með vináttu ok sáusk aldri síðan.

([*Preface:*] Now Grettir stayed with Þorsteinn through the rest of the winter and on into spring. One morning, when the brothers Þorsteinn and Grettir were lying in the sleeping loft, Grettir put his arms out from under the bedcovers. Þorsteinn was awake and saw this. After a while, Grettir woke up. [*Dramatic encounter:*] Then Þorsteinn spoke: ''I've been looking at your arms, kinsman,'' he said, ''and it doesn't surprise me that your blows seem heavy to many, for I have never seen arms like that on any man.'' ''You might have guessed,'' said Grettir, ''that I could never have accomplished what I have if I hadn't been fairly rugged.'' ''It would seem better to me,'' says Þorsteinn, ''if your arms were thinner and somewhat luckier.'' Grettir says: ''It's true, what they say, that no man creates himself. Now let me see your arms.'' Þorsteinn obliged; he was an extremely tall man and lankily built. Grettir smiled at the sight and said: ''I don't need to look any longer. Your ribs are all hooked together, and I don't think I've ever seen a set of arms more like tongs, and I doubt you have the strength of a woman.'' ''That may be,'' said Þorsteinn, ''but you should know that if your death is avenged at all, it will be by these skinny arms of mine.'' ''What can we know about how things turn out in the end?'' says Grettir. ''But I can't say that seems very likely to me.'' No more of their conversation is recorded. [*Conclusion:*] Now the spring passes. In the summer, Grettir gets aboard a ship and sails to Iceland. The brothers had a warm parting and never saw each other again.) [chap. 41]

It is not only the anecdotal quality of scenes such as this one that points to an origin in oral prehistory; it is the persistence of the fixed form in Norse narrative from the outset and over the generic range—including, significantly, the translated sagas, where a comparison with the original shows how the Norse redactors regularly add, delete, and reorder material in accordance with the tripartite template.[47] Although such scenes as the arm compari-

---

[47]The ''scenifying'' process is particularly clear in *Karlamagnús saga*, in certain of the *riddarasǫgur* (e.g., *Parcevals saga*), and, as Dietrich Hofmann's analysis suggests, in the early translations of saints' lives. See his ''Vers und Prosa in der mündlich gepflegten mittelalterlichen Erzählkunst der germanischen Länder,'' *Frühmittelalterliche Studien*, 5 (1971), esp. pp. 162–67.

son from *Grettis saga* may be literary in their received form, they may be assumed to reflect the original mnemonic unit of popular tradition.

Less neatly defined as structural entities are episodes and *þættir*, but they nonetheless stand out as formulaic elements of plot by virtue of their recurrence and predictability. Episodes are brief subplots: scenic sequences recounting thefts, seductions, litigations, weddings, horse fights, and the like. *Þættir* are recurrent stories of a detachable, hence semi-independent, nature, also describing typical action patterns (e.g., the Travel Pattern and the Feud Pattern). *Þættir* in particular show signs of a literary hand, but they, too, like scenes and episodes, have an anecdotal quality that leads one to associate them with popular tale telling at an earlier stage. It falls outside the scope of this study to reconstruct the oral saga, but one can speculate that its narrative composition was more like that of the *þættir* or the *fornaldarsǫgur* than the Icelandic saga proper.[48]

There is little "oral" about the way these narrative parts are combined in complex wholes, however.[49] Current opinion holds that interlace or stranded narration, particularly in simultaneous forms, is prima facie evidence of self-conscious literary authorship. Even without this corollary evidence, however, the Icelandic case would seem to be straightforward enough. The preclassical texts themselves dispel any notion that the form of composition in the classical sagas can be a venerable feature of popular tradition. What is striking about the early writings, particularly in

[48]Peter Buchholz contends that the *fornaldarsaga* is the most archaic and hence best surviving representative of oral saga tradition in Scandinavia. See his *Vorzeitkunde: Mündliches Erzählen und Überliefern im mittelalterlichen Skandinavien nach dem Zeugnis von Fornaldarsaga und eddischer Dichtung*, Skandinavistische Studien, 13 (Neumünster: Wachholtz, 1980).

[49]"The sagawriters did not have to import foreign rules for the construction of smaller units such as a battle scene, a goading scene, or even an entire feud episode. They did not have to learn abroad how to make the audience feel antipathy for the treacherous Loki figure or sympathy for a Siegfried figure fighting his last battle. They could use the old motifs and narrative rules which they had inherited from their ancestors; this was a heritage strong enough to resist many foreign influences even when the sagawriters were familiar with foreign literature. Their native literary grammar was too ingrown to be radically changed, but it could be modified and refined to suit new and more sophisticated literary interests, fostered by clerical minds of the thirteenth century" (Lönnroth, *Njáls Saga*, p. 103).

contrast with those of the classical period, is the degree of variation in composition from text to text (e.g., *Fagrskinna* versus *Morkinskinna*) and even within the same text (e.g., *Sverris saga*). This would hardly be the case if saga composition were in fact taken over from an oral prototype. Moreover, there is discernible in the preclassical texts a sketchy but clear development from shorter works in which stranding is an occasional and rudimentary feature to longer works in which it is a regular and elaborate one—again, not the pattern we would expect if there were an oral prototype. In other words, as far as composition is concerned, recourse to an oral unknown is unnecessary. The extant literary documents themselves provide an adequate and plausible model of the evolution of the complex saga. Oral tradition may have been instrumental in the preservation and framing of the particulars, but there is no reason to suppose that their organization in large, convoluted wholes is anything other than a literary development of the twelfth century—a development in which the Latin connection played a decisive role.[50]

Sigurður Nordal argued that Norse prose began as factual knowledge but yielded by degrees to art for purposes of entertainment, with the classical sagas representing the optimal combination. The saga "begins as fact, ends as fiction, and progresses through every shade in between," he wrote; and further, "All true saga-writing is a balance between fact and art."[51] A survey of composition during the preclassical period suggests that "art" in this case is not a thing apart from the factual sphere of chronicle and history, but itself derived directly from that sphere, and further that this development is by no means peculiar to Iceland, but is part of the larger European development. This association is important to remember in connection with sagas such as *Heiðarvíga saga, Reykdœla saga,* and even the *Legendary*

[50]Especially suggestive for the Norse case is Peter M. Schon's study of the transition, in French tradition, from chronicle prose to literary prose, "Studien zum Stil der frühen französischen Prosa," *Analecta Romanica*, 8 (1960), 1–60.

[51]Nordal, *Snorri Sturluson*, esp. p. 131; reiterated in somewhat modified form in his "Sagalitteraturen," esp. pp. 27–73. Cf. Bjarni Guðnason, *Um Skjöldungasögu* (Reykjavík: Bókaútgáfa Menningarsjóðs, 1963), esp. pp. 269–83. See also Walter Baetke, *Über die Entstehung der Isländersagas*, Berichte über der Verhandlungen der Sächsischen Akademie der Wissenschaften zu Leipzig, phil.-hist. Kl., 102, pt. 5 (1956), pp. 5–108, esp. pp. 51–54.

*Saga*—works thought by virtue of their early date to be relatively uncontaminated specimens of native narrative traditions. The year 1226 may be a watershed date in some respects, but on the level of composition Norse prose had contracted its foreign debt well before that. Latin chronicle writing played a role in the development of art prose in Scandinavia no less than on the Continent, and even the earliest sagas are too late not to have felt its influence.

## Romance and Saga

If the preceding model is correct, the composition of the classical sagas is explained as the result of a largely domestic development, one shaped in the early stages by Latin practice but evolving on its own terms after that. The question is whether this model is sufficient to explain the numerous and striking correspondences, outlined in the earlier chapters of this book, between classical saga narrative and Continental narrative, above all, the mass of cyclic literature that came to dominate the French literary picture at the same time that the saga was rising to preeminence in Iceland. In both the saga and the prose romance we are dealing with full-length imaginative works in prose. In both cases, open composition is the point of departure for their genesis and the basic principle of their construction. And in both cases, interlace is used, not merely in "practical" forms, but in gratuitously developed and extended forms. The specific patterns differ: prose romances pursue fewer lines at greater length and focus on remarkable chronological coincidences, whereas the sagas intertwine a larger number of shorter strands in the interest of tracing webs of acts and consequences in the broader social fabric. In the sagas, that is, the intervals are typically shorter but the data more numerous and the fragmentation of the plot far more extreme. But in their copiousness, their interweaving of synchronic plot lines, and their obvious delight in the aesthetic of multiplicity and recurrence, the sagas and the prose romances are so alike that it is hard to suppose that they are unrelated.

Equally intriguing are the parallels in development. Like early saga tradition, early romance tradition seems to derive in part from Latin practice the techniques and language of digression (both external and internal). Both traditions assimilate the Latin figure gradually. In the first phase (the preclassical Norse texts and the poetic romances), digression or interlace is occasional and straightforward in form. In the second phase (the classical sagas and the prose romances), it has become a regular and artful feature of the narrative. In the third phase (e.g., *Flateyjarbók* and the *Prophécies de Merlin*) it is no longer a question of composition but of gross compilation. Particularly telling is the corresponding evolution of transitional phrases: from the infrequent use of a variety of phrases directly translating the Latin *aphodoi* to the abundant use of a few standard formulas in the later period. In both cases the gradual depersonalization of these phrases gives them a colloquial flavor in the later stages that tends to obscure their bookish origins. The romance model is most immediately helpful in understanding the rapid evolution of the saga from shorter and clearer plots to the voluminous amalgams of the later period.

These correspondences may be said to constitute the circumstantial evidence for the influence on saga writing of cyclic tradition. The immense popularity of the prose romances relative to many of their verse predecessors should not be forgotten. As Vinaver points out, the *Prose Tristan* "easily superseded all the poetical versions of the legend," becoming from the thirteenth century onward "the only recognized form of the Tristan story.... Throughout Europe the *Prose Tristan* was read and imitated, and its *rifacimenti* in the various European languages often became classics in the countries in which they appeared" (e.g., Malory's *Morte Darthur* [Books 8–12] in England and *La tavola ritonda* in Italy).[52] The poetic versions dropped out of circulation until their reintroduction in 1823 and 1835 with the publication of Béroul's and Thomas's fragments respectively.[53] The equivalent popularity of the *Prose Lancelot* is attested by the survival of about a hundred manuscripts and its impact on other romances all over Europe.[54] Given the prominence of the prose

---

[52]Eugène Vinaver, "The Prose *Tristan*," in *Arthurian Literature in the Middle Ages*, ed. R. S. Loomis (Oxford: Clarendon, 1959), p. 346.

[53]Ibid., p. 346.

[54]Jean Frappier, "The Vulgate Cycle," in Loomis, *Arthurian Literature*, pp. 317–18. See also chapter 1, note 2, above.

phenomenon and the fact that it was the growth sector of medieval literature, it is hard to suppose that any Icelander at that time who knew anything at all about French literary culture could have been ignorant of it. Moreover, because the novelty of the prose romances lay less in the stories they told (most of which were known already in some form or other) than in the way they were knitted together in large, interlocking wholes, it may reasonably be supposed that "influence" in this instance would take the form of technical imitation, not necessarily plot borrowing.[55] It may indeed be argued that, given the vigor of their own literary culture and the multifarious nature of their own quasi-historical traditions, the Icelanders were particularly susceptible to this literary fashion.

Material evidence for the influence of prose romance on saga writing is harder to come by.[56] The only sure point of contact between saga and romance is the translation into Norse of such verse works as *Yvain, Erec et Enide, Perceval, Tristan,* and the *lais* of Marie de France. Commissioned in the first instance by Hákon Hákonarson, these translations appear to have found a ready audience in Scandinavia, and words and motifs from them quickly passed into general circulation, as their incorporation in sagas on native subjects attests. For the most part, recent inquiry into Franco-Norse literary relations has been limited to this and other equally demonstrable connections (e.g., *Karlamagnús saga*). The possibility of influence from untranslated works, or works not otherwise known to have been translated, remains a

[55]It is this sort of formal influence, rather than a material influence, that Heusler thought the Irish sagas might have exerted on Norse storytelling traditions. See his "Die Anfänge der isländischen Saga" in *Andreas Heusler: Kleine Schriften,* ed. Stefan Sonderegger (Berlin: de Gruyter, 1969), pp. 427–29; originally published in *Abhandlungen der Königlich Preussischen Akademie der Wissenschaften,* phil.-hist. Kl. (1913). See also Baetke, *Über die Entstehung der Isländersagas,* pp. 82–98, and Guðnason, *Um Skjöldungasögu,* pp. 243–83. Jean Rychner's systematic analysis of "articulation" techniques in the *Mort Artu* suggests a basis for the further comparison of prose romance narrative with the sagas. See his *L'articulation des phrases narratives dans la Mort Artu,* Université de Neuchâtel: Recueil de Travaux de la Faculté des lettres, 32 (Geneva: Droz, 1970).

[56]The question of just how conversant the Icelanders were with French culture was debated recently by Theodore M. Andersson, "Skalds and Troubadours," *Mediaeval Scandinavia,* 2 (1969), esp. pp. 13–16, and Bjarni Einarsson, "The Lovesick Skald: A Reply to Theodore M. Andersson," *Mediaeval Scandinavia,* 4 (1971), esp. 28–36.

largely unexplored field. There is only one claim based on the criterion of plot correspondence that a prose romance was known in Iceland, and it has been challenged.[57] Even if it is genuine, it alone is too late to have affected the early development of the saga. Because of the problems in dating the family sagas, it is hard to draw any firm conclusions about the evolution of the form during the course of the thirteenth century. In general, it would seem that the cyclic tendency is more conspicuous in the later, longer sagas of the district chronicle type than in the earlier, shorter sagas of the biographical type, but it is in any case sufficiently evident even in those sagas we regard as oldest (including *Heiðarvíga saga* and *Reykdœla saga*, a district chronicle recently redated to 1207–20)[58] that if we are to assume influence from cyclic romance, we must suppose that it began in the first or second decade of the century. This is not, strictly speaking, impossible. Like the saga, the prose romance had its preclassical phase in the years before and after 1200 in the works of Robert de Boron (whose tetralogy is dated between 1190 and 1212, probably around 1202) and the highly stranded *Perlesvaus* (the original version of which appeared between 1191 and 1212). The "classical" cyclic works, like the classical sagas, belong to the thirteenth century proper: the Vulgate Cycle is generally dated between 1215 and 1230 and the first version of the *Prose Tristan* between 1225 and 1235 (the second version comes from the latter half of the century). The early vigor of the cyclic idea is suggested by the translation into German of the *Prose Lancelot* not long after the date of its original composition. The rise of cyclic romance, in other words, is exactly contemporaneous with the rise of the saga. To claim, therefore, that the former played a critical role in the development of the latter requires us to assume (1) that the connection was unusually efficient and did not entail the usual

---

[57]In his *Skáldasögur: Um uppruna og eðli ástaskáldasagnanna fornu* (Reykjavík: Bókaútgáfa Menningarsjóðs, 1961), Bjarni Einarsson argued that the *Prose Tristan* is reflected especially in *Kormáks saga* (pp. 75–76). Cf. Andersson ("Skalds and Troubadours," pp. 38–41) and Einarsson's reply ("The Lovesick Skald," pp. 38–41).

[58]Dietrich Hofmann, "Reykdœla saga und mündliche Überlieferung," *Skandinavistik*, 2 (1972), 1–26. The highly digressive structure of *Sturlunga saga* should be noted in this connection.

time lag (compare the lapse of eighty-odd years between the time of Chrétien's original publication and the time of the Norse adaptation); (2) that the cyclic idea was adopted immediately and more or less unanimously by Norse authors; and (3) that the cyclic idea reached Scandinavia before the translation of the verse romances. None of these assumptions is in itself implausible, but taken together they depart too emphatically from some of our basic presuppositions about Norse literary history to be wholly convincing.

In light of this problematic chronology and in the absence of hard evidence, it is difficult to suppose that the prose romances played a decisive role in the formal development of the saga. The more prudent assumption is that the saga and the prose romance represent, at least in the early stages, independent responses to a common medieval aesthetic (chronicle writing, first Latin and then vernacular, being an important factor in both cases). This is not to say that the cyclic idea never penetrated Scandinavia—it is clear from *Flateyjarbók* that it did—but that it may have come later rather than earlier and that its effect was not so much formative as it was to reinforce preexisting narrative tendencies and perhaps to contribute certain technical refinements (e.g., the use of suspended animation at transition points). Such a secondary influence may explain at least some of the striking surface similarities between the two traditions. In either case, whether saga composition is to be explained as the result of independent development out of Latin practice, or as a direct imitation of prose romance, or as a combination of the two, the larger point is clear: it belongs to the general European development of the late twelfth and thirteenth centuries.

## The Two Audiences

The idea that the sagas were orally delivered to a listening public—the *sagnaskemmtun* or "saga entertainment"—enjoys a current consensus in saga studies. The evidence, conveniently collected in Hermann Pálsson's *Sagnaskemmtun Íslendinga* (1962),[59] suggests that *sagnaskemmtun* in the preliterate period

[59]Hermann Pálsson, *Sagnaskemmtun Íslendinga* (Reykjavík: Mál og Menning, 1962).

involved telling a traditional story more or less from memory, but that this practice gave way at some early point to the reading aloud of sagas from manuscripts. Just when that change took place may be disputed, as may be the question of just what form the early "told" sagas took. Generally accepted, however, is the idea that the canonical sagas were read aloud, in something like the form we have them, probably in nightly installments (*Njáls saga* would require about two weeks), in conditions not unlike those of the famous Reykjahólar wedding in 1119: at a larger farm, in connection with a special occasion, and to socially mixed company (prominent landowners, clerics, merchants, independent farmers, women).[60]

[60]"Þar var nú glaumr ok gleði mikil, skemmtan góð ok margs konar leikar, bæði dansleikar, glímur og sagnaskemmtan. Þar var sjau nætr fastar ok fullar setit at boðinu, af því at þar skyldi vera hvert sumar Óláfs-gildi, ef korn gæti at kaupa, tvau mjölsáld, á Þórsnessþingi, ok váru þar margir gildabræðr.... Frá því er nökkut sagt, er þó er lítil tilkváma, hverir þar skemmtu eða hverju skemmt var. Þat er í frásögn haft, er nú mæla margir í móti ok látast eigi vitat hafa, því at margir ganga duldir ins sanna ok hyggja þat satt, er skrökvat er, en þat logit, sem satt er: Hrólfr frá Skálmarnesi sagði sögu frá Hröngviði víkingi ok frá Óláfi Liðsmanna-konungi ok haugbroti Þráins berserks ok Hrómundi Gripssyni—ok margar vísur með. En þessari sögu var skemmt Sverri konungi, ok kallaði hann slíkar lygisögur skemmtiligstar. Ok þó kunna menn at telja ættir sínar til Hrómundar Gripssonar. Þessa sögu hafði Hrólfr sjálfr saman setta. Ingimundr prestr sagði sögu Orms Barreyjarskálds ok vísur margar ok flokk góðan við enda sögunnar, er Ingimundr hafði ortan, ok hafa þó margir fróðir menn þessa sögu fyrir satt." ("Now there were high spirits and great merriment, good entertainment and many kinds of amusements: dancing, wrestling, and storytelling. They [the guests] sat at the feast for a fixed period of seven full nights, because there was supposed to be a Feast of St. Óláfr at the Þórsnes Thing every summer during which they could purchase two meal-measures of grain, and there were many guild-brothers present. Something is told, though it is of little consequence, about those who entertained there and what the subject of the entertainment was [i.e., who told stories and what these stories were]. Stories are told, which many people now disclaim or act as if they never knew, because many are blind to the truth and regard those things as true which are fabrications and those things as lies which are true: Hrólfr from Skálmarnes told a saga about Hröngviðr the viking and about Óláfr Liðsmannakonungr and the grave robbery of Þráinn the berserk and Hrómundr Gripsson—along with many stanzas of poetry. This saga was told to King Sverrir, and he declared such lying-sagas to be most amusing. Yet people can trace their families back to Hrómundr Gripsson. Hrólfr himself had composed [lit. "put together"] this saga. Priest Ingimundr told the saga of Ormr Barreyjarskáld, with many stanzas of poetry and, at the end of the saga, a good *flokkr* which Ingimundr had made, and even so, many wise men consider this saga to be true"—*Þorgils saga ok Hafliða*, chap. 10.) On the authenticity of the passage, see Peter G. Foote, "Sagnaskemtan: Reykjahólar 1119," *Saga-Book of the Viking Society*, 14 (1955–56), 226–39.

The picture of the *sagnaskemmtun* is in agreement with the picture, generally accepted until recently, of the Middle Ages as an era when vernacular literature was orally disseminated in some way or other, even among the literate laity.[61] As Ruth Crosby put it, medieval people "read by means of the ear rather than the eye, by hearing others read or recite rather than by reading to themselves."[62] In the earlier period, oral performances took the form of the recitation or chanting of tales by professional performers (jongleurs, scops, skalds) in the halls of the nobility as well as for common people on the streets. As illiteracy gave way to oligoliteracy, oral performance, at least among the privileged classes, increasingly took the form of the reading aloud from a manuscript by someone (first a professional, later a member of the family). Two kinds of evidence are advanced for the custom of reading aloud. One is extrinsic and consists of passages actually describing the act and circumstances of such readings (e.g., Chrétien's description, in *Yvain,* of a *pucele* who reads aloud to her family from a manuscript in Old French).[63] The other kind of evidence is intrinsic and consists of phrases apostrophizing the listener, often in prologues or conclusions: "Or escoutez, granz et menour (Now listen, lords and lowborn)" or "Herkneth to me, gode men, / Wiues, maydnes, and alle men."[64] The superfluity of listener-phrases in the verse romances led an earlier generation of

[61]See in particular H. J. Chaytor, *From Script to Print: An Introduction to Medieval Literature* (Cambridge: Cambridge University Press, 1945); Ruth Crosby, "Oral Delivery in the Middle Ages," *Speculum,* 11 (1933), 88–110; Albert C. Baugh, "The Middle English Romance," *Speculum,* 42 (1967), 1–31; and Pierre Gallais, "Recherches sur la mentalité des romanciers français du moyen âge: Les formules et le vocabulaire des prologues," *Cahiers de civilisation médiévale,* 7 (1964), 479–93.

[62]Crosby, "Oral Delivery," p. 88.

[63][Yvain] apoiié voit dessor son cote / Un prodome qui se gisoit / Sor un drap de soie, et lisoit / Une pucele devant lui / An un romanz, ne sai de cui. / Et por le romanz escouter / S'i estoit venue acoter / Une dame, et c'estoit sa mere, / Et li prodon estoit ses pere, / Si se pooient esjoïr / Mout de li veoir et oir. ([Yvain] sees, reclining upon his elbow upon a silken rug, a gentleman, before whom a maiden was reading from a romance about I know not whom. There had come to recline there with them and listen to the romance a lady, who was the mother of the damsel, as the gentleman was her father; they had good reason to enjoy seeing and hearing her, for they had no other children"—vv. 5362–72).

[64]Further examples in Crosby, "Oral Delivery," and Chaytor, *From Script to Print,* Appendix B (pp. 144–47).

scholars to assume that they were the compositions of unlettered minstrels. But now that the bookish nature of the works has been firmly established, their "oral" phrases are taken rather as reflections of their intended mode of delivery. Because authors realized that their works were probably not destined for dissemination solely through the multiplication of manuscripts, they wrote, according to Albert C. Baugh, "with oral presentation in mind, adopting a style, so far as they were capable of it, natural to live presentation."[65] Circumstances required that the literary work imitate the oral form.

The question has recently been raised whether the case for oral reading has not been overstated and whether rather more medieval literature was intended for private reading than has been supposed.[66] Estimates of the degree of literacy among the laity are not much help because they vary greatly and do not distinguish the partially literate (able only to read) from the fully literate (able to read and write), not to speak of degrees of ability within those categories.[67] That some people could and did read vernacular poetry would seem to be indicated by the occurrence of references, admittedly fewer, to readers as well as listeners.[68] The

[65]Baugh, "Middle English Romance," p. 9. See also Ramón Menéndez-Pidal, *Poesía juglaresca y juglares* (Madrid: Espasa-Calpe, 1924), pp. 274–79; and Gallais, "Recherches," pp. 479–93.

[66]See especially Martín de Riquer, "Épopée jongleresque à écouter et épopée romanesque à lire," *Actes du Colloque de Liège (Sept. 1957): La technique littéraire des chansons de geste* (Paris: Société d'édition "Les Belles Lettres," 1959), pp. 75–84; G. B. Gybbon-Monypenny, "The Spanish *Mester de Clerecía* and Its Intended Public: Concerning the Validity as Evidence of Passages of Direct Address to the Audience," *Medieval Miscellany Presented to Eugène Vinaver*, ed. Frederick Whitehead et al. (Manchester: Manchester University Press, 1965), pp. 230–44; Roger Walker, "Oral Delivery or Private Reading? A Contribution to the Debate on the Dissemination of Medieval Literature," *Forum for Modern Language Studies*, 7 (1971–72), 36–42; and Ian Michael, "A Comparison of the Use of Epic Epithets in the *Poema de Mio Cid* and the *Libro de Alexandre*," *Bulletin of Hispanic Studies*, 38 (1961), 32–41.

[67]Two useful books on medieval literacy are James Westfall Thompson, *The Literacy of the Laity in the Middle Ages*, University of California Publications in Education, 9 (Berkeley: University of California Press, 1939; rpt. New York: B. Franklin, 1963), and M. T. Clanchy, *From Memory to Written Record: England, 1066–1307* (London: Edward Arnold, 1970; rpt. 1979). Further bibliography can be found in these works and in Franz H. Bäuml, "Varieties and Consequences of Medieval Literacy and Illiteracy," *Speculum*, 55 (1980), 237–65.

[68]Examples are given by Crosby, "Oral Delivery," pp. 99–100.

question is, of course, how authentic such phrases are as indi-
cators of audience. The "oral" formulas in particular may have
been part of the conventional baggage of vernacular poetry, understood by author and audience alike to be quaint remnants of
the minstrel era. This would seem to be the lesson of those examples occurring in works known to have been written for private
readers.[69] Peter M. Schon came to this conclusion about the listener formulas in early French prose: they remained part of the
author's stock in trade long after the oral situation ceased to
obtain.[70] But in either case, the likelihood that verse romances
were customarily read aloud does not detract from the likelihood
that they were also read privately and that their authors were
aware that both forms of publication were possibilities.

What, then, of prose? It is a commonplace that the rise of prose
for purposes of entertainment and edification is associated with
the spread of education. Aware of the possibility that their works
might be read privately as well as publicly, authors abandoned the
traditional vehicle of oral performance (indeed, of fiction or
legend in general), the verse form. Some literary historians assume a period of transition.[71] Others, like Schon, incline to the
view that the use of prose was by definition indicative of a significant number of private readers.[72] That the prose romances were
aimed at readers, not listeners, is suggested by the paucity of the
conventional signs of oral delivery (passages describing it and
exhortations to listeners)[73] as well as another kind of intrinsic

[69]See Gybbon-Monypenny, "The Spanish *Mester de Clerecía*"; Michael,
"Comparison of the Use of Epic Epithets," pp. 32–41; and Walker, "Oral Delivery or Private Reading?" pp. 37–38.
[70]Schon, "Studien zum Stil der frühen französischen Prosa," pp. 141–43 and
159–63. Gybbon-Monypenny ("The Spanish *Mester de Clerecía*") points out that
words such as "say" and "hear" are often used catachrestically "in the way that
a modern writer will "say" things to his readers" (pp. 242–43).
[71]E.g., Chaytor, *From Script to Print*, pp. 141–43.
[72]Schon, "Studien zum Stil der frühen französischen Prosa," pp. 141–43; also
Georges Doutrepont, *Les mises en prose des épopées et des romans chevaleresques du XIVᵉ au XVIᵉ siècle*, Mémoires de l'Académie royale de Belgique, classe
des lettres, 40 (Brussels, 1939), esp. pp. 380–441.
[73]Of the derhyming process, Doutrepont writes: "As a general rule, the epic
mechanisms and phrases disappear—that is, the call for attention or for silence;
the repetitions or the summaries, indispensable in the recitation of chansons de
geste; the epithets serving as leitmotifs. All of these economies may be explained:
the use of the mechanisms and phrases, technical concomitants of the epic genre,

evidence: their complex narrative structure. It has often been noted that narrative intended for oral delivery, even when it is written by fully literate authors, tends to have the characteristics of oral narrative. As Franz Boas once put it, "The form of modern prose is largely determined by the fact that it is read, not spoken, while primitive prose is based on the art of oral delivery and is, therefore, more closely related to modern oratory than to the printed literary style."[74] Narrative form, in other words, reveals as much about those who consume it as those who produce it; an author can finally be no more "literate" or "literary" than his or her audience. At least one critic has for this reason classified as "oral" all poetry intended for oral delivery regardless of the circumstances of its origin (a view, however, that has not met with general approval).[75]

This correspondence in form between orally composed narrative and texts written by literate authors for reading aloud may in part be the result of a deliberate effort to imitate popular practice; but it may also be an unconscious acknowledgment of something intrinsic in the act of listening, a set of limitations the situation imposes on literate and illiterate alike. The underlying idea is that the listener cannot tolerate the same degree of formal complexity as the reader, who, as H. J. Chaytor puts it, "has time to ponder the matter before him, to read a passage over as often as he pleases and to exert his critical faculties."[76] On these grounds, more than any other, the prose romance distinguishes itself from its verse predecessors. The verse romances as a group may have story lines suitable for oral delivery, but the reverse is true of the prose romance, of which it may be said (as Roger Walker said of

---

has no reason to exist once the genre itself ceases to exist. Indeed, it would have been absolutely impossible to maintain them. Another factor motivating the disappearance of the 'apparatus' of epic is that, being set in prose, they [the de-rhymed works] were not addressed to the ear but to the eye. The reader *reads;* he does not *hear*" (*Les mises en prose*, p. 565); and further: "All this more or less artificial framework [i.e., the 'oral' features] arose almost by necessity from the force of circumstances. But starting as early as the thirteenth century, it begins to disappear" (ibid., p. 685).

[74]Franz Boas, "Stylistic Aspects of Primitive Literature," *Journal of American Folk-Lore,* 38 (1925), 329–39.

[75]Ruth Finnegan, *Oral Poetry* (Cambridge: Cambridge University Press, 1977), esp. pp. 16–24.

[76]Chaytor, *From Script to Print,* p. 80.

the *Zifar*, a Spanish example from ca. 1301) that "its huge length, slow-moving plot, complex structure, high level of abstraction and constant moralizing conflict at every turn with the vivacity, actuality and concreteness that are the salient features of all mass oral literature, whether orally composed or merely orally diffused."[77] It should be remembered that there is a certain medieval authority for the idea that narrative intended for private reading may indulge more complex forms of exposition than narrative intended for oral delivery—explicitly in the form of rhetoricians' rules ("Circuitous development . . . dulls the mind of the listener by making an unsolvable labyrinth, unless the listener is very subtle") and implicitly in practice (e.g., Alcuin's differently ordered versions of the same saint's life for different audiences).[78]

The extrinsic evidence for the oral delivery of sagas has been collected elsewhere and will be discussed only briefly here.[79] It consists of a handful of medieval references to specific occasions and the more numerous accounts, from later centuries, of the practice of oral reading on Icelandic farms. The latter assume the status of evidence by virtue of the common supposition of an extraordinary degree of cultural continuity in Iceland during and after the Middle Ages.[80] The medieval descriptions proper are few and notoriously inconclusive. It is not always clear, for example, whether they refer to recitation (as is assumed to be the case in the Reykjahólar passage) or reading aloud (as the wording of the "Huldar saga" passage in *Sturlunga saga* would seem to suggest).[81] Nor are the references informative on the question of

---

[77]Walker, "Oral Delivery or Private Reading?" p. 40.

[78]See Chapter 3, esp. notes 23–27.

[79]See Pálsson, *Sagnaskemmtun Íslendinga*.

[80]In a similar way, Stefán Karlsson argues that an unusually high degree of literacy in sixteenth-century Iceland must reflect a high degree of literacy there in the Middle Ages—a view rejected by Lönnroth. See Stefán Karlsson, "Ritun Reykjarfjarðarbókar. Excursus: Bókagerð bænda," *Opuscula*, 4, Bibliotheca Arnamagnæana, 30 (Copenhagen: Munksgaard, 1970), pp. 120–40; Lönnroth, *Njáls Saga*, pp. 166–70. If we regard as evidence of its medieval currency the practice of *sagnaskemmtun* in later centuries, so we must by the same token acknowledge the unusually high incidence of Icelandic literacy in later centuries as an indication of a relatively large number of readers in medieval Iceland.

[81]Related in "Sturlu þáttr" (*Sturlunga saga*, II, 232–35). Sturla Þórðarson entertains King Magnús with the oral delivery of "Huldar saga." Pálsson (*Sagnaskemmtun Íslendinga*, p. 52) and Lönnroth (*Njáls Saga*, p. 173) assume, on grounds of the wording, that a manuscript is involved: Magnús, in requesting the

form. A rare mention of length is found in the *Morkinskinna* description of the recitation of Haraldr harðráði's *útferðar saga;* the king and the Icelander conspire to stretch the saga over the thirteen evenings of Yule by dividing it into unusually short segments.[82] A further complication lies in the uncertainty of the exact meaning of the word "saga." The possibility should be considered that the memory of the "saga," like other orally transmitted memories, was unconsciously adjusted by each generation to its own experience and that the thirteenth-century commentators were themselves in some degree unwitting heirs to and purveyors of an anachronism.[83] The mere persistence of the word "saga" is no guarantee that the thing itself did not undergo changes during the two centuries in question (modern readers may be in a better position than the medieval Icelanders to speculate on the nature of that change). Finally, of course, there is the often-noted fact that, as B. M. Ólsen put it, there is to be found in the early literature "no evidence that such saga-tellers chose family sagas as their subject matter."[84] The records mention numerous tales of a fantastic sort, as well as stories of kings and saints, but no Icelandic matter. However reasonable it may be to assume that this omission is an accident of history and that "sagas" on

---

performance, asks Sturla to "bring with him the saga about the troll-woman (hafa með sér trollkonusöguna)." Hofmann disagrees: "It is most unlikely that Sturla would have read the saga aloud [to Magnús]. In his reduced circumstances—'hafði hann nær ekki í fé [he had almost no property],' it says in connection with his departure from Iceland, and for his voyage he didn't even have his own provisions along—he would scarcely have carried a manuscript around with him, especially one of entertainment value only. Nor could it have comprised only a few leaves, because he recited the saga for the better part of the day, as the second mention indicates ('sagði mikinn hluta dags sögu')" ("Vers und Prosa," p. 168). A clear case of reading is found in *Þorgils saga skarða* (in *Sturlunga saga,* II, 218), in which Þorgils asks to have *Tómas saga erkibyskups* read to him.

[82] *Morkinskinna,* pp. 199–200. A recent discussion of this passage as it relates to other oral traditions is that of H. M. Heinrichs, "Mündlichkeit und Schriftlichkeit: Ein Problem der Sagaforschung," *Akten des V. Internationalen Germanisten-Kongresses, Cambridge 1975,* published as Ser. A, vol. 2 of *Jahrbuch für Internationale Germanistik* (Bern: Herbert Lang, 1976), 114–33.

[83] For an illuminating discussion of memory in oral tradition, see Jack Goody and Ian Watt, "The Consequences of Literacy," in *Literacy in Traditional Societies,* ed. Jack Goody (Cambridge: Cambridge University Press, 1968), pp. 27–68.

[84] Björn M. Ólsen, "Um Íslendingasögur," *Safn til sögu Íslands,* 6 (1937–39), p. 9.

local subjects must have been disseminated in more or less the same way as "sagas" on other subjects, the fact remains that there is no record to that effect. As bookprosists have often pointed out, we have no real extrinsic evidence from the medieval period that Icelandic sagas were orally delivered in any form. Also in short supply in the Icelandic sagas are the usual intrinsic signs of oral delivery, such as passages addressing the listener. As indirect evidence that they were read aloud have been cited the handful of audience exhortations found in the *riddarasǫgur* ("Hafi sá þökk, er las, og sá, er skrifaði, ok allir þeir, er til hlýða [Let him be thanked who read, him who wrote, and all those who listened]"), but these tell us more about the redactors' eagerness to imitate a foreign convention than they do about how romances actually circulated in the Norwegian court, not to say how native sagas circulated in Iceland.[85] The absence of equivalent exhortations in the Icelandic sagas may be explained as part of their narrative stance, which excludes apostrophe, but the question must then be asked whether this narrative stance is compatible with the usual requirements of oral delivery. The only "oral" phrases in the Icelandic sagas are such formulas as *nú er at segja, er frá var sagt*—phrases that may or may not be remnants of an oral stage of storytelling but in either case cannot be taken as an indication of oral delivery in and of themselves (particularly given their apparent interchangeability with "writer" phrases).[86]

[85]The example is from the end of *Rémundar saga keisarasonar*. *Elis saga ok Rósamundu* contains the following admonition: "Nú hlýðið góðgæfliga! Betra er fögur fræði en kviðar fylli; þó skal við sögu súpa, en ei ofmikið drekka. Sæmd er sögu að segja, ef heyrendur til hlýða, en tapað starfi að hafna að heyra (Now listen well! A fair tale is better than a full belly. One should sip while listening to a saga, but not drink too much. It is an honor to tell a story when the audience pays attention, but a vain effort when they stop listening)." As Damsgaard Olsen points out ("Den høviske litteratur" in *Norrøn fortællekunst*, p. 108), this is an expansion of the French *or m'escoutes signor*. See also Lönnroth, *Njáls Saga*, pp. 172–73.

[86]The significance of such phrases in the sagas has been disputed. Liestøl took them at face value as oral remnants; Baetke dismissed them as "validating" clichés, not to be taken seriously; Andersson, reviewing the evidence more systematically, concluded that a certain portion of them must constitute textual evidence of a prehistoric oral saga. To the debate may be added a modern note—the function of such phrases in establishing what Ong calls the "audience fiction." Just as the use of folktale language by H. C. Andersen and Karen Blixen is not an indication that they intended their stories to be read aloud but rather that they

But it is above all the formal structure of the saga that speaks against its having been intended solely or even mainly for oral publication. The problem is not length per se, which is attested as an "oral" possibility in living epic traditions,[87] nor is it prose per se, which is after all the vehicle of the folktale (though the combination of nonrhythmic prose and length is uncommon in the world of oral entertainment[88]). Nor is it style; the language of the sagas is a model of clarity, and even if it does not reflect an oral style as much as a literary idealization of an oral style—"more natural than nature" (Nordal) or "unnaturally natural" (Heusler)—it is in any case not "literary" in the usual sense. Nor, as I have suggested earlier, does the difficulty lie in the smaller denominations of plot—scenes, episodes, *þættir*. These, too, have an anec-

expected their readers to imagine themselves, for the duration of the narrative, in the role of children or naive listeners, so may the "oral" language of the saga be little more than an invitation to a nostalgic fiction ("Listen, my children, and you shall hear / Of the midnight ride of Paul Revere . . ."). See Knut Liestøl, *Upphavet til den islendske ættesaga* (Oslo: Aschehoug, 1929), esp. p. 36; Walter Baetke, *Über die Entstehung der Isländersagas*, esp. pp. 29–31; Theodore M. Andersson, "The Textual Evidence for an Oral Family Saga," *Arkiv för nordisk filologi*, 81 (1966), 1–23; and Walter J. Ong S.J., "The Writer's Audience Is Always a Fiction," *PMLA*, 90 (1975), 9–21.

[87]A late fourteenth-century instance of a long oral reading is described by Froissart in his *Dit du Florin*. He tells how he read his poetic romance *Méliador* (more than 30,000 lines long) to Gaston Phébus. Even Chaytor doubts comprehensibility under the circumstances (*From Script to Print*, pp. 103–4).

[88]Two recent attempts to see saga literature in the context of larger oral tradition are, with reference to the Icelandic sagas, Heinrichs, "Mündlichkeit und Schriftlichkeit," and, with reference to the *fornaldarsǫgur* (legendary sagas), Buchholz, *Vorzeitkunde*. The difficulty in both cases is that the majority of cited evidence is from poetic traditions, for the reason that oral narrative is almost by definition poetic narrative. As Robert Scholes and Robert Kellogg summarize: "It is the universal experience of mankind that the oral composition of prose sentences is more difficult than the oral composition of metrically perfect verse. Some critics believe that prose cannot develop orally because of the difficulty of controlling the logical and syntactic rhythm of the prose sentence. They have restricted illiterate man to the esthetic use of verse" (*The Nature of Narrative* [New York: Oxford University Press, 1966], pp. 50–51). Such prose traditions as do exist appear to be markedly rhythmic and repetitive (see Finnegan, *Oral Poetry*, pp. 24–28 and 50–51, and Boas, "Stylistic Aspects of Primitive Literature"). An exception to the rule of verse, cited by both Heinrichs and Buchholz as possibly pertinent to the saga case, are prose traditions in central Asia (see esp. Buchholz, *Vorzeitkunde*, pp. 29–30); Buchholz also refers to Welsh, Scottish, and Irish traditions. Unfortunately for saga scholars, oral prose has not been given the same attention as oral verse, with the result that its "poetics" are poorly understood.

dotal stamp and must represent an oral layer. The problem lies rather in the larger composition of the whole. The component parts may be perfectly lucid, but the way they are put together, not to say the sheer number of them, is not. At this level, even the freeprosists agree, the saga is a literary creation. Heusler's statement about Snorri's *Óláfs saga helga* is worth repeating, for it applies to the classical sagas in general: "[It] meshes complex and polycentric narrative masses into a whole that advances chronologically in such a way that a thread is interrupted and resumed several pages later. This sophisticated procedure lies far beyond the capacity of the preliterary saga tellers. In addition, the narrative parameters, the scope of the work, exceed the limit of oral performance."[89]

But what of the audience? Heusler, like Olrik and others who have pronounced on the literary nature of saga composition, stopped short of the next logical step. The question is whether those features of the saga which are "far beyond the capacity of the preliterary saga tellers" were not also in some sense beyond the capacity of listeners—whether, that is, a literary form that presupposes a sophisticated author does not by the same token presuppose a sophisticated audience. In Vinaver's view, appreciation of interlace structure in prose romance was limited not only to a reader but only the cleverest reader: "So delicate an architecture presupposed in the reader and the writer an unusual discipline of mind and a span of attention which even in the thirteenth century could not have been the privilege of many."[90] One saga critic who recognized that the convoluted structure of the saga was hard to reconcile with the concept of oral delivery was Hollander, but his implicit trust in the doctrine of *sagnaskemmtun* kept him from taking his own analysis to its logical conclusion. Rather than asking whether literary composition might not imply a literate audience, he posited a uniquely gifted group of listeners:

> The modern reader, with a neatly printed text before him, can, to be sure, leaf back at his leisure to disentangle the skein of interbraided

[89]See chapter 2, note 6.
[90]Eugène Vinaver, *The Rise of Romance* (New York: Oxford University Press, 1971), pp. 92–93.

events. But one marvels at the mental alertness of Icelandic listeners, ancient and modern, who could do this, and seeks refuge in the rather lame consideration that, after all, listening, like intelligent reading, is an art which can be acquired; also, that Icelanders heard these stories over and over again as our forebears heard the Biblical stories read to them, day in and day out. Even so, the sagas, and more especially this one [*Eyrbyggja saga*], cannot be read quasi-passively, as can a unilateral story or a modern novel, but require a certain amount of co-operation on the part of the reader which, *exempla docent,* our scholars have not shown in this instance.[91]

As prefaces to popular editions of the sagas repeatedly point out, the Icelanders must have known a great deal about the particulars (genealogies, place names, anecdotes) that formed the historical matrix of the saga and contribute to the confusion of the modern reader. But familiarity with particulars is one thing and convoluted arrangement another—particularly when that arrangement strongly resembles the patterns of other contemporary European narrative of an unhistorical sort. (Nor, it should be added, were the plots and the imaginary world of Arthurian romance unfamiliar to the European reader of the thirteenth century.) The idea that saga listeners transcended the normal limits of the oral situation by dint of sheer repetition has two disadvantages: it posits Iceland as a society where the majority evidence ends and the minority evidence begins, and it presupposes a period and kind of evolution of which no historical record remains.

It is a tribute to the appeal of the *sagnaskemmtun* doctrine that, despite what is generally conceded to be an unusually high degree of literacy in medieval Iceland,[92] the existence of a sophisticated

[91]Lee M. Hollander, "The Structure of Eyrbyggja saga," *Journal of English and Germanic Philology,* 58 (1959), 226–27.

[92]The classic contribution is that of Sigurður Nordal, "Tid och kalvskinn," *Scripta Islandica,* 5 (1954), 5–18; translated as "Time and Vellum," *MHRA: Annual Bulletin of the Modern Humanities Research Association,* 24 (1952), 15–26. See also Einar Ólafur Sveinsson, "Lestrarkunnátta Íslendinga í fornöld," *Skírnir,* 118 (1944), 173–97; rpt. in his *Við uppspretturnar* (Reykjavík: Helgafell, 1956), pp. 166–92; and Karlsson, "Ritun Reykjarfjarðarbókar." A contrary view was argued by Lars Lönnroth, "Tesen om de två kulturerna: Kritiska studier i den isländska sagaskrivningens sociala förutsättningar," *Scripta Islandica,* 15 (1964), esp. pp. 52–77; and his *Njáls Saga,* pp. 166–70. See note 80 above.

readership of the sagas has never been cited as an explanation for
their manifestly literary characteristics. There are two reasons for
supposing that the thirteenth-century Icelandic reader might have
grown impatient with the traditional forms of native storytelling
and so indirectly contributed to their literary mutation. One is
that by the mere fact of their literacy, readers were able to take in
more numerous narrative data in more complex forms. The other
is that, again by virtue of their literacy, readers had been exposed
in varying degrees to foreign culture and thus had glimpsed a new
range of literary possibilities. The Continental orientation of this
elite readership is obvious both from the translating activity and
from the incorporation into native sagas of learned and foreign
matter. Narrative habit is harder to pin down, but the fact remains
that the Icelanders developed the same taste for baroque exposition as their European neighbors—a literary development and a
specifically medieval one, however the coincidence is to be explained.

Just how large this literate subgroup was can only be guessed
at. It must have included clerics, wealthier people, and whatever
other individuals had acquired the skill of reading and a taste for
literature—including, of course, the saga authors themselves.
There were, after all, at least as many readers in Iceland as there
were writers, and that is already more than a few. Whatever other
audience they had in mind, saga authors must also have been
writing for each other. To concede the literary artistry of the saga
is to concede a self-conscious artist, one who presumably studied
the work of others with an eye to imitation or improvement. Just
as, according to *Egils saga*, Einarr skálaglamm and Egill Skallagrímsson met at the Althing and conversed at length and pleasur-
ably on the subject of poetry, "a topic they both found enjoy-
able,"[93] so must saga authors have known one another and
formed their own literary society. At some level, each individual

---

[93]"Einarr gekk til búðar Egils Skalla-Grímssonar, ok tókusk þeir at orðum, ok
kom þar brátt talinu, at þeir rœddu um skáldskap; þótti hvárumtveggja þær rœður
skemmtiligar. Síðan vanðisk Einarr optliga at ganga til tals við Egil; gerðisk þar
vinátta mikil (Einarr went to Egill Skallagrímson's booth and they started talking.
Their conversation quickly turned to poetry, a topic they both found highly enjoy-
able. After that Einarr made it a habit of often going to talk with Egill, and they
formed a close friendship"—*Egils saga*, chap. 78).

saga is a response to the sagas preceding it and a standard for
those to come. One cannot but wonder whether the Atlantic Interlude of *Njáls saga* is not to some extent artists' art, written
primarily for the edification of other practitioners of the craft.
However small the number of authors and readers in thirteenth-
century Iceland, they must by virtue of their literacy have formed
a subgroup that for the individual author would have been a significant minority indeed. Like art prose in France, art prose in Iceland seems, as Georges Doutrepont said, to address itself "less
and less to groups and more and more to individuals. It is created
for particular people and not for the masses. One might even say
that it [art prose] becomes, if we may agree on the meaning of the
word, individualistic."[94] This is not to deny that the sagas were
performed orally, but to suggest that even if the oral audience was
the larger and more common one, it was not the only one—nor,
by the thirteenth century, was it the primary or authoritative one
so far as the composing artist was concerned. The obvious explanation for the often-noted fact that the Icelandic sagas combine
oral tradition with literary innovation is to suppose that their
authors intended them for both forms of publication. It is first and
foremost to the anecdotes of the sagas—the wit and lapidary
phrasing of which seem ideally suited for performance—that the
listening audience must have responded in the saga read aloud,
exactly as their forebears had in the saga told more or less from
memory. The listening audience must also have followed the general drift of the plot (with which they were presumably familiar in
some degree). But especially given the fact that the sagas were
read in installments, the listening audience is unlikely to have
appreciated the literary niceties of the larger plot—the precise
relation of all the interlocking subplots, the long-range forecasts
and correspondences, or the factor of time in simultaneous passages. These are the sagas' literary features, intended for the
enjoyment of their private readers, for whom, as for the readers
of the prose romances, the "exercise of memory was itself a
pleasurable pursuit which carried with it its own reward."[95]
    It is probably simplistic to draw such a sharp distinction be-

[94]Doutrepont, *Les mises en prose,* p. 685.
[95]Vinaver, *Rise of Romance,* p. 83.

tween the two audiences of the saga. In reality, there must have been degrees of sophistication among those who could read and degrees of comprehension among the listening audience. But if there is no fixed line between literate and illiterate, there are roughly zones, the acknowledgment of which in the sagas is crucial not only to the appreciation of their aesthetics, but to an understanding of the peculiar place they occupy in medieval literary history. The usual pattern in oligoliterate societies is for the literate and the illiterate sectors to part ways, each pursuing its own tastes in narrative entertainment. Something like this must have happened in Norway, with the development of a relatively sophisticated court literature on one hand and an unknown quantity of popular tradition on the other—unknown precisely because literate people were not there to cultivate or record it. But in Iceland, which had no court and where the literary forum was distinctly mixed by virtue of social circumstances (as Walter Baetke in particular has emphasized),[96] there was no such opportunity for a radical split; the literate and the illiterate did not diverge, but necessarily cooperated on a form of narrative that accommodated both of them. That narrative had oral origins, and it retained its oral characteristics sufficiently to entertain a listening audience. But the literary elite was in the meantime reshaping native traditions into forms that are identifiably literary and strikingly similar to those found in other European literature from the same period. Like other unnatural unions, this one between literate and illiterate in Iceland produced a hybrid. Where there was no such union, as in Norway and Denmark, there was no classical saga; and when, as in Iceland itself during the following centuries, there was a waning of the specifically literary vitality (for reasons perhaps having to do with the cultural isolation in the post-medieval period), the balance was disturbed, and saga art reverted to a more popular idiom.

Saga scholarship has made much of the importance of historical traditions, in particular genealogical traditions, in determining the compositional shape of the sagas. In Heusler's words, their "fourfold multiplicity—in plot, space, time, cast of characters—points toward a derivation in a matter-laden chronicle of

---

[96]Baetke, *Über die Entstehung der Isländersagas*, pp. 99–108.

events."[97] The line of continuity between *Landnámabók* and the individual Icelandic sagas and, further, such compilations as *Mǫðruvallabók* and *Sturlunga saga,* is a very clear one. But to say, as Ker does, that the form of the saga is for this reason largely indebted to circumstances outside of art[98] ignores the fact that a large proportion of European narrative, including traditions unencumbered by genealogical concerns or indeed historical concerns of any kind, displays a very similar sort of art. The sagas are non-Aristotelian in much the same way that their European neighbors are non-Aristotelian. Open composition, compound structure, internal digression, abundance of particulars, cyclic tendencies, simultaneous narration, and the pursuit of multiplicity for its own sake are medieval characteristics, not just saga peculiarities. The question is not of theme determining matter, but of matter being brought into the thematic sphere. The underlying principle is not that of unity in the classical sense, but rather of the "irritatingly enigmatic" logic of cohesion preferred by medieval authors, particularly in the French tradition.[99] This is not to deny the role played by local historical traditions in determining the composition of the Icelandic saga, but to suggest that the aesthetic climate of thirteenth-century Europe favored the use of complex and digressive forms (not to speak of prose) in imaginative literature; if the subject matter was inherently digressive to begin with, as Icelandic local traditions in particular must have been, so much the better. The sagas themselves, and the manuscripts in which they are contained, offer prima facie evidence that this literary climate was by no means restricted to Continental authors, but prevailed in Scandinavia as well. That saga composition was influenced by Latin history writing is clear. Whether it also received reinforcing secondary impulses from French prose romance is not clear, though circumstantial evidence points in that direction. In either case, it is with the prose romances, not with epic, that the sagas bear formal comparison. However dis-

---

[97]Andreas Heusler, *Die altgermanische Dichtung,* 2d ed. rev. (Potsdam: Athenaion, 1941), p. 221. All of Heusler's "proofs" of the chronicle impulse in the Icelandic family sagas stand as descriptions of interlace composition.

[98]W. P. Ker, *Epic and Romance,* 2d ed. (London: Macmillan, 1906; rpt. New York: Dover, 1957), p. 184.

[99]Albert Pauphilet, *Le legs du moyen âge: Etudes de littérature médiévale* (Melun: Libraire d'Argences, 1950), p. 214.

tinctive the style and sober vision of the sagas, and however much their temper seems to associate them with heroic traditions, their composition, especially their extended and gratuitous interweaving of plots, associates them with those books of chivalry the Renaissance critics found distastefully digressive and the Canon of Toledo condemned as multilimbed monsters.[100] From the perspective of medieval aesthetics, it is of some interest that interlace literature has a substantial representation in the north. From the perspective of Scandinavian cultural history, it is correspondingly important to understand that in the central aspect of their composition the sagas are not so anomalous as they are often taken to be, but belong to the common enterprise.

[100]See chapter 1, note 79, above.

# Editions Consulted

This list includes primary sources quoted or cited in the text. In quoting from Latin, Old Norse–Icelandic, and Old French works, I have often ignored paragraph and chapter divisions. Unless otherwise indicated, all translations appearing in the text but not on this list are my own.

*ÍF* = *Íslenzk fornrit* editions, vols. 1–14 and 26–28 (Reykjavík: Hið íslenzka fornritafélag, 1933–68).

ADAM OF BREMEN. Bernhard Schmeidler, ed., *Adam von Bremen, Hamburgische Kirchengeschichte* [*Gesta hammaburgensis ecclesiae pontificum*], Scriptores rerum germanicarum, 3d ed. (Hanover: Hahn, 1917).

AD HERENNIUM. Harry Caplan, ed., *Rhetorica ad Herennium*, Loeb Classical Library (Cambridge, Mass.: Harvard University Press, 1954).

ÁGRIP. Finnur Jónsson, ed., *Ágrip af Nóregs konunga sǫgum*, Altnordische Saga-bibliothek, 18 (Halle/Saale: Niemeyer, 1929).

ALCUIN. Karl Halm, ed., *Disputatio de rhetorica et de virtutibus sapientissimi regis Karli et Albini magistri*, Rhetores latini minores (Leipzig, 1863).

———. Wilhelm Wattenbach and Ernst Ludwig Dümmler, eds., *Alcuini vita sancti Willibrordi*, Bibliotheca rerum germanicarum, 6 (Berlin: Weidmann, 1878).

ALISCANS. Erich Wienbeck, Wilhelm Hartnacke, and Paul Rasch, eds., *Aliscans: Kritischer Text* (Halle/Saale: Niemeyer, 1903).

AMADÍS DE GAULA. Edwin B. Place, ed., *Amadís de Gaula*, 4 vols. (Madrid: Consejo Superior de Investigaciones Científicas, 1959–69).

———. Edwin B. Place and Herbert C. Behm, trs., *Amadis of Gaul* (Lexington, Kentucky: University of Kentucky Press, 1974).

ARIOSTO. Santorre Debenedetti, ed., *Lodovico Ariosto: Orlando furioso* (Bari: Laterza, 1928).

ARISTOTLE. W. D. Ross, ed., *The Works of Aristotle Translated into English*, 12 vols. (Oxford: Clarendon, 1906–52).

ARI ÞORGILSSON. *ÍF* I (1968).

ÁRNA SAGA BISKUPS. Jón Sigurðsson and Guðbrandr Vigfússon, eds., *Biskupa sögur*, 2 vols. (Copenhagen: Møller, 1858–1878), vol. I.

BANDAMANNA SAGA. *ÍF* VII (1936).

BEOWULF. Fr. Klaeber, ed., *Beowulf and the Fight at Finnsburg*, 3d ed. (Boston: D. C. Heath, 1950).

BÉROUL. Ernest Muret, ed., *Le roman de Tristan, poème du XII^e siècle par Béroul*, 4th rev. ed., Les classiques français du moyen âge, 12 (Paris: Champion, 1967).

BÓSA SAGA. Otto Luitpold Jiriczek, ed., *Die Bósa-saga in zwei Fassungen, nebst Proben aus den Bósa-rímur* (Strasbourg: Trübner, 1893).

BRENNU-NJÁLS SAGA. See *Njáls saga*.

CHANSON DE GUILLAUME. Duncan McMillan, ed., *La chanson de Guillaume*, Société des anciens textes français (Paris: Picard, 1949–50).

CHANSON DE ROLAND. Gerard J. Brault, ed. and tr., *The Song of Roland: An Analytical Edition*, 2 vols. (University Park, Pa.: Pennsylvania State University Press, 1978).

CHAUCER, GEOFFREY, F. N. Robinson, ed., *The Works of Geoffrey Chaucer*, 2d ed. (Boston: Houghton Mifflin, 1957).

LA CHEVALERIE D'OGIER DE DANEMARCHE. Mario Eusebi, ed., *La chevalerie d'Ogier de Danemarche* (Milan: Cisalpino, 1963).

CHRÉTIEN DE TROYES. Alexandre Micha, ed., *Cligès* (Paris: Champion, 1957).

———. Mario Louis Roques, ed., *Erec et Enide*, Les classiques français du moyen âge, 80 (Paris: Champion, 1953).

———. Alfons Hilka, ed., *Der Percevalroman (Li contes del graal)* (Halle/Saale: Niemeyer, 1932).

———. Mario Louis Roques, ed., *Le chevalier au lion (Yvain)*, Les classiques français du moyen âge, 89 (Paris: Champion, 1960).

———. W. W. Comfort, tr., *Chrétien de Troyes: Arthurian Romances* (New York: Dutton, 1975).

CODEX REGIUS. See *Edda*.

DROPLAUGARSONA SAGA. *ÍF* XI (1950).

EDDA. Gustav Neckel and Hans Kuhn, eds., *Edda: Die Lieder des Codex Regius nebst verwandten Denkmälern* (Heidelberg: Carl Winter, 1962).

EGILS SAGA. *ÍF* II (1933).

EILHART. Hadumod Bussmann, ed., *Tristant von Eilhart von Oberg.*
*Synoptischer Druck der ergänzten Fragmente mit der gesamten Paral-*
*lelüberlieferung,* Altdeutsche Textbibliothek, 70 (Tübingen: Niemeyer,
1969).

EIRSPENNILL. See *Sverris saga.*

EREX SAGA. Gustaf Cederschiöld, ed., *Erex saga,* Samfund til udgivelse
af gammel nordisk litteratur, III (Copenhagen: Møller, 1880).

———. Foster W. Blaisdell, ed., *Erex saga artuskappa,* Editiones Arnamagnæanæ, Series B, vol. 19 (Copenhagen: Munksgaard, 1965).

ESTOIRE DEL SAINT GRAAL. See Vulgate Cycle.

EYRBYGGJA SAGA. *ÍF* IV (1935).

FAGRSKINNA. Finnur Jónsson, ed., *Fagrskinna. Nóregs kononga tal*
(Copenhagen: Møller, 1902–3).

FLATEYJARBÓK. Guðbrandur Vigfússon and C. R. Unger, *Flateyjarbók,*
3 vols., Norsk historisk kildeskriftfonds skriften, 4 (Oslo: P. T. Mal-
ling, 1860–68).

———. Sigurður Nordal, ed., *Flateyjarbók,* 4 vols. (Akranes: Prentverk
Akranes, 1944–45).

FLORIS AND BLANCHEFLOUR. Walter French and Charles B. Hale, eds.,
*Middle English Metrical Romances* (New York: Prentice-Hall, 1930).

FÓSTBRŒÐRA SAGA. *ÍF* VI (1943).

FROISSART. Simeon Luce et al., eds., *Froissart: Chroniques,* 15 vols.,
Société de l'histoire de France (Paris: Renouard, 1869–1975).

GAMELYN. Walter French and Charles B. Hale, eds., *Middle English*
*Metrical Romances* (New York: Prentice-Hall, 1930).

GAUTREKS SAGA. Wilhelm Ranisch, ed., *Gautreks saga,* Palaestra, 11
(1900).

GAWAIN AND THE GREEN KNIGHT. J. R. R. Tolkien and E. V. Gordon,
eds., *Sir Gawain and the Green Knight,* 2d rev. ed. (Oxford: Clarendon, 1968).

GEOFFREY OF VINSAUF. *Documentum de modo et arte dictandi et ver-*
*sificandi* and *Poetria nova,* in Edmond Faral, eds., *Les arts poétiques*
*du XIIᵉ et du XIIIᵉ siècle* (Paris: Champion, 1958).

———. Jane Baltzell Kopp, tr., *Poetria nova,* in James J. Murphy, ed.,
*Three Medieval Rhetorical Arts* (Berkeley: University of California
Press, 1971).

GÍSLA SAGA. *ÍF* VI (1943).

GREAT SAGA OF SAINT ÓLÁFR. Oscar Albert Johnsen and Jón Helgason,
eds., *Den store saga om Olav den hellige efter pergamenthåndskrift i*
*Kungliga Biblioteket i Stockholm Nr. 2 4ᵗᵒ med varianter fra andre*
*håndskrifter,* 2 vols. (Oslo: Jacob Dybwad, 1930–33).

GRETTIS SAGA. *ÍF* VII (1936).

GUILLAUME D'ANGLETERRE. Maurice Wilmotte, ed., *Guillaume d'Angleterre: Roman du XIIᵉ siècle*, Les classiques français du moyen âge (Paris: Champion, 1927).

GUNNLAUGS SAGA. *ÍF* III (1938).

HALLFREÐAR SAGA. *ÍF* VIII (1939).

HÁVARÐAR SAGA ÍSFIRDINGS. *ÍF* VI (1943).

HEIDARVÍGA SAGA. *ÍF* III (1938).

HEIMSKRINGLA. *ÍF* XXVI–XXVIII (1941–51).

HISTOIRE DE SAINT LOUIS. See Joinville.

HISTORIA NORWEGIÆ. Gustav Storm, ed., *Monumenta historica Norvegiæ* (Christiania: Brøgger, 1880).

HŒNSA-ÞÓRIS SAGA. *ÍF* III (1938).

HORACE. H. Rushton Fairclough, *Horace: Satires, Epistles, and Ars poetica*, Loeb Classical Library (Cambridge, Mass.: Harvard University Press; London: Heinemann, 1929, rpt. 1970).

HRAFNKELS SAGA. *ÍF* XI (1950).

HUGH OF ST. VICTOR. Charles Henry Buttimer, ed., *Didascalion de studio legendi*, Studies in Medieval and Renaissance Latin, 10 (Washington, D.C.: Catholic University Press, 1939).

ÍSLENDINGABÓK. See Ari Þorgilsson.

ÍSLENDINGASAGA. See *Sturlunga saga*.

JOHN OF GARLAND. *Poetria,* in Edmond Faral, ed., *Les arts poétiques du XIIᵉ et du XIIIᵉ siècle* (Paris: Champion, 1958).

JOINVILLE. Natalis de Wailly, ed., *Jean de Joinville: Histoire de Saint Louis* (Paris: Didot, 1874).

JÓMSVÍKINGA SAGA. Ólafur Halldórsson, ed., *Jómsvíkinga saga* [AM 291 4°] (Reykjavík: Jón Helgason, 1969).

―――. N. F. Blake, ed., *Jómsvíkinga saga/The Saga of the Jomsvikings* [Cod. Holm. 7 4°] (London: Thomas Nelson, 1962).

JÓNS SAGA HELGA. Jón Sigurðsson and Guðbrandur Vigfússon, eds., *Biskupa sögur,* I (Copenhagen: Møller, 1858).

JORDANES. Theodor Mommsen, ed., *Iordanis romana et getica,* Monumenta Germaniae historica (Berlin: Weidmann, 1882).

KARLAMAGNÚS SAGA. C. R. Unger, ed., *Karlamagnús saga ok kappa hans* (Christiania: H. J. Jensen, 1860).

KJALNESINGA SAGA. *ÍF* XIV (1959).

KÖNIG ROTHER. Theodor Frings and Joachim Kuhnt, eds. *König Rother* (Halle/Saale: Niemeyer, 1922).

KORMÁKS SAGA. *ÍF* VIII (1939).

LANDNÁMABÓK. *ÍF* I (1968).

LAXDŒLA SAGA: *ÍF* V (1934).

LEGENDARY SAGA. Oscar Albert Johnsen, *Olafs saga hins helga efter pergamenthaandskrift i Uppsala Universitetsbibliotek Delagardieske samling nr. 5* (Oslo: Dybwad, 1922).

LIVRE D'ARTUS. See Vulgate Cycle.

LJÓSVETNINGA SAGA. *ÍF* X (1940).

LONGEST SAGA. Ólafur Halldórsson, ed., *Óláfs saga Tryggvasonar en mesta*, Editiones Arnamagnæanæ, Series A, vols. 1–2 (Copenhagen: Munksgaard, 1958–61).

MALORY, THOMAS. Eugène Vinaver, ed., *The Works of Sir Thomas Malory*, 3 vols. (Oxford: Clarendon, 1947).

MARIE DE FRANCE. Alfred Ewert, ed., *Lais* (Oxford: Blackwell, 1944).

MARTIANUS CAPELLA. *De Rhetorica*, in Karl Halm, ed., Rhetores latini minores (Leipzig: Teubner, 1863).

MATTHEW OF VENDÔME. *Ars versificatoria*, in Edmond Faral, ed., *Les arts poétiques du XII^e et du XIII^e siècle* (Paris: Champion, 1958).

MORKINSKINNA. Finnur Jónsson, ed., *Morkinskinna*, Samfund til udgivelse af gammel nordisk litteratur (Copenhagen: Jørgensen, 1932).

MORT ARTU. See Vulgate Cycle.

MǪDRUVALLABÓK. *Codex Möðruvallensis*, Corpus codicum islandicorum medii aevi, 5 [Early Icelandic Manuscripts in Facsimile] (Copenhagen: Levin and Munksgaard, 1933).

NIBELUNGENLIED. Karl Bartsch and Helmut de Boor, eds., *Das Nibelungenlied*, 20th ed. (Wiesbaden: Brockhaus, 1972).

NJÁLS SAGA. *ÍF* XII (1954).

ODDR SNORRASON. Finnur Jónsson, ed., *Saga Óláfs Tryggvasonar af Oddr Snorrason munk* (Copenhagen: Gad, 1932).

OLDEST SAGA. Gustav Storm, *Otte brudstykker af den ældste saga om Olav den hellige*, Norsk historisk kildeskriftfond (Oslo: Grøndahl, 1893).

ORKNEYINGA SAGA. *ÍF* XXXIV (1965).

PARCEVALS SAGA. E. Kölbing, *Riddarasögur* (Strasbourg: Trübner, 1872).

PAUL THE DEACON. Ludwig C. Bethmann and Georg Waitz, eds., *Pauli Historia Langobardorum*, Monumenta Germaniae historica, Scriptores rerum langobardicarum et italicarum (Hannover: Hahn, 1878; rpt. 1964).

PRESTSSAGA GUÐMUNDAR GÓÐA. See *Sturlunga saga*.

PROFECTIO DANORUM. M. Cl. Gertz, ed., *De profectione Danorum in Hierosolymam*, Scriptores minores historiæ Danicæ medii ævi, 2 vols. (Copenhagen: Gad, 1918–20; rpt. Copenhagen: Munksgaard, 1970), vol. I.

PROPHÉCIES DE MERLIN. Lucy Allen Paton, ed., *Les prophécies de Merlin*, 2 vols. (New York: D. C. Heath, 1926–27).

PROSE LANCELOT. See Vulgate Cycle.

PROSE TRISTAN. Eilert Löseth, *Le roman en prose de Tristan, roman de Palamède et la compilation de Rusticien de Pise: Analyse critique d'après les manuscrits de Paris,* Bibliothèque de l'Ecole des Hautes Etudes (Paris: Bouillon, 1890).

QUESTE DEL SAINT GRAAL. See Vulgate Cycle.

REYKDŒLA SAGA. *ÍF* X (1940).

ROBERT OF BASEVORN. *Forma praedicandi,* in Th.-M. Charland, ed., *Artes praedicandi: Contribution à l'histoire de la rhétorique au moyen âge* (Paris: J. Vrin, 1936).

————. Leopold Krul O.S.B., tr., "The Form of Preaching," in James J. Murphy, ed., *Three Medieval Rhetorical Arts* (Berkeley: University of California Press, 1971).

ROMAN D'ENÉAS. J.-J. Salverda de Grave, ed., *Enéas: Roman du XII<sup>e</sup> siècle,* 2 vols., Les classiques français du moyen âge, 44 & 62 (Paris: Champion, 1925–29).

ROMAN DE TROIE. Léopold Constans, ed., *Le roman de Troie par Benoît de Sainte-Maure,* 6 vols., Société des anciens textes français (Paris: Didot, 1904–12).

SAXO GRAMMATICUS. C. Knabe and Paul Herrmann, eds., *Saxonis Gesta Danorum,* rev. Jørgen Olrik and Hans H. Raeder (Copenhagen: Levin and Munksgaard, 1931).

SCHOLIA VINDOBONENSIA. Joseph Zechmeister, ed., *Scholia vindobonensia ad Horatii artem poeticam* (Vienna: Apud C. Geroldum Filium Bibliopolam, 1877).

SEPARATE SAGA. See *Great Saga.*

SQUIRE OF LOW DEGREE. Walter French and Charles B. Hale, eds., *Middle English Metrical Romances* (New York: Prentice-Hall, 1930).

STURLUNGA SAGA. Jón Jóhannesson, Magnús Finnbogason, and Kristján Eldjárn, eds. *Sturlunga saga,* 2 vols. (Reykjavík, 1946).

SULPITIUS VICTOR. *Institutiones oratoriae,* in Karl Halm, ed., *Rhetores latini minores* (Leipzig: Teubner, 1863).

SVERRIS SAGA. Gustav Ludvig Indrebø, *Sverris saga* [AM 327 4°], Norsk historisk kjeldeskrift-fondet: Skrifter, 46 (Oslo: Dybwad, 1920).

————. Finnur Jónsson, ed., *Eirspennill* [AM 47 fol.], Norsk historisk kildeskriftkommission: Skrifter, 42 (Oslo: Thømte, 1916).

TASSO. Luigi Poma, ed., *Torquato Tasso: Discorsi dell'arte poetica e del poema eroico* (Bari: Laterza, 1964).

————. Mariella Cavalchini and Irene Samuel, trs., *Discourses on the Heroic Poem* (Oxford: Clarendon, 1973).

THEODORICUS. *Historia de antiquitate regum Norwagiensium,* in Gustav Storm, ed., *Monumenta historica Norvegiæ* (Oslo: Brøgger, 1880).

THOMAS. Bartina H. Wind, ed., *Les fragments du roman de Tristan,* *poème du XII<sup>e</sup> siècle*, Textes littéraires français, 92 (Geneva: Droz, 1960).

TRISTAN. See Béroul, Eilhart, and Thomas.

TRISTRAMS SAGA. Gísli G. Brynjúlfson, ed., *Saga af Tristram ok Ísönd, samt Möttuls saga* (Copenhagen: Thiele, 1878).

VIE DE SAINT ALEXIS. Jean-Marie Meunier, ed., *La vie de Saint Alexis, poème français du XI<sup>e</sup> siècle* (Paris: Droz, 1933).

VÍGA-GLÚMS SAGA. *ÍF* IX (1956).

VILLEHARDOUIN. Edmond Faral, ed. and tr., *Geoffroi de Villehardouin: La conquête de Constantinople*, 2 vols., Les classiques de l'histoire de France au moyen âge, 18–19 (Paris: Société d'édition "Les belles lettres," 1938–39).

VULGATE CYCLE. Heinrich Oskar Sommer, ed., *The Vulgate Version of the Arthurian Romances*, 7 vols. + index (Washington: Carnegie Institution, 1908–16).

_____. W. A. Nitze, ed., *Le roman de l'estoire dou graal* (Paris: Champion, 1927).

_____. Alexandre Micha, ed., *Lancelot, roman en prose du XIII<sup>e</sup> siècle*, 3 vols., Textes littéraires français, 247, 249, & 262 (Paris: Droz, 1978–79).

_____. Albert Pauphilet, ed., *La queste del saint graal: Roman du XIII<sup>e</sup> siècle* (Paris: Champion, 1923 and 1949).

_____. Jean Frappier, ed., *La mort le roi Artu: Roman du XIII<sup>e</sup> siècle*, Textes littéraires français (Geneva: Droz, 1964).

_____. P. M. Matarasso, tr., *The Quest of the Holy Grail* (Harmondsworth, Middlesex: Penguin, 1969).

_____. James Cable, ed., *The Death of King Arthur* (Harmondsworth, Middlesex: Penguin, 1971).

VQLSUNGA SAGA. R. G. Finch, ed., *Vǫlsunga saga/The Saga of the Volsungs* (London: Thomas Nelson, 1965).

WOLFRAM VON ESCHENBACH. Albert Leitzmann, *Wolfram von Eschenbach: Parzival*, Altdeutsche Textbibliothek, 12–14 (Halle: Niemeyer, 1902–3).

_____. Helen M. Mustard and Charles E. Passage, trs., *Wolfram von Eschenbach: Parzival* (New York: Vintage, 1961).

ÞÓRÐAR SAGA KAKALA. See *Sturlunga saga*.

ÞORSTEINS SAGA HVÍTA. *ÍF* XI (1950).

ÞORSTEINS ÞÁTTR STANGARHǪGGS. *ÍF* XI (1950).

# Index

*Library of Congress Cataloging in Publication Data*

Clover, Carol.
  The medieval saga.

  Bibliography: p.
  Includes index.
  1. Sagas—History and criticism.  I. Title.
PT7183.C56      839'.63      81-17432
ISBN 0-8014-1447-4          AACR2